D0443113

The Study
of Public
Policy

The Bobbs-Merrill Policy Analysis Series

The Study of Public Policy

Richard I. Hofferbert

THE BOBBS-MERRILL COMPANY, INC.
Indianapolis · New York

Thomas R. Dye
Florida State University
GENERAL EDITOR, *The Bobbs-Merrill Policy Analysis Series*

UNIVERSITY LIBRARY
Lethbridge, Alberta
99554

Library of Congress Cataloging in Publication Data

Hofferbert, Richard I.   1937-
  The study of public policy.

  (The Bobbs-Merrill policy analysis series)
  1. United States—Politics and government.
2. Policy sciences. I. Title.
JK271.H7   309.1'73   73-9826
ISBN 0-672-51455-9
ISBN 0-672-61062-0 (pbk.)

Copyright © 1974 by The Bobbs-Merrill Company, Inc.
Printed in the United States of America
First Printing

To Rose, for a decade and a half of patience

Foreword

The aim of the Policy Analysis Series is the systematic explanation of the content of public policy. The focus of the series is on public-policy choices of national, state, and local governments, and the forces that operate to shape policy decisions.

Books in the Policy Analysis Series are not concerned with what policies governments *ought* to pursue, but rather with *why* governments pursue the policies that they do. Public policies are not debated or argued in these volumes; rather, they are assembled, described, and explained in a systematic fashion.

The Study of Public Policy organizes, describes, and analyzes policy research in the social sciences—approaches, theories, methods, and results. It summarizes studies of legislatures, bureaucracies, executives, and courts in policy formation, as well as studies of informal power centers which operate outside of the governmental structure. Using Stephen K. Bailey's pioneering study of the Full Employment Act; the Bauer, Pool, and Dexter landmark study of foreign-trade policy; and A. Lee Fritschler's revealing study of the F.T.C.'s decision to ban cigarette advertising, Professor Hofferbert assesses the contribution of case studies to our understanding of policy-making. His comprehensive and critical review of the systematic, comparative research on the social, economic, and political determinants of public policy at the state and local level provides a valuable overview of the field. Professor Hofferbert himself has made many important contributions to the state policy research literature, and he writes with authority and insight on the problems of comparative systematic policy research.

The Study of Public Policy is an important addition to the Policy Analysis Series. Previous volumes in the series focused atteniton on particular areas of public policy—civil rights, education, taxing and spending, economic development, consumer protection, and urban affairs. Professor Hofferbert in this book provides a comprehensive survey, analysis, and critique of public-policy research. He tells us how scholars have approached the complex questions involved in determining the causes and consequences of public policy, and, more importantly, he offers important suggestions for the future of policy research.

Thomas R. Dye

Contents

Tables

Figures

PREFACE

This book has two themes, one implicit, the other explicit. The implicit theme is that students of politics and public affairs would do well to expand their understanding of how public policies are formulated. Of the various matters to which they might turn their attention, the processes of policy formation are certainly one of the most fascinating and fruitful.

The explicit theme is that the study of public policy can be pursued in a more productive manner than it has often been in the past. The comparative analysis of policy systems and of the political and social contexts within which public policies are formed will yield the most interesting results—interesting for the social scientist and interesting for the citizen concerned about the conditions of public policy.

A comprehensive survey of public-policy studies—what policy is, how it is made, and what it does—would cover all that is commonly thought of as "politics." This book is not a general treatment of politics. Therefore, it is necessary to state clearly what its objectives are. It summarizes and criticizes how scholars (especially political scientists) have viewed public policy as an object of study, and it

analyzes, in a rather summary fashion, some of the general conclusions reached by those who have studied public policy.

One of the leaders in the development of modern political science
has stated: "It has always seemed to me that the process by which
knowledge about politics, or anything else, is created is as important
from the teaching point of view as such knowledge itself."[1] If we
can learn something about the state of knowledge regarding public
policy, we will then be better equipped to do a number of things.
Students will be able to evaluate more critically what they learn
about politics, researchers will be able to improve their inquiry, and
citizens will be better able to judge between alternative policies.

Much that is presumably "known" about public policy and the
operation of American policy-forming processes is not knowledge at
all. Many misconceptions exist about the forces that produce policy—
misconceptions that have cumulated and been accepted in lieu of
systematic testing and verification. My objective is to evaluate
the methods and material that inform our knowledge about policy
formation.

A good deal of the policy-making activity in America takes place
at the state and local level. All too often major studies of policy do
not take systematic account of subnational activity. Yet a considerable amount of promising analysis, in terms of potentially valid
scientific findings, has focused on the state and local levels. This book
seeks to integrate these subnational studies into a general examination
of policy formation.

The summaries, analyses, criticisms, and suggestions offered here
form a framework for the rest of the Bobbs-Merrill Policy Analysis
Series. The series has been designed both to include a variety of
approaches to analyzing policy and to consider a number of substantive aspects of policy. This book provides an overview of these
approaches—the enterprise pursued in the other volumes of the
Policy Analysis Series.

[1]Heinz Eulau, *The Behavioral Persuasion in Politics* (New York: Random
House, 1963), p. vii.

ACKNOWLEDGMENTS

Several friends and I have discussed policy analysis for many years. I doubt that they would want me to credit them publicly with having influenced my thinking. I believe they have. But to insist upon it would place far too great a burden upon them. In any event, discussions with Thomas R. Dye, Heinz Eulau, John Grumm, and Ira Sharkansky have been fun. I hope they continue. Three of my students have unquestionably influenced my thinking, and, given their dependent status, they cannot evade the responsibility. My research and conceptions of politics will never recover from the impact of David Cameron, Stefanie Hecht Cameron, and J. Stephen Hendricks. Mrs. Cameron has provided critical substantive guidance and help, without which it is doubtful that the book would ever have been completed. The preparation of the manuscript was hastened by the able efforts of Linda Sobkowski and Jane Willer.

Throughout, I have borrowed rather liberally from my articles published previously in the *American Political Science Review,* the *Midwest Journal of Political Science,* and *Polity.* Some of the discussion also appeared in the *Political Science Annual,* vol. III (Indianapolis: Bobbs-Merrill, 1972).

   Though this book did not cost much to write, I have received material support from a number of sources in recent years for my research activity. The book has been affected by that research experience. I greatly appreciate the support of the Committee on Governmental and Legal Processes of the Social Science Research Council, the Comparative Political Behavior Program of the Cornell University Center for International Studies, and the Inter-university Consortium for Political Research. The last, in addition to being my current employer, was the sponsor of two research conferences—one in 1966 and one in 1968—that were vital in orienting my thinking about policy analysis.
   The intellectual and rhetorical quality of the manuscript, whatever its final shortcomings, has been vastly improved by the suggestions of Allan Rosenbaum and by the truly extraordinary editorial work of William Hoth.
   My largest debt is acknowledged elsewhere.

                                                    Richard I. Hofferbert

Ann Arbor, Michigan
December, 1973

The Study
of Public
Policy

chapter I

The Study of Public Policy in America

What Is Public Policy?

Two hundred adults and three hundred children gather in City Park to watch fireworks. Everyone stands, and some sturdy souls sing along as the high-school band gallantly plays the national anthem. A former state representative and local commander of the American Legion speaks of the necessity to remember our heritage, to protect our way of life, and to aid in the "defense of freedom in faraway lands." Is this public policy? The *Washington Post* reports from a "reliable source" that the United States will shortly increase its sales of jet aircraft to Israel. Is either the *Washington Post* or the "reliable source" making public policy?

The Fourth of July celebration is a manifestation of political actions; it is a widely expected product of the local political system. Foreign leaders and domestic publics react to news of impending decisions as though they mattered. And in *human* affairs, if people react to something, it matters. If people leave the fireworks display feeling a little more confident of America's purposes as manifested in her actions, is that not a reaction that matters? If Arab leaders read the *Washington Post* and increase their combat readiness, is

that not a reaction that matters? We could define public policy as
purposive action taken for or to the public. Taken by whom? And
for or to which part or parts of the "public"?

What about formal rule-making? Is a constitutional convention
a policy-making body? Is a constitution "policy"? Is a clarification
and application of the Constitution by the Supreme Court "policy"?
Some would argue that constitutional politics is policy-making at
its most basic.[1]

Going further, is policy the action taken or the reaction obtained? We do not have any definitional trouble with some indicators
of public policy. A tax schedule, a welfare check, a new school, a
defense budget, or a mission to the moon are the *visible products of
decisions taken by identifiable actors for public purposes.* These
visible products indicate public policies, clearly and deliberately. But
examples do not make definitions. Definitions of social concepts are
often like a dart board without a bull's-eye. If one has enough darts,
he can accumulate points equal to one bull's-eye. If we have enough
examples of a social phenomenon we can get a sense of what is at
its center—without ever hitting a bull's-eye. Many "visible products
of decisions taken by identifiable actors for public purposes" might
reasonably be excluded from a definition of public policy. A vege-
table stand on a farmer's lawn would qualify. Many students of
public policy, however, choose to narrow their concern to attributes
of the activities of legal governments. Heinz Eulau and Robert
Eyestone, for example, define policy as "the relationship of a governmental unit to its environment."[2] Their definition hardly improves
the recognizability of "public policy," for as Eulau and Eyestone
note:

> It finds expression in general programs and specific decisions,
> or in policy declarations of decisionmakers. But because a
> policy need not be declared to be a policy, analysis cannot

[1] See discussion by Robert H. Salisbury, "The Analysis of Public Policy: A
Search for Theories and Roles," in *Political Science and Public Policy,* ed.
Austin Ranney (Chicago: Markham Publishing Co., 1968), pp. 153-154.
[2] Heinz Eulau and Robert Eyestone, "Policy Maps of City Councils and Policy
Outcomes: A Developmental Analysis," *American Political Science Review*
62 (1968): 126.

rely on manifest statements or overt decisions alone but must concern itself with policy outcomes.[3]

"Public policy" can be indicated by the framework of governmental formation and deliberation, the intentions of political actors, the formal statements of public activity, or the consequences of this activity for society.[4] The *public* component of "public policy" can be considered in at least two ways: it can signify action taken by "public authorities"—that is, governmental officials—or it can signify action done to or for the public, regardless of who is performing it. Eulau and Eyestone's orientation is useful for the direction it provides; it tells us to look for the *products* of governmental activity. Many students of politics spend a lot of time on elections and rules of selection—on how governments are formed. Others focus their attention on the rules and inner workings of official and unofficial political organizations—on legislatures and interest groups.

The concern of this book is with the products of political systems. It is concerned with the formation and inner workings of governments only insofar as they may help us understand these products. True, ambiguous and controversial elements are contained within this orientation. For instance, what about nongovernmental activities, such as corporate pricing, that directly alter the impact of governmental decisions? Do we include as policy the inattention of public officials to a situation that could possibly be changed— "actions" in the form of "nondecisions"?[5] These problems will be considered at various points throughout the book. But the reader is alerted here that our main concern is with understanding the *substance* of what governments produce rather than the processes by which they produce it. We must also distinguish this substance from the ends sought—that is, the "goals" of policy-makers and from the results—that is, the "impacts" of public policy.

The indicators of policy are legislative enactments, executive orders, administrative regulations, tax dollars spent, and the like.

[3]Ibid.

[4]See Salisbury, "Analysis of Public Policy," for a lucid discussion of alternative conceptions and definitions of policy.

[5]See Peter Bachrach and Morton S. Baratz, "Decisions and Non-Decisions: An Analytic Framework," *American Political Science Review* 57 (1963): 632-642.

These are all provided by employees of formal government. Often called "outputs," these indicators are not to be confused with the goals and social effects of governmental action, which would be included under a fuller definition of "public policy." In the long run, policy analysts will no doubt turn their attention to the systematic explanation of the impact and consequences of public policies.[6] But a good case is to be made for trying to explain why outputs are different from one place or time to another before we try to explain why the impacts of a policy differ from one setting to another.

Still, outputs of political systems cannot be explained if they are viewed in isolation. Policy seen as the relationship between governments and their environments focuses attention on the intersection of the political system and the society around it. As Eulau and Eyestone point out, public policy is "a response of government to challenges or pressures from the physical and social environment."[7] Some political philosophers would label as "policy" any action taken by the "state." The political theorist David Easton speaks of the "authoritative allocation of values for society."[8] These formulations and most others are satisfactory for present purposes, so long as the reader bears in mind that the study of public policy is, in a specialized way, the study of politics in society. The purpose of citing these observations is to emphasize the interactions between society and politics, between the social structure and the state.

Problems always exist at the fringes of definitions. Some nongovernmental actions look like public policy and must be accommodated in any comparison of policies as they affect people's lives. Private schools educate children in a way similar to public schools. Electricity produced by the Tennessee Valley Authority (a government corporation) runs a washing machine the same as electricity from Detroit Edison (a private corporation). Charities do in some places what public welfare does in others. Many private activities have the appearance of being products of public policy if for no

[6]See, for example, Thomas R. Dye, ed., *The Measurement of Policy Impact* (Tallahassee: Florida State University, 1971).
[7]Eulau and Eyestone, "Policy Maps," p. 126.
[8]David Easton, *The Political System* (New York: Alfred A. Knopf, 1953).

other reason than that they are tolerated by governmental decision-makers; moreover, they are often encouraged through tax incentives and through public recognition and regulation. These examples illustrate the problem of definition: anything in society can be considered a public policy because public officials allow it to exist. We could speak of *deliberate* governmental action or tolerance, but we may wish to consider nondeliberate non-actions of some policy-makers. Some policy-makers do not care to change social circumstances or to expand their list of options. These people are called "conservatives," and they are an interesting part of the policy process.

To look at only the substance of governmental outputs, therefore, does not let us see all that might reasonably be included in the study of public policy. Yet the consideration of outputs is a manageable starting point. Interesting questions can be asked in a scientifically respectable manner about substantive outputs. A good deal of variation is evident in policies conceived in this manner. The substance of policy can change dramatically over time within a single jurisdiction. Cities tear down and reconstruct public buildings. The national government changes its policies on environmental protection. States change their laws on billboards. Furthermore, the substance of policy on a particular matter can differ from one jurisdiction to another. It is to these kinds of differences in the substance of policy from one setting (time, jurisdiction, and so forth) to another that can constitute and has constituted the research focus for a growing number of social scientists.

In this volume, policies are the things to be explained. Why do kids in one state go to one kind of school and kids in other states go to a different kind? Why at one point in time does the federal government seem to do everything it can to help the tobacco industry and then later begin to put on the squeeze? Our interest in explaining policy differences and changes will lead to an interest in who and what influences policy.

To focus upon policy as an object of study is to focus on the product side of the political equation. Instead of being concerned primarily with what affects government, or with what goes on inside political institutions, we are *primarily* interested in what comes out of the process. Politicians are central to the policy process; so, too, may be political parties, protest groups, labor unions, and corporation executives. Students of the policy process are interested in politicians and parties and corporate executives, but not in and of themselves. Rather, they are interested in them as they affect policy. Botanists choose plants as their dependent variable without denying the relevance of the hydrologic cycle. Climatologists know how important plants are to weather patterns, but climatologists are not botanists.

So, this book is concerned with policy—what we know about it and how it has been studied. More specifically it is concerned with progress toward the scientific explanation of why policies vary from one part of the country to another and from one time to another. Political scientists have found many matters relevant to these concerns, but in most cases their findings relevant to policy have been by-products of other scientific concerns.

Political Science and the Policy Process

It is only in the last generation that some political scientists have turned deliberately and self-consciously to the study of substantive public policy as a primary scholarly activity. Previously, the interest of the discipline centered upon the moral and ethical bases of civil society, the legal structures of government, the relations between nation-states, and, particularly in the American setting, the constitutional implications of judicial decisions. Though the fruits of these endeavors sometimes contained insights helpful in an understanding of policy, such insights were usually unintended by-products that failed to cumulate in a coherent manner. A brief glance at the course listings of most university political-science departments would demonstrate, even today, the persistence of older conceptions of the structure of the discipline. Now I do not wish to argue that political philosophy, governmental structures, or judicial pronouncements are irrelevant to policy. The point is, rather, that the policy consequences of such considerations have not been the central interest of those who have studied them most assiduously. Policy has not been the primary focus of their intellectual stance. Indicators of substantive policy have not been the central dependent variables for most political scientists.

With the development of more rigorous techniques for observing and measuring political actions and with a recognition of the scientific benefits of comparative inquiry, however, scholarly interest in public policy has grown. Scientific generalizations usually rest upon comparative observations. And we have discovered that policy can be measured, albeit sometimes crudely, in order to allow for comparison of patterns between political systems. Aspects of political systems other than public policy can also be measured and compared, but the problems are often more imposing than in comparing policies. Political parties, electoral activity, or legislatures, for example, may be quite different from one society to another. In many ways the only similarity between the Communist Party of Bulgaria and the Democratic Party of Nebraska is the inclusion of the word "party" in the labels. The same may be said for the Supreme Soviet and the House of Commons. But Nebraska, Bulgaria, England, and the U.S.S.R. also have many patterns and areas of substantive policy that can be conceptualized in fairly common language. They all have public schools, pension programs for the aged, highways, sewer systems, economic regulatory plans, and a host of governmentally supported programs of remarkably comparable substantive and administrative content. The differences between many policies in these countries are matters for explanation rather than definition. In recent years the technical and conceptual tools of political science have been sharpened to allow a start on the process of explaining why such policies differ from one place or time to another. That dramatic differences in some policy areas obtain from one political system to another does not obviate the potential for comparative research.

In the United States, however, it is not only methodological and conceptual progress that has spurred interest in the systematic study of public policy. A major reason for the changing stance of some political scientists in recent decades has been the changing role of government in American society. Although the tenacity with which laissez-faire ideas held in check policy-makers of the nineteenth century has often been overestimated, the scope of governmental action in the last generation or so has clearly been expanded and extended relative to other sectors of the social order. Figure I-1 illustrates, for example, the changing ratio of governmental spending

Figure I-1

RATIO OF TOTAL FEDERAL, STATE, AND LOCAL SPENDING TO GROSS NATIONAL PRODUCT: 1900-1970

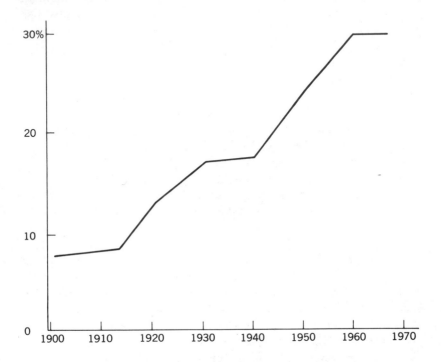

SOURCE: U.S. Bureau of the Census, *Historical Statistics of the United States, Colonial Times to 1957* (Washington, D.C., U.S. Government Printing Office, 1960); idem, *Statistical Abstract of the United States: 1971*, 22nd ed. (Washington, D.C., U.S. Government Printing Office, 1971).

to gross national product between 1900 and 1970—a vivid illustration of the ever-larger part played by public policy in our society. Political scientists are also social scientists, and as such they quite naturally focus their attention on the circumstances that matter most in society. Increasingly, policies made by public—primarily governmental—decision-makers have come to constitute a key directional force in our collective and individual lives.

Public Policy and Social Life

The magnitude and emphasis of governmental involvement in society has changed from era to era. At one time, much of what government now does would have been considered none of its business. For decades, legislators, jurists, and critical citizens debated the propriety of laws regulating the hours and wages of working children. Not too long ago it would have been thought incredible that local governments could tell a man what he could build or what he could not build on his own land, let alone what kind of materials he must use in his house. The chief business of nineteenth-century government was, at least at the national level, to keep out obnoxious intruders, both military and economic.

Yet beneath the apparently placid surface of policy inaction—and well before the apparent surge in governmental action during the 1930s—new forms for public involvement in the affairs of society could be glimpsed. Compulsory school attendance was required by Massachusetts in 1852, to be followed by the other states in reasonably short order.[9] In the 1860s, long before the Sherman Antitrust Act, Illinois was setting railroad rates for the shipment of certain commodities. Examples of early state regulatory experimentation in health, economic development, education, and natural resources could be cited.[10]

For the most part, public attention today focuses on policy innovation and activity at the national level. Nonetheless, much of the experimentation in public control and services, after as well as before the Depression, has taken place in the state capitols and city halls. While it is reasonable to wonder about the rationale of state and local jurisdictions as they have been constituted, strong evidence exists to support their claim to prominence in the processes of public-policy formation in America. Our subnational policy structures are more than mere legal forms or political habits. Federalism is a vital facet of American policy-making, and a major portion of inquiry into the policy processes has centered on subnational activity.

[9]Thomas R. Dye, *Politics, Economics, and the Public* (Chicago: Rand McNally, 1966), p. 75.

[10]See the discussion by Daniel J. Elazar, *The American Partnership* (Chicago: University of Chicago Press, 1962).

Federalism and Policy-Making by State and Local Governments[11]

One might argue that the American states and their local units have little impact upon our lives. Some points can be scored for that argument, but ultimately it must be rejected. Legal forms and political practices, regardless of their initial functional justification, do affect behavior and condition the processes by which patterns of human interaction evolve. To be sure, there may have been no reason relevant to initial patterns of social intercourse for drawing the Idaho-Nevada boundary at the 42nd parallel. And it is unlikely that anyone unassisted by maps or legal descriptions would be able to answer the question "Why Rhode Island?" In some cases the initial decisions as to what land should constitute which states may have been arbitrary and even capricious, having been ultimately settled on the basis of such temporarily relevant or ephemeral considerations as local politics and family interests. More often than not, however, the states did have a rational identity, though their boundaries are no more "natural" than are local jurisdictional limits.

Much of the diversity that exists within the United States and which, for reasons of statistical convenience, is often described in reference to particular states, is regional in character and due to factors largely outside the unique attributes or control of a particular state.[12] We know, for instance, that the difference in per capita income between the South and the North is not wholly unique to particular states within each region. In 1967, per capita income ranged from $1,895 in Mississippi to $3,865 in Connecticut. Population density ranged from .5 persons per square mile in Alaska to 930 per square mile in New Jersey. And in 1960, 42 per cent of the people in Mississippi were black, compared with only .1 per cent in Vermont. These differences could be cited as evidence of the diversity of the states. But we know that the Plains constitute a sparsely populated region; that more blacks live in the South than in upper New England; that many more people are crammed into a smaller

[11]This subsection is an elaboration of points made in Richard I. Hofferbert and Ira Sharkansky, eds., *State and Urban Politics* (Boston: Little, Brown and Co., 1971), pp. 1-9.

[12]See Ira Sharkansky's *Regionalism in American Politics* (Indianapolis: Bobbs-Merrill, 1970).

space in the East than they are in the West. Such figures do not make a strong case for studying individual state politics, although they do point to the possibility for comparative analyses.[13]

A visual examination of individual states goes even further to bear out the regional nature of many of the significant social dimensions of the American polity and the lack of sociological sense in many state boundaries. Certainly an east-west drive across Kansas and Colorado does not reveal the state line. The rolling, sparsely populated cattle and wheat country rising from Topeka westward comes to an abrupt halt not at the Colorado line but at the foot of the Rocky Mountains—midway through Colorado. The differences in interaction patterns, social mores, and political beliefs within the past and present mining centers of the western slope of Colorado —towns like Steamboat Springs, Leadville, and Rifle—contrast sharply with the social patterns found in the semi-arid, irrigated communities of the southern and eastern parts of the state. The differences in life-style are strikingly revealed in the manner of dress, modes of speaking, forms of political discourse, and a host of other conspicuous behavioral traits.

A further example of the baffling social and economic composition of the states themselves would be seen by a traveler bisecting Indiana from the southeast to the northwest. He would be presented with a varied panorama closely approximating a miniature of the entire nation—rolling hills and marginal farmlands; the commercial-agricultural complex in and around Indianapolis; rich, flat prairies; and, finally, the large industrial-shipping center on the Lake Michigan shore.

A geological map of the United States would provide great insight into the politics of any region—without ever indicating state lines. The scenic beauty of the rocky fields of New England stands in stark contrast with the niggardliness of the land in yielding a livelihood. The impact of such natural phenomena on the lives of Americans and their politics, therefore, is readily apparent. We do not have to know anything at all about specific state or local politics to understand these phenomena.

[13]Even the South, which is so often referred to in the singular, is remarkably diverse internally, a point well made long ago by V. O. Key, Jr., in *Southern Politics* (New York: Alfred A. Knopf, 1949).

What is not readily apparent to the occasional traveler or the casual scholar, however, is the kind of diversity within regions that is due exclusively to the decision-making power of those participating in the state and local political systems. Many of the differences in the life-styles of people in the United States are due to the manipulative powers existing in the states as semi-autonomous, legal-political entities—that is, to their capacity to make public policy.

The impact upon individual lives of the states' continued existence as policy-making entities cannot be ignored. Nor can one ignore the impact of such legal and political entities upon behavior patterns, which are centrally relevant to understanding the functioning of the larger, national political system. The states are significant arenas for much of the meaningful political activity that takes place in this country. State political systems, for example, provide the recruitment base for the majority of national decision-makers. When congressmen contemplate the acceptability of national policy alternatives, they ask themselves, "How will this go over in X or Y?" X or Y are almost invariably states.

If we listen to much political oratory or consume the rhetoric of many journalistic critics, we may be led to believe that the American states have fallen on idle or evil days. Those on the right decry the demise of the states as arenas of self-government; those on the left bemoan the continued potency of the states as a barrier to the arrival of the New Jerusalem. To hear the complaints of many state political figures, the states have been denied their birthright; such constitutional protections of state "sovereignty" as the Tenth Amendment are but tattered shreds of once glorious instruments of liberty. The federal government has so completely entered jurisdictional fields formerly reserved to the states that the latter have been left no significant functions. On the other hand, impatient critics of state sovereignty point to the power of states as a hindrance to progress. Their role is seen as one of obstruction, of inhibition, and of personal exploitation of public substance.

It is not necessary to defend or to attack state political systems in order to appreciate and measure their relevance as policy-making entities. Differences in policies from one state to another are also measures of the importance of state political systems. And because of the consequentiality of state and local political systems as producers of policy, they have captivated the attention of an increasing number of policy analysts. Even a cursory glance at the range of involvement of state and local governments in social life reveals why this has happened.

When the "typical American" is born, he enters a life intimately and extensively affected by state governmental actions, laws, and processes. His entry into the world is with the aid of a doctor licensed by the state, assisted by a nurse certified by the state, in a hospital inspected by the state. The milk in his bottle has been processed in accordance with state regulations, and, in many cases, sold at a price closely controlled by state law. In the normal course of events, this typical American enters a public school, which is supported by state funds, staffed by teachers licensed by the state—and probably educated at a state university or college—and operated by a local school board in accordance with state regulations and under the direction of the state board of education.

If this "typical American" becomes ill, he will buy his medicine from the corner druggist who holds a license from the state. Should his illness be psychosomatic or a manifestation of deep-seated psychic irregularities requiring the facilities of a mental institution, the chances are high that he will enter a state-owned or assisted facility.

Everything done by the "typical American's" town, county, city, township, school district, fire department, planning commission, police force, zoning board, and cemetery authority is subject to state law. The very existence of local governmental units and the actions taken by them are at the sufferance of the states within which they are located.

The assassination of a president is a violation of a *state* law; the assassin is prosecuted in *state* courts. The man who complains that the federal social-security program or minimum-wage laws are denials of his "freedom" ought to reflect for a moment upon the tyranny wrought upon him by local government. In most communities, he is prohibited from building a garage or installing a wall socket without permission from a body authorized by the state. He can be required by other local government authorities to remove a billboard or the family privy, regardless of their sentimental value or the "privateness" of his property.

For a number of reasons—most of them pertaining to international conflicts—greater public attention seems to have been given in recent years to innovations in governmental programs at the national level. But the innovative role of the states has not yet been eliminated. One of the standard defenses of the federal system has been the usefulness of the states as laboratories for public policies. Of course, most politicians who have complained vociferously about the abrogation of "states' rights" have been the least prone to innovate at home.

While glaring examples can be cited of states refusing to use their resources to meet some of the most pressing needs of their citizens, other, and sometimes more dramatic, examples exist of states providing models and valuable experiments in new areas of public policy—to the ultimate benefit of their own citizens, their fellow states, and the federal government. The entire structure of primary, secondary, and—outside the East—most higher education in this country has been erected either through direct state action or through local initiatives deliberately allowed and encouraged by the states. Without question, the hand of the federal government has been felt in higher education, particularly through the land-grant college program established in 1862. Educational variations between states, however, are more than ample evidence of the continued potency of subnational decisions.

Numerous states passed civil-rights laws long before the federal government got into the act seriously during the 1950s and 1960s. Women had the right to vote in many states before it was guaranteed them by the national Constitution. Minimum wages were set, hours regulated, working conditions supervised by many states long before the Supreme Court decided it was cricket for the national government to pass labor regulations, too. Louisiana has had a program of widespread public medical assistance for more than three decades—preceding by a generation comparable national programs. In 1965 Massachusetts moved well ahead of other states and the federal government in passing legislation designed to alleviate racial imbalance in the public schools.

Perennially, the two most significant functions of the states, at least in terms of dollars spent, have related to highways and education. To be sure, federal involvement in both roads and schools has been growing in recent years. Yet the rate of federal expansion hardly challenges the pre-eminent position of the states and their local dependencies. Figures on the state and local share of expenditures in certain major areas of public policy are instructive: in 1969, of the more than $50 billion spent for education, funds raised by state and local governments accounted for 85 per cent of the total; for highways, the percentage was 70; for health and hospitals, 67; for public welfare, 40 per cent.[14] In all instances, the percentages exclude federal grants to the state and local governments. In earlier years, the state and local share was even bigger.

While the financial mix varies, therefore, from one policy area to another, the states and their local governments, for all intents and purposes, have footed the bulk of the bill for the "welfare state" as we know it in America. Admittedly, a hefty federal nudge has occurred here and there in the process. Even so, the overall rate of expansion of state and local spending compared with federal domestic expenditures has been substantially greater since World War II. Total domestic expenditures—excluding defense and international spending —increased between 1946 and 1964 from $29 billion to $149 billion, or 414 per cent. The federal share increased from $16 billion to $74 billion, or 363 per cent. In the same period, state and local spending increased from $13 billion to $75 billion, or 477 per cent. When one considers further that a major portion of the federal domestic spending is channeled through the states and appropriated to specific functions by them, an excuse for ringing the death knell on the heirs of the American colonies is hardly creditable.

The impact of the states as policy-making entities upon individual life-styles also cannot be ignored. Nor can one ignore the impact of their status as policy-producers upon behavior patterns that are of central relevance to understanding the functioning of the larger, national system. The states are significant arenas for much of the consequential political activity that takes place in the United States.

In many significant ways the inhabitants of Newark and of New York City have more common problems than the people of Ithaca and the Bronx; nevertheless, separate statehood has major implica-

---

[14]These points are elaborated in Hofferbert and Sharkansky, *State and Urban Politics*, pp. 1-8.

tions for the manner in which solutions to these problems are conceived. Newarkites look to Trenton and New Yorkers look to Albany
for answers to the difficulties that surpass the capabilities of their
cities. They each pay different taxes and enjoy preferential tuition
rates at their respective state-assisted universities and colleges. And
they each pay different prices for gasoline, cigarettes, and gin because
of state-enacted policies. The accident of birth on one side or the other
of a state line can also make a tremendous difference in the quality of
education a child receives, in the size of an unemployment check,
and in the care of the mentally ill—whether they are incarcerated in
a custodial institution or receive expert remedial treatment in a technically sophisticated community mental-health center. It used to make
the difference of life or death in the event of conviction for certain
severe crimes.

And without reference to the policy-making powers and actions
of the several states, what student of American politics—surveying
it from the time the first black slaves arrived in 1619 to the present—
could possibly explain the single most important dimension of our
domestic conflict: the problem of accommodating large numbers of
whites and blacks within a single society? What but the independent
policy-making power of the states could explain the fact that ten
years after *Brown* v. *Board of Education* only .03 per cent of the
black children in Alabama were in schools with whites; for Mississippi
the figure was even lower. What but separate state decisional auton-
omy could explain the average monthly payment of $54 per depen-
dent child in New York compared with $7 in Mississippi?

Regionally unique differences do not sufficiently explain these
disparities. In a host of interesting ways, geographically contiguous
states have adopted policies that differ radically from one another and
yet touch the roots of social organization. Such differences in public
policy have a distinctive impact upon the way of life of each state's
inhabitants. This being the case, political scientists would be remiss if
they ignored the vital middle of the American political system—the
states. Fortunately, they have not done so.

Much of the variance in American public policy results from
the operation of a federal system. But the federal system has itself
been changing. Much of the initiative and a good deal of the direct
support for the expanded relevance of public policy in our lives is

because of changes in the role played by the federal government. And one reason for these changes is the Great Depression; it practically bankrupted local governments.

Changing Roles in the Federal System

Of all the levels of government, local governments were the most severely affected by the Depression, partly because of their heavy reliance upon local property taxes. In a nation with widespread property ownership, a general devaluation of property dramatically and quickly influences the revenue of governments relying mainly upon it as their tax base. State and federal governments have traditionally exploited somewhat more resilient tax sources. During the Depression, many states adopted retail sales or personal income taxes, or both. Further, the higher the level of government—township, city, county, state, national—the greater the proportional debt capacity seemed to be of the particular governmental unit. Management of the monetary system and adjustment of fiscal policy in line with modern economic principles are almost exclusively the options of large central governments. By the thirties, industrialization and the development of a nationally integrated economy had removed virtually all remnants of local economic self-sufficiency. And self-sufficiency is accompanied by the possibility of utilizing the public treasury for purposes of effective economic management.

For these and other reasons, the greatest result of the Depression was to undercut—for all time, it would seem—the pre-eminence of local governments in the field of American public spending. We must conclude, therefore, that a substantial readjustment has taken place in the level of government responsible for spending the public's money. Figure I-2 illustrates this development. It portrays the percentage of total domestic spending for each level of government from 1902 to 1970.

As these data show, the events and circumstances of the Depression had a definite, centralizing effect upon governmental activity in the United States. This development could not have been fully predicted on the basis of trends in earlier years. Between 1902 and 1927 we do see some indication of an increase in the share of domestic dollars spent by the states and by the federal government.

Figure I-2

PERCENTAGE OF DOMESTIC EXPENDITURES BY LEVEL OF GOVERNMENT: 1902-1970

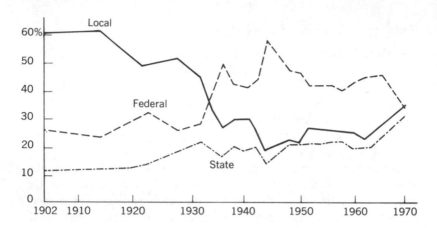

SOURCE: U.S. Bureau of the Census, *Statistical Abstract of the United States* (Washington, D.C., U.S. Government Printing Office, various years).

But the plunge taken by local governments during the Depression changed the distribution of responsibilities within the federal system. Nevertheless, some common assumptions may have to be amended by the historical facts.

Patterns of Centralization

It might be assumed that events of national consequence, such as the Depression and World War II, coupled with the nationalization of the economy and the increasing interdependence of life-styles, would bring in their wake across-the-board centralization of governmental activities. That is, we might have expected the processes of centralization to be evident at all levels—the local governments' share of the public treasury dropping in favor of states'; the states' share dropping in favor of the federal government's. Figure I-2 supports the former statement, but not the latter. The vitality of the states in the federal system appears to have a high degree of persistence. The big losers in the competition for the management of public services—to the extent that this competition is indicated by expenditures—have been local governments, although recent data show they are holding their own for the present. Far from merely maintaining their relative position, the states have actually increased their share of the treasury. The long-term decline in the local share of domestic spending has not been made up by increased federal activities. Rather, the local "loss" has been accommodated by equal rates of expansion in both state and federal spending. The percentage of domestic expenditures by local governments dropped between 1902 and 1970 from 61 pr cent of 35 per cent. The federal percentage rose from 27 to 34.1. Likewise the state share more than doubled, increasing from 12 per cent to 31.9. The political effects of the Depression then, were felt in terms of redistribution upward of governmental responsibilities —from local to both state and federal. And the states were scarcely the losers in the bargain.[15]

Between 1932 and 1936, federal domestic spending jumped from $3.5 billion to $8.2 billion, an increase of more than 134 per cent. This rate of increase is unmatched in any previous four-year period for any level of government, in the aggregate. In these four years, the federal share of all domestic spending rose from 30 per cent to 52 per cent. Considered in the light of later history, the increase, which illustrates a shift in governmental responsibilities, was minor. But viewed in terms of the perceptions and actions of specific policy-makers in Washington, it warrants singling out as a substantial departure from earlier patterns. The same might be said for particular state decision-makers; their actions in many specific instances, which are not revealed by the aggregate figures, were comparable to the federal model. And, in reverse fashion, the unavoidable decisions to cut buck services at the local level must be viewed as monumental for the particular people involved.

---

[15]The specific long-term effects of the Depression, even on federal-level activities alone, has been devalued by the economic historian Slade Kendrick. Kendrick calculates the amount of "Depression induced" federal spending. While such activity accounts for an average of 36.2 per cent of federal spending between 1930 and 1941, it is responsible for only 5.5 per cent from 1942 to 1951. M. Slade Kendrick, *A Century and a Half of Federal Expenditures* (New York: National Bureau of Economic Research, 1955), pp. 32-33.

The most significant changes wrought by the Depression, therefore, are not seen in the level of public spending, but rather in the
level of government doing the spending. A considerable shift took
place in the management of public services from the municipal governments to the state and federal governments. This movement of
the decision-making process from lower to higher governmental levels
brought with it pressures for standardization. And centralization
means bureaucratization. Bureaucratization implies depersonalization.
Hierarchy erodes localism, parochialism, and the community. Re-
adjustments of this type cause qualitative changes in kind as well as
degree.

While the states have more than held their own in the sharing
of public-policy activity, we must not minimize the impact on the
states of the federal government's larger role in public spending.
The federal government has gained in importance not only as a
funding agency, but also as a definer and stimulator of common
policy activities within and between the states. States often enter
programs because of the temptation of federal matching funds. No
other form of investment promises such high interest in states' funds.
And in these programs, the federal authorities define general standards, promote administrative models, and establish centralized program goals. The goals, of course, are no small task for policy-
makers contemplating the allocation of scarce revenues. Thus the
actual centralization, in terms of standards and programs, may be
far greater than apparent from the simple picture painted by spending records.

The movement toward centrally defined goals and methods,
however, is partly counterbalanced by the fact that much of the
money placed in the federal column in the preceding analysis is
allocated and spent by and through state or local policy-making
machinery. This distribution of federal funds provides the opportunity
for a broad variation in the final content of ostensibly national service activities. A brief examination of state welfare practices, for
instance, would amply substantiate this variation. V. O. Key, Jr., summarized the general pattern several years ago: "Along with the
growth in the scale of its operations, the state has come to occupy
a new and pivotal administrative and fiscal position in the govern-

mental structure."[16] After discussing both the channeling of federally collected funds through the states and state collected funds through local governments, Key observed further: "The seeds for the conversion of the states into governments that spend money they do not raise and raise money they do not spend existed . . . even in 1920. Yet the change since that time has been so great as to be one of kind rather than of degree."[17]

Expenditure patterns are not the only clues to the changed role of the national government. We find more and more instances in which services are being provided in direct response to articulated demands of highly motivated groups and in which policy-makers are seeking out widespread but organized interests. "Truth-in-lending" laws are designed to protect the gullible or careless borrower. Federal control over the wholesomeness of meat—whether or not it is sold in interstate commerce—is being established. While promise has greatly exceeded performance, concern about the quality of life for succeeding generations has found expression in federal antipollution and conservation legislation.

In the kinds of policies represented by these examples, we find a difference—qualitative and in degree only, to be sure—from the regulatory and service policies nationalized during the New Deal. The extension of governmental influence, and consequently the social relevance of public-policy formation, has reached nearly every facet of individual and collective life.

Conclusion

Policy is made in a variety of contexts. Different contexts produce different policies. As the preceding discussion demonstrates, the level of government is one critical contextual variant for policy activity. So is the national economic context. Changes in the level of government responsible for certain tasks or changes in the overall economic climate lead to variations in policies produced. These variations are

[16]V. O. Key, Jr., *American State Politics: An Introduction* (New York: Alfred A. Knopf, 1956), p. 7.
[17]Ibid.

amenable to explanation by social scientists. Given the directions taken by public policy-makers in the past generation or so, it is not surprising that scholarly interest has grown in the processes and substance of public policy. But as yet no clear theory or methodology for the study of policy has evolved. Some comparative studies have begun to link up with a few strands of social theory, but the bulk of policy-related research follows either the older, institutional approach or the case-study approach.

This is not to say that the institutional or the case-study approaches cannot yield valuable insights into the policy process. They can, as the next two chapters will illustrate. Chapters II and III examine the study of political actors from several perspectives. Most political scientists still think of themselves as specialists in either an area of the world, a particular set of institutionally defined actors—legislators, executives, judges—or specific types of politically relevant action —voting, political socialization. All these elements can be examined in terms of how they affect policy or how policy affects them. But for our purposes it is the study of actors within certain institutional or areal boundaries that produces the most interesting questions and findings. Formal, legal settings are a relevant context for policy activity. Chapter II, therefore, discusses studies of legislators, executives, judges, and community leaders. Community leaders as policy-makers are a special branch of the study, but for reasons to be presented later, they fit well within the other studies focusing on actors in the policy process.

chapter II
The Behavior
of Policy-Makers

Who Makes Policy?

Deciding who makes policy is almost as difficult as defining "policy" itself. In the history of political science the question, "What determines policy?" has not often been asked exactly that way; scholars' questions about the policy process, as I indicated in the previous chapter, have had a different cast to them. The policy process is most often personified in the form of visible actors doing things that look like policy-making. The actors in the process are identified by their institutional context, and the questions become: "What is the job of president?" "What makes legislators—or judges or bureaucrats or lobbyists—act the way they do?" "Who has power?" "Who makes the decisions of public consequence?" These are the questions that have been systematically investigated.

Questions about the holders of formal offices—as well as their associates in the policy process, such as lobbyists—are relevant to the study of policy only if we can assume or demonstrate that certain of these officeholders are important in making policy. Students of policy-making usually begin where the traces of the policy-making process are clearest—around legislators, executives, and other holders of formal office. Studying their relationship to policies finally enacted may indicate what affects policy. Though the original researchers of the policy process may not have been concerned with the question of what affects policy, we can try to extract an answer from their material. With these studies as a starting point, we can attempt to determine the extent of involvement of governmental personnel, the influence and effect of nongovernmental persons and groups, and the impact of the socioeconomic environment on the policy process.

We must not assume too much, however, in reviewing these studies. Many people and situations outside formal offices influence policies. Private citizens express their grievances in many visible ways that are important to those who work full time at shaping policy. Some private citizens are more influential than others, and one of the things that has intrigued—and often frustrated—political scientists has been the job of figuring out how people outside the halls of government make their mark on the policies with which we all must live. Nongovernmental influence is brought to bear in a multitude of ways: through the organizational solidarity of interest groups; through the ballot box; through money; through the demonstration of expertise; through riots. The variety of influences upon the policy process makes it difficult to identify extragovernmental influence. And in a nation that considers itself more or less "democratic," questions of extragovernmental pressures have naturally captivated many students of politics. The answers these students have put forth have generated more than a little controversy.

The controversy over the roots and forms of nongovernmental political involvement, over just how relevant to policy much nongovernmental involvement is, has been conditioned in no small way by ideological commitments. This ideological component is not easy to dispel. Much of the political argument in contemporary society, both scholarly and otherwise, is over how we can honestly assert that we have a government of the people and by the people.[1]

[1] Yehezkel Dror, in an intriguing table labeled "An Integrated Evaluation of Public Policymaking in Modern Democratic Countries," evaluates several aspects of the roles played by eleven categories of participants in the policy process. He includes private individuals, intellectuals, political leaders, legislative bodies, political executives, civil servants, courts, parties, universities, interest groups, and "other relevant units: special thinking units, e.g., RAND

Given the nature of the research upon which we must draw, it makes sense to begin by looking at studies of those people located fairly clearly within the formal governmental context—the people making the most distinct tracks on the policy-process path. Later, I shall discuss a rather impressive body of research that seeks to assess the relative importance of formal governmental officeholders versus nongovernmental elites in the policy process.

The traditional objects of concern in American political science are nowhere more apparent than in the study of public officeholders. Patterns of inquiry have evolved from the analysis of legal texts and philosophic pronouncements to the fairly systematic observation and cataloging of actions and attitudes of real people. But the "scientific" stance—the theoretical underpinning—is not as dissimilar from former days as some modern researchers might want us to believe. Every high-school student is taught that "we have a system of separated powers, with constitutional checks and balances." Montesquieu's theory of the separation of powers has been a standard starting point for political analysis. It is a rare university catalog that does not find a prominent listing for courses on "The Presidency," "The Congress," and "Constitutional Law." Texts on state and local politics seldom veer from a similar list. Montesquieu would be proud.

A mode of inquiry is not intrinsically wrong simply because it is old. But I would argue that the types of questions being asked today by, for example, students of Congress, are not basically different from those asked in 1885 by Woodrow Wilson in *Congressional Government*. Current inquiry often falls short of the theoretical breadth urged by Lord Bryce in his *American Commonwealth*.[2] But modern statistical techniques of inquiry are more reliable and far more impressive than the tools used in the nineteenth century. We can now begin to know what we formerly suspected. We have swept out a few misconceptions. Yet the intellectual stance is still roughly the same. Most students of legislatures, executives, or other governmental actors want to know what affects the actors—not primarily

---

and planning bodies." See his *Public Policymaking Reexamined* (San Francisco: Chandler Publishing Co., 1968), Appendix A, Table I.

[2]James B. Bryce, *American Commonwealth,* 3 vols. (New York: AMS Press, Inc., 1888).

what the actors affect. Contemporary research, however, offers occasional answers to questions about the products of the system and why these products are as they are.

Certainly the most imposing and impressive body of studies of public officers is that which deals with legislative behavior.

Legislators and Public Policy[3]

Of all the "official" contexts within which political actors act, the legislature has come under the closest scrutiny.[4] Several reasons account for the popularity of legislative studies among political scientists. One is the accessibility of legislatures for observation and analysis; few scholars are located beyond driving distance of a statehouse. And legislators, being less pressed than executives by the immediacy of daily events, are often willing to talk about their jobs. One further reason for the popularity of legislative research is the public nature and significance of legislative deliberation. Most major issues of public policy come before the legislature, and when they do it is often the only visible official arena for joining the various forces involved in the process of policy initiation and formation. This is not to say that legislatures count for more than other governmental

[3]Several ably written bibliographic and review essays concerning legislative-behavior research have been published in recent years. I would especially recommend Heinz Eulau and Katherine Hinckley, "Legislative Institutions and Processes," in *Political Science Annual*, vol. I, ed. James A. Robinson (Indianapolis: Bobbs-Merrill, 1966), pp. 85-189. See also Malcolm Jewell's *The State Legislature: Politics and Practice*, rev. ed. (New York: Random House, 1969); John C. Wahlke, "Behavioral Analysis of Representative Bodies," in *Essays on the Behavioral Study of Politics*, ed. Austin Ranney (Urbana: University of Illinois Press, 1962); Thomas R. Dye, "State Legislative Politics," in *Politics in the American States*, ed. Herbert Jacob and Kenneth N. Vines (Boston: Little, Brown and Co., 1961); William J. Keefe and Morris S. Ogul, *The American Legislative Process* (Englewood Cliffs, N. J.: Prentice-Hall, 1964); and Malcolm E. Jewell and Samuel C. Patterson, *The Legislative Process in the United States* (New York: Random House, 1966).

[4]A selected bibliography on state legislatures published in 1968 lists 844 articles and books. This concerns only *state* legislatures and excludes studies of foreign legislatures or the United States Congress. Citizens Conference on State Legislatures, *Selected Bibliography on State Legislatures* (Kansas City, 1966).

entities. Congress started neither racial integration of the schools nor the war in Vietnam. But few if any highly controversial proposals for new policies or changes in old policies are resolved without some public exposure of conflicting positions in the legislative context. This public exposure, of course, follows from and reinforces the traditional democratic theory's preoccupation with the nature of representation and the role of the representative as an instrument of popular control.

Political scientists would be less than candid, however, if they were not willing to admit that one reason for studying legislatures and legislators is their amenability to sophisticated techniques of social scientific inquiry. This opportunity helps explain why many of the legislative studies in the American context have focused upon state legislatures.

Although I have argued in the last chapter that the states are a highly significant and consequential part of the general policy-making structure of American government, that fact alone is insufficient to justify the amount of attention political scientists have given to state legislatures. Rather, their attention has centered upon state legislatures, as opposed to the national Congress, not only because of the access they enjoy, but because it is possible to conduct various types of comparative inquiries in state legislatures. There are fifty state legislatures and infinite subsets of data pertaining to them that can be examined by scholars. But there is only one Congress. Firm generalizations about the contexts of a set of data are not easy to make when the set has only one member. But with state legislatures, comparisons can be made between one- and two-party legislatures, between legislatures in highly industrialized and in primarily agrarian polities, between large and small legislatures, between highly professionalized and amateur legislatures, and between strongly led and pluralistic legislatures. Where comparative analysis is practical, both the range of possible questions and the reliability of findings are substantially greater than when one is conducting what is, at best, an elaborate case study.

Part of the problem in conducting a systematic analysis of congressional behavior can be overcome by looking at similar activities in the past. When this long-range view has been applied, however, the results indicate that the changed external circumstances in which the different Congresses met were so consequential that they made controlled observation impossible.[5] Hence, even careful attempts at moving beyond simple descriptions of idiosyncratic events and personal factors do little more than demonstrate their complexity. These difficulties nearly preclude testing of general hypotheses.

Difficulties also exist in the context of comparative state legislative analysis. The costs and problems of inquiry, for example, have prevented comparative analysis of more than a handful of legislative situations in a limited time perspective.[6] Many of the problems of relating legislative analysis to the policy process, however, do not concern techniques or costs of research. They have to do with the theoretical orientation of the research itself. Discussions of the policy role of the legislature tend to be either procedural or behavioral. Procedurally, we have such statements as "The legislature reviews the budget," "The Senate confirms appointments," "The committees oversee administrative practices."[7] Behavioral studies ask why legislators act the way they do.

Procedural Studies

Many of what I am calling "procedural studies" are decidedly reformist in tone and intent. Legislatures, especially state legislatures, have come in for their share of harsh criticism. A number of concerned observers blame legislative procedures and organization for the apparent inability of the political system, at whatever level, to solve our major social ills.

Many contemporary critics see the operation of the legislature as inextricably tied to the nature of the American party system. Their

[5]Leroy N. Rieselbach, "The Demography of the Congressional Vote on Foreign Aid," *American Political Science Review* 58 (1964): 577-588.

[6]See, for example, David R. Derge, "Metropolitan and Outstate Alignments in the Illinois and Missouri Legislative Delegations," *American Political Science Review* 52 (1958): 1052-1065; William J. Keefe, "Comparative Study of the Role of Political Parties in State Legislatures," *Western Political Quarterly* 9 (1956): 726-742. See as a noteworthy exception, however, Wayne L. Francis, *Legislative Issues in the Fifty States* (Chicago: Rand McNally, 1967).

[7]For example, see Jewell, *State Legislature,* pp. 125-128; or, despite the section title "Legislative Outputs: Consequences," most of the items cited by Eulau and Hinckley, "Legislative Institutions," pp. 170-179.

criticisms emanate from a theory of popular government that posits certain central relationships.[8] This theory is an amalgam of elements extracted from British parliamentary practice and idealizations of American experience. It views the political process as a confrontation of men and programs before an articulate, active electorate. Candidates, clearly labeled by the programs they approve, stand for office. Institutional arrangements are such that all possible alternative programs and men subscribing thereto are reduced to two— symbolized by their respective party labels. These alternatives — and they must be discernibly different—are presented for review and preview by an electorate able and motivated to choose between them. After the election, formal and personal behaviors are so structured that the policy projections of the winners are enacted into law and administered as promised. Those men whose programs fail to gain majority approval from the electorate retain a conspicuous place in the system and wait in the hope that the voters will subsequently choose their alternative, or its future refinements, in the next election. The exercise of electoral choice at one point in time does not thereby preclude a change of mind or a choice of a new alternative at a future date.

Although the "responsible two-party system" approach, as this theoretical stance is usually termed,[9] is by no means universally accepted as valid for American practice, the lines of argument it sets forth have tended to structure a good deal of the inquiry into legislative behavior. This is especially true of what I am here calling "procedural" studies. The concern of even the most objective students of legislative practice has been directed, by the thrust of the responsi-

[8]One of the most articulate examples of this approach, with respect to Congress, is James MacGregor Burns' *The Deadlock of Democracy* (Englewood Cliffs, N. J.: Prentice-Hall, 1963), especially chap. 14. At the state level, see works by V. O. Key, Jr., especially his *American State Politics: An Introduction* (New York: Alfred A. Knopf, 1956). See also E. E. Schattschneider, *The Semi-Sovereign People* (New York: Holt, Rinehart and Winston, 1960); Jewell, *State Legislature;* and Joseph S. Clark, ed., *Congressional Reform: Problems and Prospects* (New York: Thomas Y. Crowell, 1965).

[9]In recognition of the Report of the Committee on Political Parties of the American Political Science Association, "Toward a More Responsible Two-Party System" (special supplement to *American Political Science Review,* September, 1950).

ble-parties argument, to investigate at great length the role and functions of parties in the operation of legislatures and the attitudes of their members.[10]

The aspect of American legislative practices most disturbing to the proponents of more responsible parties is the fragmentation of leadership in the policy process. Policy planning and coordination between executive and legislature are seen as collaborative at best but more often as competitive. Instead of unified policy formation, the proponents of more responsible parties view the legislature and the executive—at both the state and national levels—as serving dissimilar constituencies. Presidents and governors are elected by the nation or a particular state; congressmen and legislators are elected by districts. Cooperation among branches rests on compromise and bargaining rather than upon "leadership" and "rational" rules of decision-making.

Within the legislatures, especially in the U.S. Congress, further devolution and fragmentation occurs through the committee system and the seniority rule.[11] Each committee has a virtual veto and a constrictive hold on policy initiative in its own substantive jurisdiction. And the rules of committee membership and authority offer no guarantee of representation for interests affected by policies over which it has authority.

A more potent party system, presumably, would provide the coordinating muscle to overcome these impulses toward the atomizing of policy-making authority. At the state level, staggered timing of elections and the direct primary serve to reduce the chances for party potency and unity between branches of the government and

---

[10]See, for example, David Truman, *The Congressional Party* (New York: John Wiley and Sons, 1959); Duncan MacRae, Jr., "The Relation Between Roll-Call Votes and Constituencies in the Massachusetts House of Representatives," *American Political Science Review* 44 (1952): 1046-1055; Thomas R. Dye, "A Comparison of Constituency Influences in the Upper and Lower Chambers of a State Legislature," *Western Political Quarterly* 14 (1961): 473-480; Samuel C. Patterson, "The Role of the Deviant in the State Legislative System: The Wisconsin Assembly," *Western Political Quarterly* 14 (1961): 460-472.

[11]"Congressional politics is committee politics," states one student of the subject. See James A. Robinson, *The House Rules Committee* (Indianapolis: Bobbs-Merrill, 1963), quoted by Eulau and Hinckley, "Legislative Institutions," p. 93.

among members of the legislature.[12] At the national level James McGregor Burns' recommendations are fairly typical of the procedural reforms designed to invigorate the two-party system and thereby superimpose over the scattered centers of authority a common bond and a center of interdependence. His recommendations include: a system of national election laws; development of formal membership parties at the local level; ballot reorganization to place candidates for president, Senate, and House of Representatives together; internal congressional reform—for example, committee assignments by leadership appointment instead of seniority; centralization of party finances; and invigoration of the national opposition party.[13] With a number of similar reforms, it is projected that the parties would become the focal points of policy formation. Instead of a system of pluralistic accommodation, whereby certain partial interests exercise a specialized veto, policy-making would be truly nationalized. Programs aimed at solving national problems, such as federal assistance to inner-city schools, would not be subject to emasculation by congressional spokesmen for small, contrary interests.

A serious problem with the procedural criticisms of legislative practices lies in the central concepts of the underlying theory. What is "responsibility" or "the national interest" or "rational policy formation"? These concepts tend to be used either as disguises for individual policy preferences or as surrogates for "centralized leadership." We may laud the policy goals, but decry the state of our intelligence. An enduring liberal tradition holds to the premise that centralized leadership will be "in the public interest." Parochial fiefdoms, such as congressional committees or malapportioned legislatures, will be overridden and liberal policies enacted if the proper tools are given to chief executives. If one defines such terms as "responsibilities" and "national interest" procedurally as activity stemming from centralized authority, the argument is circular. Rational policies are those formed by centralized leadership. We do not have such a leadership structure; therefore, we do not have the formation of rational policy.

[12]Key, *American State Politics,* chap. 3.
[13]Burns, *Deadlock of Democracy,* pp. 327ff.

Propositions of this type do not lend themselves to scientific testing. In any contest it is tempting to consider changing the rules when the outcome is not to one's liking. And the substance of such recommendations for change will be guided by one's conception of what makes the contest—that is, by one's theory about it. In the absence of demonstrations to prove the soundness of conceptions, however, recommendations for change cannot pass as the results of scientific inquiry. When careful observations reveal facts and relationships that contradict a scientific theory, the scientist questions his theory; he does not condemn the facts or the circumstances that generated it. When a nonscientific but morally sensitive man sees facts of which he disapproves, he sets out to correct them and to prevent their recurrence; he is at a distinct disadvantage by his own standards, though, if his conceptions are poorly informed regarding the generative forces behind those facts to which he objects. And, unfortunately, for all of the discussion about legislative procedures, very little research has thus far posed the questions: "What difference does it make for policy that there are differences in procedures?" "Does centralized leadership produce policies that are different from those proposed by fragmented leadership?" To answer the second question, different leadership situations and the policies produced by them must be examined. Later chapters will review some preliminary studies that have tried to tackle the problems of policy procedure in this way; their admittedly fragile findings do not support the expectation of dramatic changes in policy from procedural reforms.

Behavioral Studies

Although some theoretical similarity exists between the procedural and behavioral studies, the latter have tended to be less reform oriented and designed more for the purpose of yielding empirical explanations of legislative activity. None of the techniques of inquiry used by students of legislative behavior is without flaws, but taken together the techniques represent a major increment in social-scientific knowledge. Attitude tests and carefully constructed questionnaires have been administered to hundreds of legislators and congressmen. The roll-call vote—taken as a publicly visible statement of preference at a central stage of the policy process—

has been studied with highly complex statistical techniques, and much has been written about the technology of roll-call vote analysis.[14] Coupled with studies that match the socioeconomic and political characteristics of a legislator's constituency with his roll-call votes, an impressive body of systematic inquiry is available.

In their comprehensive review of studies in the field, Eulau and Hinckley have divided legislative studies into those following "inside" and "outside" models. Both are potentially relevant to the policy process. The inside model examines such factors as committee structure, leadership patterns, and voting blocs as they determine the rules of intralegislative behavior. From a policy standpoint, we would want to know how these variables shape and mold the policy preferences of legislators and how these preferences structure the products of legislative activity. The outside model examines the relationships between extralegislative forces—constituency claims, interest-group activity, gubernatorial and administrative pressure, party influence, and so forth—upon the legislators' perceptions and actions. This line of analysis is most likely to place the legislature in an environmental context. And policies are presumably designed in response to and to influence the social context within which the legislature operates.

Adopting for the moment the inside model, what are some of the intra-institutional matters that affect legislative behavior? When the typical citizen thinks of his legislature, he conjures up an image of dozens or hundreds of men, usually in a semicircle, facing a raised podium, and volubly discussing affairs of state. We know, however, that the down-to-earth business of legislative bodies is normally conducted in much smaller, face-to-face meetings. Committees and informal groups of voluntarily affiliated people tend to structure the activity of the whole body in such a way that the publicly conspicuous

[14]See the discussion and citations in Duncan MacRae, Jr., "A Method for Identifying Issues and Factions from Legislative Votes," *American Political Science Review 59* (1965); 909-926. In order to help meet the needs of scholars utilizing roll-call votes in various types of research, the Inter-university Consortium for Political Research (Ann Arbor, Michigan) has compiled in machine-readable form all the roll-call votes of the United States Congress from 1790 to the present. The ICPR also maintains a current file of all United Nations roll-call votes.

activity on the floor of the legislature is but a crude index of the entire legislative process. Many students of legislatures, cognizant of the decentralized nature of the process, have adopted the research stance used in other social sciences to study small groups.[15]

The formal organization of legislatures has directed many scholars to study the effects of committee membership, leadership influence, and, in the U.S. Congress, state delegations.[16] The most consequential internal determinants of patterns of legislator behavior appear to be informal norms of conduct. Richard Fenno, Jr., for example, has elaborated several such norms for members of the House Appropriations Committee.[17] He found that committee members are expected to specialize in particular policy areas, to cooperate and support the committee's recommendations on the floor, to reciprocate favors from nonmembers, and to act without undue partisanship. None of these rules is written, but all are familiar guiding principles heeded by the committee members.

Donald Matthews' study of the U.S. Senate revealed similar "folkways."[18] New senators are expected to serve an apprenticeship —to work hard and to speak rarely. They are expected to specialize in one or two policy areas and to avoid dilettantism. Courtesy to one's colleagues is demanded, regardless of party or policy differences. And, finally, senators are expected to be absolutely loyal to the Senate as an institution. Samuel Patterson observes similar informal rules at the state level.[19]

All these studies tell us a good deal about the demeanor of our various legislative bodies. They offer considerable insight into what

---

[15]See, for example, Richard F. Fenno, Jr., *The Power of the Purse: Appropriations Politics in Congress* (Boston: Little, Brown and Co., 1966).

[16]See Eulau and Hinckley's summary and critique, "Legislative Institutions," pp. 88-114.

[17]Fenno, *Power of the Purse*.

[18]Donald R. Matthews, "The Folkways of the United States Senate: Conformity to Group Norms and Legislative Effectiveness," *American Political Science Review* 53 (1959): 1064-1089. For a partial alternative and elaboration, see Ralph K. Huitt, "The Outsider in the Senate: An Alternative Role," *American Political Science Review* 55 (1961): 566-575.

[19]Patterson, "Role of the Deviant."

life inside them is like. But they tell us little about how policy would differ if informal norms were different. At best we can conclude that such norms have a conservatizing effect. They all tend to inhibit the innovator. They guard against rocking the boat. They reward accommodation and gradualism. But to be sure that this is their effect we ought to examine a number of legislatures with differing norms and compare these to the pattern of policy produced from different normatively ordered legislatures. Unfortunately, such research has not been done.

Most of the outside studies of legislative behavior have concentrated upon two aspects of the legislative environment: the impact of party and the impact of constituency. This attention to party and constituency is not surprising, given the theoretical heritage of American political science. Our tradition of popular control sparks an interest in the mechanisms by which popular preferences get translated into legislative action. The concern with more responsible parties—which reached its apex at the time when modern methods of legislative analysis were first being applied—links quite easily into a concern with the effects of party identification and organization upon legislative activity.

No single observable characteristic of legislative organization has been discovered that is more consequential than party membership. Any other means of classifying legislators finds less constant voting groups than party-membership blocs.[20] Lawyers seldom vote as a bloc.[21] Urban legislators rarely align against rural legislators, or rural representatives against their city colleagues.[22] This last finding is particularly surprising in view of the widespread distress over malapportionment, which for so long has characterized legislative districting in many states.

Some evidence has been obtained of the multiple effects of party and constituency in roll-call voting. Although party is the most im-

[20]Julius Turner, *Party and Constituency* (Baltimore: Johns Hopkins University Press, 1951).

[21]David R. Derge, "The Lawyer as Decision-Maker in the American State Legislature," *Journal of Politics* 21 (1959): 426-431.

[22]Derge, "Metropolitan and Outstate Alignments"; Robert S. Friedman, "The Urban-Rural Conflict Revisited," *Western Political Quarterly* 14 (1961): 481-495.

portant bond within the legislature, not all Democrats or Republicans always vote as their fellow partisans do. On those votes where party seems to be important—as measured by most Democrats opposing most Republicans—what accounts for defection? Duncan MacRae has found that the Massachusetts legislators most likely to desert their party are Democrats from "normally Republican" districts and Republicans from "usually Democratic" districts.[23] "Normality" is identified by the socioeconomic composition of the district, with Republican districts having a tendency to be better off economically. Representatives from politically atypical districts are more likely to deviate on party votes. MacRae also found that the chances of deviating are increased when the legislator won by a close vote. Thomas R. Dye discovered similar patterns of conformity and deviation in Pennsylvania's house of representatives, but not in its senate.[24]

Patterson took this line of inquiry one step further and studied the dimensions of conformity in the one-party Oklahoma legislature.[25] If party is the most salient dimension of legislative voting, what happens when party differences are virtually eliminated? Does some other axis exist around which reasonably stable alignments can be structured? Patterson's answer is no. To the extent that structures of voting blocs in Oklahoma can be uncovered at all, he determined that they are usually loose and adaptive:

> Where party organization or even stable factional alignments are not available to the legislator to refer to for voting standards, the patterns of voting in the legislature are likely to be compartmentalized. And, in the absence of party as a reference group, the legislator is likely, consciously or unconsciously, to respond to different pressures in different voting areas.[26]

The point of these and similar studies is to confirm the wisdom of a party theory of legislative behavior—with legislative behavior as a dependent variable.

[23]MacRae, "Relation Between Roll-Call Votes and Constituencies."
[24]Thomas R. Dye, "A Comparison of Constituency Influences," pp. 473-480.
[25]Samuel C. Patterson, "Dimensions of Voting in a One-Party State Legislature," *Public Opinion Quarterly* 26 (1962): 185-200.
[26]Ibid., p. 200.

So far as legislative behavior is concerned, we have an impressive list of generalizations. But, by and large, these generalizations concern the legislature as a self-contained entity. To the extent that external factors are examined at all, they are likely to be chosen on the basis of manifest relevance to legislative behavior rather than as alternative or independent components of the policy process. Gubernatorial behavior, for example, is studied by students of legislatures as an impact and constraint on legislators. Party is studied either as an internally operating cue system or as an external restraint through the electoral process within legislative constituencies. Socioeconomic characteristics are studied not as inputs in a total policy process but as constituency characteristics somehow reflected in intralegislative groups.

A clear indicator of the stance taken by students of legislative behavior is the manner in which they have treated unanimous roll-call votes. In nearly every study, the researcher has eliminated all unanimous votes and often those on which no more than, for example, 10 per cent dissented. If one is interested only in the behavior of legislative officeholders—that is, only in the internal operations of the legislature where the dependent variable is the behavior of the legislators themselves—then this procedure makes some sense. We will not discover anything by reviewing unanimous votes because variance is absent, and where no variance is registered comparative analysis is impossible. All the unanimous vote says is that the legislature was in agreement. To discover the issues over which there are consequential differences, attention must be concentrated on those over which behavior differs. This is a fairly elementary rule of scientific inquiry.

If our interest, however, is not exclusively in the behavior of legislators but rather in the relationship of the legislators and the legislature to the patterns, structure, and levels of public-policy activity, then the unanimous roll-call vote is a vital piece of information. To be sure, in the context of a single state unanimous votes, as just noted, tell us nothing because there is no variance. But if we were to construct a map of the variations in what is and what is not unanimously regarded between states, we would determine a great deal about the nature of the political culture, the policy consensus,

and perhaps the relevance of the legislature to the policy-making
process in the states.

Most political theorists and a great many people who have
studied comparative politics argue that no society can maintain its
structure of internal order without a substantial body of agreed-upon
principles of action. The term most often applied to these agreed-
upon principles of action is "consensus." What is the nature of the
consensus of a society? Many have struggled with this question, and
it would be useful to know the answer. Upon what do the policy-
makers of a particular civil system agree? I would hypothesize that
the issues upon which unanimous or nearly unanimous agreement
exists are not the same in all fifty states or in all the thousands of
city councils in this country or even, for that matter, from one
Congress to another. Quite the contrary. I would argue that what
constitutes a base of universal agreement in New York State is quite
different from what constitutes a base of universal agreement in
Iowa, Wyoming, or Arkansas. Further, that which constituted a base
of universal agreement in the Congress of 1945 or 1950 is substantially different from what constitutes the content of universal agreement in Congress today.

The elimination of unanimous roll-call votes from their behavioral analysis is a reflection of the position that has been taken
by students of legislatures. It illustrates graphically their concern
with the legislative act and the legislators' actions rather than with
the role of the legislator and legislature in the total policy-making
process.

A careful tabulation of tested or testable hypotheses from a
comprehensive review of state legislative studies produced twenty-
eight general hypotheses (ignoring for present purposes several minor
alterations that could be considered subhypotheses).[27] Of these
twenty-eight, one concerned the extent of legislative activity, five
related to the relative strength of governors versus legislatures, five
pertained to the geographic base of members, four referred to social
backgrounds and career patterns of legislators, eleven had to do

[27]This is my own computation based on a reading of Dye's "State Legislative
Politics."

with party control, and one dealt with the attitudes of legislators toward their job. Only one hypothesis concerned the policy consequences of differences between legislatures.

The findings of procedural and behavioral legislative studies are not necessarily consequential beyond the specicfic institutional setting. In an entire chapter entitled "Legislative Outputs," one of the foremost students of legislative behavior presents no evidence of how differences between legislatures lead to differences in the policies produced.[28] He suggests that with better apportionment, the legislatures will come to care more about cities, though he offers no hard evidence to test this prediction. He also suggests that increased federal participation in the affairs of our cities will further circumscribe the options open to state legislators, thereby further reducing their relevance in the policy process. Everybody knows the House of Lords does not figure in a mighty way in British policy-making— at least on those matters that count most. But the question is infrequently asked, and even more rarely studied carefully, with regard to American legislative bodies: Do legislatures have a noticeable impact on policy?

The point of my criticisms is not that inquiry into legislative behavior is meaningless. Legislatures and legislators are there. They are a conspicuous part of the political process. As such, they deserve the attention they have received and more. My argument is, rather, that this impressive body of literature is of limited use in the business of explaining policies and the reasons that policies evolve from the legislative process as they do. All we know about legislative behavior tells us next to nothing about the course of welfare legislation from the enactment of the Social Security Act of 1935 to the present day. This literature could in no way allow one to predict the course of legislation affecting the cities—optimism inspired by reapportionment notwithstanding. We cannot, by means of this storehouse of inquiry into legislative behavior, explain why Oklahoma is so far ahead of other states in welfare benefits and so far behind in support for education. We have to look elsewhere for that kind of guidance.

One place to look is in the executive offices.

---

[28]Jewell, *State Legislature*, pp. 125-136.

Executive Behavior and Public Policy

Within the category "executive studies," I am including inquiry into
the roles of both the chief executives—presidents and governors—
and the occupants of bureaucratic or "administrative" posts. There
is a conventional usage with which this coupling is consistent, even
though it may not be empirically the best approach in terms of long-
range conceptual precision. Politically, of course, we think in terms
of elected chief executives as heading up "the administration," the
bureaucracies included. Legally, this is more or less the case, although
large portions of the administrative structures—for example, regulatory commissions and licensing boards—are, for all practical purposes, legally isolated from any short-range impact by elected leaders.
And any long-range impact of a president or governor on such governmental structures is indirect and difficult to measure, primarily
because the impact is somewhat deflected through periodic appointments or general budgetary restraints. In addition to those administrative structures relatively insulated by law, others have managed, by a
variety of developments such as strong clientele support, to become
virtually invulnerable politically.[29] One further risk is run by putting
the policy behavior of elected executives and established bureaucracies
into a single "executive studies" category: it involves tenure. An executive rarely stays in office more than a few years; in four states he is
constitutionally limited to a maximum of four years, compared with
eight for the president. Bureaucracies, on the other hand, are often
staffed in the middle and lower echelons by civil servants whose
tenure is protected by law. Moreover, the structure of bureaucratic
activity is such that fairly regularized relationships exist between
central offices, regional units, and clientele groups. Communication
patterns between contractors and the Department of Defense, between

[29]The Colorado Fish and Game Commission, for example, enjoys much support
among that portion of the populace interested in hunting, fishing, and conservation. The commission derives a lucrative income from various fees earmarked by law for its activities. Over the years, governors and legislators
have come to view the commission's budget as simply outside their purview
because of the widespread and vocal support the commission can generate
whenever a suggestion is made that its funds might be in excess of its needs.

truckers and the Bureau of Roads, between the Sierra Club and the Forest Service, for example, survive the tenure of any particular elected official.

Despite these operational differences between elected executives and their bureaucratic "appendages," the mode in which their policy-making roles has been studied justifies their common treatment. This mode of study may be a shortcoming of research rather than a conceptually defensible approach. But this volume is reporting on the research that exists rather than contributing directly to a storehouse of information based upon novel forms of inquiry.

Studies of executive behavior have less technical similarity than the behavioral studies of legislators and legislatures. And though the executive studies have a greater dispersion of technical and methodological focus, literature on executive behavior has perhaps greater theoretical potential for explanations of policy than that on the legislative branch. Those who have studied and reflected upon the role of modern political executives have usually concentrated much of their attention on "leadership." The political executive is viewed as a key link connecting society and its problems to the workings of government. More so than the legislature, the executive has been treated as an·actor in the larger sociopolitical context.

While students of legislative behavior have seldom asked the big question, "Of what importance is the legislature anyway?" there seems to be general agreement that the legislative branch is slipping in influence relative to the executive. More and more, it is the executive who seems to be setting the agenda for other participants in the policy process.

One fundamental point about the policy-making process—namely, the origin of policy—needs to be mentioned here. Often the process is assumed to be the mechanical operation of the charts on "How a Bill Becomes a Law." Once a proposal is on the agenda for public deliberation, how does it get improved, hooked down, and finally accepted or rejected? This is a challenging question, and it has been carefully explored in several interesting case studies.[30] But

[30]See, for example, Daniel M. Berman, *A Bill Becomes a Law: The Civil Rights Act of 1960* (New York: Macmillan, 1962); Stephen K. Bailey, *Congress Makes a Law* (New York: Columbia University Press, 1950).

these studies do not get directly at the fundamental question that asks, "Where does the bill come from?"—or, more generally, "How does the political system get its cues and set its priorities?"

Where is policy initiated? The process is analogous to the nomination of presidential candidates. Several million Americans are constitutionally qualified to be president of the United States. Yet some element in the political system filters down all these potential candidates to something close to two, between whom the populace must decide. This is a tremendous reduction in alternatives for us ordinary citizens—from several million to two!

Policies also go through a "nominating process," although it is somewhat more mysterious and more subtle than primary elections or political conventions. An infinitude of possible issues is always on hand about which policy-makers can think and argue. Today congressmen and federal administrators deliberate over space exploration. Why was that not on the agenda in 1900? Pretty silly question, obviously. The Wright brothers did not get off the ground until 1903. But a profound suggestion is embedded in this otherwise silly question. Technology, largely outside the direct control of formal officeholders, has so structured society that it can affect the policy agenda of officeholders. In other words, we would have to say that technological change is a part of the policy "nominating process." It is vital to the context of policy-making. Technological and scientific progress were an essential part of putting a man on the moon in 1969. This progress was essential to the attainment of a policy objective. A more dramatic set of decisions does not exist in the annals of modern policy-making. The moon program was consciously scheduled by President John F. Kennedy and supported by massive legislative and administrative commitments. Scientific conditions and political decisions had to mesh in a symbiotic way to put men on the moon.

In 1957 an especially violent and nasty strike took place in Indiana. The legislature was besieged with pleas to "do something." Conservative groups across the nation had been agitating for years for "right-to-work" legislation—a mechanism designed to weaken union power. The combination of an external political context and internal problems visibly influenced the agenda of Indiana legislators. They enacted a "right-to-work" law. A few years later, with a switch in party control of the legislature—and calmer times—the law was repealed with far less fanfare than at the time it was enacted.

In both these instances, we see events outside the legislature structuring the range of its options—nominating policies, as it were. Rarely does a legislator, or, collectively, the legislature, "nominate" the major policy considerations that consume most of the legislative calendar. Outside forces are essential attributes of the context in which the policy agenda is set by legislators. And executives are one of those outside forces. When the president speaks, Congress listens. It may not agree with what it hears, but it hears all the same. Most state legislative time is spent on legislation suggested by the governor. The focal point of appropriations discussion is usually "the governor's budget." Not all of the legislative agenda is executively determined, of course. But virtually all executive preferences get on it, either formally or informally. Without the drama of President Kennedy's publicly stated goal, it is doubtful American footprints would have been on the moon in the 1960s.

A paradox lies within the common use of the term "executive," for "to execute" means to carry out. Yet political executives are—today, at least—the primary initiators in the policy process. They have a strong command over the policy-nominating process. It might be possible, therefore, to define "executive" in terms of the range of policy options open to an official. Governmental practice in the United States has made available to most political executives an assortment of research apparatuses and "idea" producers. Further, most elected executives are chosen from a comprehensive con- stituency, one including an entire jurisdiction—city, state, nation— rather than a small district containing a poor replica of the larger polity. The executive view is consequently "nationalized." The struc- ture of electoral coalitions in America is so tenuous that no executive can entirely ignore any potentially rebellious segment of his support base. His stance toward policy is likely to be more anticipatory than reactive when compared with that of a "typical" legislator.[31]

Any inquiry into executive behavior and public policy must in- clude—in addition to the political views and proposal-generating

[31]See Sarah P. McCally, "The Governor and His Legislative Party," *American Political Science Review* 60 (1966): 923-942.

mechanisms of the elected executive—a study of the professional, administrative bureaucracies. Once a particular function of government reaches a certain level of routinization, structures for its performance and continuance are set up; the process is called "bureaucratization." Professional specialists replace political appointees. Relationships with clientele groups become standardized. And the administrative organization develops a set of supportive interactions and communication lines to segments of the society outside the government proper. By virtue of their direct involvement with the immediate receivers or targets of public policy, lower-level bureaucrats are able to communicate with superiors in terms of the needs of clients and the inadequacies of established practice. The professional pride and standards of bureaucratic leaders move them to want to do a good job, as judged by several reference groups—policy clientele, administrative subordinates, their professional peers across the nation, and the elected executive to whom they formally report. Consequently, built into the normal bureaucratic structure is an impetus for policy improvement and initiation. Policy nomination is automated to the extent that changes enhance but do not fundamentally challenge existing structures.

The normal bureaucracy, therefore, is a source of nearly constant impulses for policy expansion and modification, and the elected executive is usually in a position to survey many programmatic suggestions emanating from the established agencies. Even in the eyes of a conservative executive, the agency that never proposes anything is apt to be viewed with some scorn. Most executives assume that their department heads or agency personnel are alert to potential problems. If a crisis should arise in an administrative department and the executive has not been forewarned, he is likely to consider that particular administrative leadership as derelict.

Not all policy initiation flowing from the offices of elected executives, of course, has its genesis in the established administrative structures. No one would argue that we have cast a bureaucratic blanket over *all* possible human needs and desires. But executives, by virtue of their electoral base and their public visibility, are in a position to be at the focal point of *most* visible discontents and aspirations of people within their political jurisdiction. From the standpoint of understanding policy processes, we should be interested in the form and inclusiveness of the mechanisms for articulating these public discontents and aspirations; from the standpoint of explaining executive behavior, we may or may not be satisfied with an examination of the means by which executives choose to take action on the specific needs and desires of their electorate—to the various inputs to which they are exposed.

The examination of these means is the usual research tack adopted by students of executive behavior. From a policy-science standpoint, this tack is inconclusive, but informative all the same. Executives have a pretty firm grip on the agenda-setting mechanisms of most policy-making processes; their role, therefore, is vital to the operation of the policy-process system.

We have available for our guidance two general types of inquiry: (a) a series of expository descriptions of the structure and functions of executive roles, and (b) a series of case studies of executive policy-making.

Structure and Function of Executive Roles

Most descriptions of executive behavior, whether at the local, state, or national level, conclude that modern executives are the central actors in the policy-making process. They work in an atmosphere of complexity, shaped significantly by events beyond their own control. Rarely, despite strong legal authority, can they accomplish any consequential policy objectives by means of edict or command. Their principal instrument of policy impact is their ability to choose when to make a policy decision and when to employ various instruments of bargaining with other actors in the policy process. The study of executive behavior in the policy process is the study of *leadership*. And those who study modern executives have implicitly or explicitly asked, "What are the means and object of leadership?" "What do leaders do and how do they do it?" "What is the 'function' and what is the 'structure' of the executive?"

The structure and functions of the modern political executive have been explored most frequently via quasi-historical studies of the presidency. Perhaps the most well-known treatment is Clinton

48

Rossiter's *The American Presidency*.[32] Rossiter's discussion, in addition to being eminently lucid, has an advantage over earlier literature on the subject by going beyond the simple listing of constitutional characteristics of the office. He sees the practicing president as "Chief" of ten analytically separable jobs. Some of these are clearly mandated by the formal, constitutionally specified nature of the post. Others derive from the evolution of the office and the actions of its occupants in the modern sociopolitical setting. Although Rossiter's discussion is confined to the national chief executive, most of his functional categories apply equally well to the smaller setting of state capitols and city halls.[33]

As "Chief of State," the president is the nation's ceremonial leader. He issues proclamations, greets dignitaries, distributes honors, and generally acts as a substitute for royalty. He performs what in Walter Bagehot's term would be the "dignified" functions of government.[34] But unlike a monarch, the president also performs what Bagehot calls the "efficient" functions of government. He is "Chief Executive" directing the entire formal administrative structure of the national government. He is "Commander-in-Chief" of the armed forces. He is "Chief Diplomat" and, as such, represents the United States in relations with other nations. He clearly occupies center stage in the formulation of foreign policy,[35] though foreign affairs are not the only issues over which the president appears to be at the crossroads, if not the starting point, of policy-making. As "Chief Legislator," he is the most visible initiator of most major policies considered within the total context of the national government. Many of the president's functions are traceable to his constitutionally prescribed options, but the majority of them can be ascribed to the exigencies of modern policy-making in a complex society.

[32]Clinton Rossiter, *The American Presidency* (New York: Harcourt, Brace and World, 1956). See also Louis Koenig, *The Chief Executive* (New York: Harcourt, Brace and World, 1964); Coleman B. Ransone, Jr., *The Office of Governor in the United States* (University: University of Alabama Press, 1956).

[33]See, for example, Koenig, *The Chief Executive*, chap. 16.

[34]Walter Bagehot, *The English Constitution* (London: World's Classics Edition, 1955).

[35]See James A. Robinson, *Congress and Foreign Policy-Making* (Homewood, Ill.: Dorsey Press, 1962).

Less formally, but of equal significance, are some functions that lie outside the constitutionally suggested realm of presidential activities. He is "Chief of Party," and thereby has the central role in projecting the image of his party and in leading its components. Rossiter also lays great stress on the role of the president as "Voice of the People." While he may not as such be the personal embodiment of Rousseau's general will, the president is in a more advantageous position than anyone else, collectively or individually, to act as national spokesman—as mirror if not manipulator of American opinion. In recent years he has often had to demonstrate his ability to embody the popular will, but in a way leading to direct action and not merely moral leadership. He is "Protector of the Peace." The fabric of order rips apart from time to time. Natural disaster hits the Mississippi River Valley. Race riots break out in Detroit. The president is looked to as the ultimate source of action in remedying the most critical breakdowns in the social and natural order. Crises, however, are not the only aspects of domestic need that require and receive the presidential impress. As "Manager of Prosperity," the president will presumably foster proposals and operate programs designed to maintain the upward trend of our affluent society. Indeed, the Employment Act of 1946 formally mandates to him the specific task of initiating policies to maintain the full vitality of a prosperous economy.[36]

In the community of nations, the president, while he may be vilified in some quarters and ridiculed in others, is nonetheless a "World Leader." President Richard Nixon dramatized this presidential role in initiating a "State of the World" message to Congress and the people. How many national executives in the past would have taken such a step without being excoriated for either colossal egotism or foolishness?

The cliché invariably applied at election time is that the president of the United States occupies the "most powerful elective office on earth." We may deplore or applaud this circumstance, but it is difficult to deny. His statements on economic matters are reflected in the money markets of Europe. The benefits and costs of a visit to him are weighed with care by holders and seekers of office throughout

[36]See Bailey, *Congress Makes a Law*, and the extended discussion of Bailey's book in chap. III of this volume.

the world. His power in international trade can make or break the economies of many smaller nations.

While many ways are available in which the power of the president—and other modern executives—can be conceptualized, this sample listing of functions is representative of one view of how the office can be examined. Yet Rossiter's treatment, as is true generally of most studies of executive offices, is not intended to address the specific policy-making activities of executives. The focus of concern is the office rather than the consequences of its incumbent's actions. Executive actions are usually touched upon, but indirectly through a description of the office itself. For example, Rossiter follows his discussion of presidential functions with a detailed qualitative evaluation and ranking of the presidents from Washington to Eisenhower. If Rossiter's central concern were the same as mine, he would probably have looked at a series of policies and ranked them by degree of presidential impact. This is not to say that one approach is superior to the other; an evaluation along that line depends upon one's main interest. Our interest here is in offices as they may inform an understanding of the policy process.

Case Studies of Executive Policy Activity

One way to help clarify the role of executives in the determination of policy is to examine their activities in specific instances rather than to consider an overall characterization of their function. Several case studies look at executives from the vantage of decisions they have made.

For several years, numerous scholars were convinced that the appropriate course for political science generally should be the study of decisions about policy. It was hoped that the "decision-making" approach would constitute an efficient and theoretically powerful orientation for understanding most of what we conceive of as politics.[37] The current concern for focusing on policy as a prime object of study has been shaped by the suggestions offered by "decision

---

[37]See Richard C. Snyder, "A Decision-Making Approach to the Study of Political Phenomena," in *Approaches to the Study of Politics,* ed. Roland Young (Evanston: Northwestern University Press, 1958).

theorists." This mode of political inquiry has taken many forms, from simple narratives to remarkably elegant mathematical constructs —complete with deductive models.[38] The common assumption of these inquiries is that policy-making can be advantageously studied by examining the men, individually and collectively, who make the political "decisions." Decisions are made when one chooses a particular course of action in the presence of options, and it would certainly appear that an examination of decision-makers themselves would be a most opportune way in which to study the policy-making behavior of political executives. Indeed, a brief examination of some examples of these studies does reveal certain common elements in the processes of executive participation in policy-making.

Insight into executive decision-making, however, can be gained only by looking at the impact of events, the complexities of the process, and the resources and alternatives available to the participants. Political executives do not create the heavens and the earth, either in seven days or in seventy years. They must work with found objects. And the context of events within which they must act often severely limits their options. Also, the moment of decision must sometimes await the evolution of events in order for an executive to take a long-desired course of action. The executive who understands the ramifications of the "opportune moment" is said to have "good timing." In commenting upon the process of deciding American policy in Vietnam, Eugene Eidenberg notes, "The need to decide, as well as the content of the decisions, was directly influenced by . . . external circumstances. The picture that emerges is of a relatively lonely president making occasional basic decisions, often forced on him, and arrived at by filtering a continuous stream of events, public opinion polls, and congressional attitudes." Eidenberg quotes former Under Secretary of State George Ball as observing, "Vietnam was a product of slowly-building pressures, both external and internal to American government and to the real situation in Southeast Asia."[39]

[38]Howard Raiffa, *Decision Analysis: Introduction to Making Choices Under Uncertainty* (Reading, Mass.: Addison-Wesley Publishing Co., 1968).

[39]Eugene Eidenberg, "The Presidency: Americanizing the War in Vietnam," in *American Political Institutions and Public Policy,* ed. Allan P. Sindler (Boston: Little, Brown and Co., 1969), p. 119.

In a slightly different vein, President Harry Truman was able to gain influence in Eastern Europe and to move toward a more open international relationship by taking advantage of "favorable" events. A disastrous harvest in Yugoslavia had made external aid essential if famine was to be avoided. By exploiting events not of his making, the president "made a moderate departure in the American foreign aid policy as it had been defined between 1948 and 1950. He carried Congress along with him with a minimum of kicking and screaming from his implacable critics."[40]

Similar limitations on and opportunities for executive decision provided by external events may be seen at the state and local level. Theodore Mitau shows how the actions of Minnesota's Governor Orville Freeman in regard to a violent strike were almost entirely constructed by circumstances outside his purview.[41] Freeman's latitude for decision was severely curtailed because the choice to act or not to act was removed. On the other hand, a scandal in New Jersey prisons provided an opportunity for decision and allowed Governor Robert B. Meyner to begin the process of major administrative reorganization.[42]

Not only are the occasions for decision most often provided by events beyond executive control, they rarely offer neat, clear options with price tags attached. Human beings are fickle, and the results of their actions are difficult to predict, no matter how carefully weighed in advance. Governor Meyner's efforts to reorganize the structure of New Jersey's penal institutions, for example, ran aground for several reasons. He had some choice as to whether or not institutional reform should be a major policy issue. That he chose to set up an attention-getting, blue-ribbon commission was evidence that he did decide penal reform was a major policy issue—and evidence that the policy decision entailed a certain risk. In this case, the

[40]Louis W. Koenig, "Foreign Aid to Spain and Yugoslavia: Harry Truman Does His Duty," in *The Uses of Power: Seven Cases in American Politics,* ed. Alan F. Westin (New York: Harcourt, Brace and World, 1962), p. 113.

[41]G. Theodore Mitau, "The Governor and the Strike," in *Cases in State and Local Government,* ed. Richard T. Frost (Englewood Cliffs, N. J.: Prentice-Hall, 1962).

[42]Richard T. Frost, "The New Jersey Institutions Case," in *Cases in State and Local Government.*

risk backfired. His commission failed to produce the recommendations he had hoped to obtain. Meyner had not been able ahead of time to assess the extent and intensity of preferences represented by those whom he had enlisted ostensibly to legitimize his own anticipated course of action.

As this instance reveals, the processes of executive decision-making are seldom one-man shows. Executive departments, individual bureaucrats, and appointees, presumably under the direction and control of the chief executive, can significantly alter his priorities whether he so desires or not.[43] In foreign policy, where the common assumption is that the president has extensive latitude, the collective constraints are perhaps most rigorous. Eidenberg says: "The president of the United States must confront the powerful forces of Congress, public opinion, advisors of strong will and talent, and foreign governments in making his decisions. All limit his freedom to act. . . ."[44]

Nowhere is the collective and complex nature of executive decision-making more profoundly obvious than in the budgetary process. Aaron Wildavsky characterizes a budget as the product of "a network of communications in which information is continuously being generated and fed back to the participants."[45] Although the final document presented to Congress is the "President's budget," the process, says Wildavsky, "turns out to be . . . incremental . . ., proceeding from a historical base, guided by accepted notions of fair shares, in which decisions are fragmented, made in sequence by specialized bodies, and coordinated through repeated attacks on problems and through multiple feedback mechanisms."[46] The executive's power to make decisions is restricted by the context in which a particular decision is made. Indeed, the decision-making process as revealed by Wildavsky's budget example raises questions as to whether it is useful to talk of "decisions" at all. The demarcation of a decision is akin to

[43]Koenig notes in regard to the Yugoslavian aid question, "The Executive departments and agencies   bear the brunt of a good deal of the initiative, so much so that policy appears almost to develop automatically. "Foreign Aid to Spain and Yugoslavia," p. 90.

[44]Eidenberg, "The Presidency," p. 123.

[45]Aaron Wildavsky, *The Politics of the Budgetary Process* (Boston: Little, Brown and Co., 1964), p. 3.

[46]Ibid., p. 62.

dating the invention of the wheel. We can speak of a decision process or the accretion of components of action, but I question whether in the real world it makes much sense to try to understand policy-making by breaking down the process into some kind of units called "decisions." For purposes of reconstructing events, it is often convenient to center attention on activities within a circumscribed time period and label them. And "decisions" may be as good a label as any. There are accelerations in activity, shifts in opinion, alterations in direction that result from a cumulation of preceding and external phenomena. But to dwell primarily upon a set of behaviors isolated artifactually and call it a "decision" can lead to vast oversimplification of the policy process.

If there are no "decisions," but only cumulative acts that add up to a policy direction, what is the nature of executive leadership? The preceding paragraphs, while summary in nature, leave us with a rather constrained view of political executives—as little more than conduits or clerks in the policy-making process. The discussion of the functions of modern executives presented by Rossiter and others, however, would suggest that this rather narrow and determined view gives an inadequate and one-sided picture. To the built-in restrictions on decisional options must also be added some awareness of the resources available to executives.

A most engaging book that considers these questions is Richard Neustadt's *Presidential Power*.[47] Neustadt takes a major step toward the development of a leadership theory by adopting a modest but self-consciously comparative approach. He compares both policies and presidents by looking at instances of "presidential power" as exercised by Truman and Eisenhower. He concentrates not on policy as such, but—as is true of the other studies cited in this chapter—on the actor and his actions.

The president, Neustadt asserts, is uniquely situated to take "action that makes for enlightenment." His position provides him with the opportunity and the situation for leadership. As other commentators usually note, presidential leadership goes beyond the legal, formal, ambiguous items of authority granted in the Constitution.

[47]Richard Neustadt, *Presidential Power: The Politics of Leadership* (New York: John Wiley and Sons, 1960).

Although it has the appearance of a cliché, Neustadt's assertion that "Presidential *power* is the power to persuade" has some explanatory force. It is the power to get people to do things they might not otherwise have done, and to get them to do them in some manner compatible with the hopes and expectations of the president.

Presidents—and lesser executives—can, from time to time, command and be obeyed. But commands are usually evidence of the failure of less drastic methods of persuasion, and they usually signal the fact that orders have only a short-run success. In 1951 Truman commanded General Douglas MacArthur to come back from Korea. In 1957 Eisenhower commanded troops to go into Little Rock and escort black children to school.[48] Both commands were obeyed. But did the removal of MacArthur accelerate the successful culmination of the United Nations mission in Korea? Did the presence of the troops significantly lower the obstacles to school integration nationally? Or did both actions signify a mire into which overall policy had slipped? Executive commands testify to the drastic exercise of short-term authority; as demonstrations of leadership, their worth is dubious.

What does the president normally substitute for command as the chief manifestation of his leadership? Neustadt insists it is persuasion. My personal observation of governors confirms the general applicability of Neustadt's thesis. And the persuasive capacity of executives is enhanced by several factors, not the least of which is the ever-present possibility that executives can resort to strictly defined authority. Military officers are aware of the sanctions ultimately available if they disobey an order. Consequently, they rarely have to be ordered. Suggestion is usually sufficient. The same holds true for others with whom the political executive interacts.

The authority of the office, in other words, constitutes yet another aspect of executive persuasive capacity. Deference is given to high officials. Governors, mayors, and presidents are eminent men. Their offices are usually grand in physical appearance. It takes a callous and confident man to approach without humility the flag-framed desk bearing the presidential seal, regardless of the personality of the man behind the desk. I have observed many discussions

48Ibid., chap. 2.

between a midwestern governor and other state officials. An aura of respect and deference is the norm on the part of those who seek out the chief executive, no matter how deep their personal antipathy toward the man himself may be. Despite egalitarian pretensions, we still surround our executives with considerable majesty. And we seldom take for granted their humanity. We are moved by pictures of the president showing tenderness toward his children. We are disappointed in an executive who occasionally displays such normal human shortcomings as anger or indecisiveness. The aura of authority is also a persuasive resource for all executives.

The authority of the office and the potential for leadership is further underscored by the ongoing nature of the relationships between executives and those with whom they interact in the policy-making process. "Leadership" or "power" must be placed in a time perspective in order to be comprehended. People who bargain with executives realize that any one issue is not the last in their relationship. Those who support what the executive seeks know that the day will come when they will be the seekers of support. The last card is never drawn.

"Leadership," seen as persuasiveness, of course, has its limits. The more an individual's status and authority stems from sources independent of the executive, the stronger will be his potential pressure on the executive and the greater his capacity to resist executive importunings. This consideration may well have been overlooked by those who predicted an appointment for Nelson Rockefeller in the Nixon cabinet. No office Nixon could have offered the New Yorker would have been sufficient in itself to undercut Rockefeller's independent, external base of support.

The job of persuasion is not simply a matter of pointing out the results of a logical examination of alternatives. Especially in public affairs, reasonable men may differ. There is no guarantee of clarity or logical consistency in any single interpretation of what is "rational" or "in the national interest." Neustadt illustrates this point with the example of the Truman-MacArthur controversy:

> The men who share in governing this country frequently appear to act as though they were in business for themselves. So, in a real though not entire sense, they are and have to be. When

Truman and MacArthur fell to quarreling, for example, the stakes were no less than the substance of American foreign policy, the risks of greater war or military stalemate, the prerogative of presidents and field commanders, the pride of a pro-consul and his place in history. Intertwined, inevitably, were other stakes as well: political stakes for men and factions of both parties; power stakes for interest groups with which they were or wished to be affiliated. And every stake was raised by the apparent discontent in the American public mood. There is no reason to suppose that in such circumstances men of large but differing responsibilities will see all things through the same glasses. On the contrary, it is to be expected that their views of what ought to be done and what they then should do will vary with the differing perspectives their particular responsibilties evoke.[49]

Although today's political executive is bound by events and the sheer magnitude of problems confronting modern society, it would appear that through it all the generating point for most policy formation resides within his range of perspective. Burns's remarks on the president apply as well to executives at lower levels in the federal system. He notes:

Presidential government is a superb planning institution. The president has the attention of the country, the administrative tools, the command of information, and the fiscal resources that are necessary for intelligent planning, and he is gaining the institutional power that will make such planning operational. Better than any other human instrumentality he can order the relations of his ends and means, alter existing institutions and procedures or create new ones, calculate the consequences of different policies, experiment with various methods, control the timing of action, anticipate the reactions of affected interests, and conciliate them or at least mediate among them.[50]

These observations help considerably in informing our expectations about executive offices and the men who occupy them. They do not, however, tell us very much about policy differences that

[49]Ibid., pp. 43-44.
[50]James MacGregor Burns, *Presidential Government: The Crucible of Leadership* (Boston: Houghton Mifflin, 1965), p. 339.

changes in the offices and the men who occupy them will bring about. We have in America several thousand "modern" executives. Thousands more have occupied executive offices in the past. The offices are structured differently. Some governors have more formal power than others. Some mayors have "weak" structures and others have "strong" structures. Some incumbents belong to one party, some to another party. The length of their terms, the mode of their election, the structure of their administrations differ. Do these elements have a bearing on the policies produced in a particular system of governance? If we grant the centrality of the modern executive in the policy-making process, we must be concerned with the factors that produce the list of options from which he sets his own priorities. How are the ranges of potential action set? Do the visible structural differences in executive offices, such as those just mentioned, influence either the options available or the choices taken?

Unfortunately, most of the literature dealing with executives has not been based upon approaches designed to demonstrate the consequences for policy of differences between offices or officeholders. The low priority given to policy, as with legislative studies, is a function of the stance taken by those who have conducted the inquiry. We will see in Chapter VII that some steps have been initiated to remedy this situation.

The study of legislatures and executives, moreover, does not exhaust the list of inquiries into the behavior of people in particular governmental slots. Following the constitutional trinity, one must also review studies of courts and judges.

Courts, Judges, and Policy-Making

No moderately informed observer of American politics could deny the historical importance of our courts in the policy process. A series of injunctive rulings in recent years by the United States Supreme Court has done much to shape the course of major national policies. The Court has said: "Thou shalt not segregate children by race in the public schools," "Thou shalt not try a man without the assistance of counsel," "Thou shalt not elect legislators from districts that vary significantly in population." In none of these rulings has the Court provided goods or services directly for public consumption. Nor has it established formal governmental structures for the regulation of behavior. But it has produced pronouncements of law. It has taken a stand on particular issues coming before it for determination. In each of these well-publicized cases, it has added the weight of judicial legitimacy to one side of an ongoing dispute.

If the executive sets the agenda of legislators, and if external events present as well as constrain options for executives, what is the environment of the judiciary? Certainly the courts of America do their work within a number of contexts. For example, courts work continually within the confines of their own prior interpretations of relevant restraints and authority. In their enunciations, courts must also consider the political environment of a particular place and time. Courts necessarily deal with the complexities of society, encountering, as do the other instruments of policy-making, the difficult facets of social change and conflict between groups and persons. In addition, judges have their own standards of professional excellence to meet, whether as members of the bar or as occupants of the bench. And, in a way more visible perhaps than any other branch of government, courts work within the confines of their own institutional traditions.[51]

Inquiry into the policies, or politics, of the judiciary has taken several odd turns. Scholarship, in one sense, seems to have shifted from an explicit concern with policy consequences to a concern with intra-institutional matters. Inquiry has moved from "constitutional law" to "judicial behavior." In a limited sense, the former is more occupied than the latter with the policy consequences of governmental activity. Although macroscopic characterizations of scholarly activity are risky, recent inquiry into the inner workings of the judiciary are consistent with the point made by Jack Peltason: "The concern is with process rather than product."[52]

[51]See Glendon Schubert, *Judicial Policy Making* (Glenview, Ill.: Scott, Foresman and Co., 1965), chap. 1.

[52]Jack Peltason, *Federal Courts in the Political Process* (Garden City, N. Y.: Doubleday, 1955), p. 1. See also Glendon Schubert's demonstration of the multidimensionality of the study of inquiry in his "Academic Ideology and the Study of Adjudication," *American Political Science Review* 61 (1967): 106-129.

By any reasonable definition of the term, courts are "political" institutions. They are the arenas in which disputes take place over the application of the law. Even more dramatically than in the voting booth, man as *politicus* is revealed in the courtroom. If, as asserted in Chapter I, the study of politics is the study of the intersection of government and society, nowhere is this crossing more visible than in the activities of the judiciary. Within the context of an ordered society, people making contrary claims upon one another seek resolution in the courts. It is through the mouths and pens of judges that general rules are fitted to individual cases.

The resolution of interpersonal conflicts and the specific application of general rules, of course, are not the exclusive preserve of the judiciary. Executives, legislators, and administrators make such decisions all of the time.[53] But particular and peculiar types of conflicts find their way into the courts. And the response of judges has a philosophic and moral cast that gives their action a special twist of its own. It has been said that the Supreme Court translates political philosophy into public policy, and philosophers and jurists have had a habit of citing one another from time to time. From the scholar's standpoint, courts of general jurisdiction are interesting not only because they produce authoritative policy, they are doubly interesting because of the frequency with which their actions are justified in writing. Only in the very recent past have political scientists turned their attention in a systematic manner to the activities of the lower, specialized courts.[54] And, further, only in recent years has anything other than written opinions or the biographies of individual jurists been employed as data in explaining the functioning and consequences of the judiciary.

That most attention has been given to the activities and pronouncements of the U.S. Supreme Court is of considerable consequence for the progress of inquiry in the field of judicial policymaking. The Supreme Court's written record of opinions on major issues from the founding of the Republic to the present has been

---

[53]See the discussion in chap. III of the role of the Federal Trade Commission in consumer protection.

[54]See essays and citations in James R. Klonoski and Robert I. Mendelsohn, eds., *The Politics of Local Justice* (Boston: Little, Brown and Co., 1970).

such a tempting source of information that students of constitutional history have had more than sufficient fuel with which to fire their scholarly activities. Regardless of the approach taken to explain the Supreme Court's role in American society, however, all scholars agree that its substantive involvement in policy has tended to vary with the times.

The early nineteenth century was an era of growing national identification. The legitimate boundaries of competing spheres of authority within the federal system had to be staked out. Decisions of the Supreme Court dwelt principally upon the nature of federalism, the respective authority of governmental branches, and the overall domain of government. The Supreme Court spent much of its time helping to define the nation's political system. The latter half of the nineteenth century and the first third of the twentieth were spent accommodating the political system to an industrial society. The Court, like Congress, had to confront dislocations brought about by socioeconomic change. Since the era of the New Deal, the Court has concentrated primarily upon redefining the rules of the new democratic society. Problems of citizenship—racial equality, equality before the law, equality of political membership—that were earlier subordinated to the problems of nation-building and industrialization have occupied the Court for the past quarter century.

As the role of the Court in society and the form of policy produced by the Court have altered, so have the approaches to the study of judicial policy-making. Glendon Schubert has produced a variety of classifications of analysis in this field, but his most useful may be his three-part classification of judicial studies: "traditional," "conventional," and "behavioral."[55]

The "traditional" method of studying activities of the Supreme Court, says Schubert, is manifested in the classroom with the study of Court opinions in particular cases, arranged topically and chronologically. Scholar and teacher try to find the *law,* explicit or implicit, in the verbalizations of judges. In such major segments of society as civil liberties, commerce, and federal relations, their objective is to trace the evolution of major *doctrines* in the history of the Su-

[55]Schubert, *Judicial Policy Making,* chap. 7.

preme Court. Coupled with this exercise, customarily called "constitutional history," is the study of judicial biography. At one time or
another in their careers, many of the great names in constitutional
history—also called constitutional law and public law—have also
produced one or more important works in judicial biography.[56]
While the biographers and students of constitutional history have
often been intrigued by the personalities and foibles of particular
justices, they share an assumption about their scholarly enterprise
and about the activities of judges that tends to downgrade the importance of an individual justice's idiosyncracies. The guiding assumption of traditional inquiry is that something called the *law*
evolves in a real and consequential manner through the opinions
of the justices.

"Conventional" inquiry, as labeled by Schubert, views the
judicial process as one of several aspects of the policy-making instruments of society.[57] The courts are seen as occupying one intersection of pressures and conflicts. They work from a set of procedures, admittedly different from those of other policy-makers, that
weigh and respond to the conflicting policy objectives of various
groups in the society. Conventional scholars place less emphasis
upon doctrine in history and more on the mechanisms that generate
the conflicting claims in the judicial arena. In this respect, conventional inquiries into judicial politics are akin to studies of the legislative process.

The "behavioral" method of judicial study examines the attitudes of judges and, presumably, the consequences of these attitudes.
The assumption of judicial behaviorists is that the pronouncements
and policies of courts can best be explained in terms of the attitudinal propensities of the participants in the judicial process, with
special emphasis upon the personal preferences and biases of the
judges themselves.

Each approach, read in its best light, could have much to say
to students of the judicial policy-making process. Perhaps more so

[56]The biographies authored by Edward S. Corwin and by Alpheus T. Mason
are superb examples.
[57]See, for example, Peltason, *Federal Courts;* or Walter F. Murphy, *Wiretapping
on Trial: A Case Study in the Judicial Process* (New York: Random House,
1965).

than any other field of traditional inquiry, the constitutional historians exhibit an overt concern with public policy. Despite their emphasis on the philosophic implications and doctrinal content of judicial pronouncements, the stuff of their analysis is the authoritative statements on conflict resolution that emerge from the judicial process. The conventional, or what might be called "political," analysis of the judicial process should alert us to the legal consequences of changing group structures in the society. These changing structures obviously have implications for the patterns of policy established by judicial activity. And, if the attitudes of participants in the policy process have consequence for policy outputs, there is some prima facie justification for the behavioral approach to the judicial process.

The brief historical sketch of the relationship of the Supreme Court to social change given above is readily supported by an analysis of particular cases and the varying doctrines employed by incumbents of the Supreme Court throughout our history. The evolution of judicial doctrines can also be seen as a response to the inflections in political articulation by different groups in the society. Certainly the Court of the late nineteenth century, for example, was responsive to the emerging business interests of American society. The Court of the 1950s and '60s revealed its sensitivity to the increasingly vocal claims of black people for equal rights, as presented before it by such groups as the National Association for the Advancement of Colored People (NAACP) and its Legal Defense Fund. Particularly in view of the number of five-to-four decisions on such issues as criminal procedure, the balance of judicial opinion in the latter years of the Warren Court shows the possible consequences of particular preferences and attitudinal orientations of individual justices. John Marshall's landmark decisions staking out and legitimizing a significant range of federal authority in the early years of our constitutional structure can also be read as a response to doctrinal interpretations of the Constitution, as a reflection of the vicissitudes of competing political claims, or as a demonstration of Marshall's own firm belief in the necessity for a strong national government within a vital federal system.

That the same phenomena can be interpreted in different ways through traditional, conventional, and behavioral methods of inquiry does not alter the fact, however, that students of the Court today are asking different questions and writing in a different style from those of a period as recent as the nineteen fifties. Quantitative techniques, content analysis, and the language of social science are now much more commonly encountered than are the philosophic and historical reflections found in earlier writing about the Supreme Court. Further, although the balance of emphasis is still on the Supreme Court, there is today an expansion and redefinition of interest in the lower federal courts, state trial and appellate courts, and in local courts as a part of the total complex of law-enforcement agencies.[58] These shifts in the stance and style of scholarship parallel the shifts that have taken place in most other areas of political science.

Despite the growth of more rigorous scientific techniques, however, students of the judicial process and its policy-making functions still have to accommodate themselves to the peculiarities of the judicial milieu. From the standpoint of their policy-making role, the courts clearly operate in an odd manner. Nevertheless, it should be emphasized that the differences between judicial policy-making and policy-making by other governmental instrumentalities are matters of degree rather than of kind. Robert Salisbury, for example, points to the pre-eminent role the Court plays in making what he calls "constitutional policy," as opposed to "substantive policy."[59] By constitutional policy, Salisbury is referring to "decisional rules by which subsequent policy actions are determined." These contrast with "decisions that directly confer material or expressive benefits upon one or another contending group."[60] By this distinction, Salisbury does not maintain that the rules on *how* decisions are to be made do not in one way or another lead to biases that benefit particular groups and ultimately lead to the differential dispensation of goods, services, and symbols. But he is pointing out a valid distinction—a distinction that becomes even clearer when viewed in terms of the history of political inquiry. Courts—particularly lower

[58]Klonoski and Mendelsohn, *Politics of Local Justice.*
[59]Robert H. Salisbury, "The Analysis of Public Policy: A Search for Theories and Roles," in *Political Science and Public Policy,* ed. Austin Ranney (Chicago: Markham Publishing Co., 1968), p. 160.
[60]Ibid., p. 159.

courts—do indeed make decisions that confer differential benefits upon particular groups. And other instrumentalities of the political system, such as legislatures and executives, are involved in constitutional policy. What Salisbury is highlighting is a balance of activity rather than an exclusive mode of action. Courts are responsive rather than initiative. They speak through the vehicle of decisions in particular cases and controversies rather than upon their own legislative initiative.

Courts operate rather differently from other policy-making bodies. Although, in terms of consequences, one should not make too much of it, courts follow a peculiar and somewhat formalized (if not mysterious) set of procedures in making their decisions. Membership on the courts tends to be the exclusive preserve of a particular profession—namely, the legal profession. Control over what is brought to the courts is only in part self-determined. And the means for executing decisions are dependent upon cooperation from other governmental agencies. These differences, however, should not be used as an excuse for the development of specific and special modes of inquiry. Contemporary students of the judicial process have demonstrated if not the validity of specific generalizations at least the credibility of rigorous, systematic social-scientific inquiry into the judicial process.

Unfortunately, the amount of methodological reflection contained within contemporary literature on the judicial process is likely to be somewhat out of proportion to the body of verified generalizations. A relatively small body of systematic research has been classified and categorized, and this, too, is somewhat out of proportion to the merit of its content. It is useful, nonetheless, to examine some of the classifications of inquiry and their research content.

Within the contemporary structure of judicial research, Schubert, for instance, finds four subcategories of inquiry.[61] He divides modern judicial inquiry into (a) group-interaction studies, (b) small-group research, (c) socialization studies, and (d) attitudinal research.

[61]Glendon Schubert, "Behavioral Research in Public Law," *American Political Science Review* 57 (1963): 433-445. This system of categorization precedes his traditional, conventional, and behavioral trichotomy. Nevertheless, it continues to comprise a useful taxonomy for contemporary inquiry.

The group-interaction approach fits what Schubert labels "conventional" inquiry. He includes in this category of inquiry Frank Sorauf's study of the response to the case of *Zorach* v. *Clausen,* one of the landmark decisions on the separation of church and state. Sorauf in his research examines the differential response of school systems throughout the country to the Court's limitations upon the use of public-school resources for religious instruction. He finds a remarkably varied pattern of acquiescence to the Supreme Court's ruling.[62] Other studies have examined the relationship between the American Bar Association, the Court, and such entities as the Legal Defense Fund of the NAACP.[63]

Sorauf's studies, Schubert points out, had the initial advantage in the 1950s and '60s of taking the student of the Court out of the library and putting him into the field. If they did not produce a large body of verified generalizations, at least they made students of judicial behavior sensitive to the political environment within which the Court works—an environment that includes the activities of interest groups. The studies of the interaction between the courts and interest groups are largely descriptive rather than explanatory. But they are moderately comparative in the sense that they show the relevance of courts along with other institutions in the public-policy process.

The small-group method of studying judicial behavior has borrowed primarily from social psychology and has used such theoretical orientations as role analysis and such technical devices as the analysis of voting blocs and leadership structures. Herman Pritchett,[64] in many respects, was the progenitor of contemporary quantitative studies of the Supreme Court in his bloc analyses published in the nineteen forties. His studies and the later inquiry by others show not only

[62]Frank Sorauf, "Zorach v. Clausen: The Impact of a Supreme Court Decision," *American Political Science Review* 53 (1959): 777-791.

[63]Clement Vose, "Interest Groups, Judicial Review, and Local Government," *Western Political Quarterly* 19 (1966): 85-100; Walter Murphy and R. H. Birkby, "Interest Group Conflict in the Judicial Arena: The First Amendment and Group Access to the Courts," *Texas Law Review* 42 (1964): 1018-1048; see also works cited in Gerald Rigby and James Witt, "Behavioral Research in Public Law: 1963-1967," *Western Political Quarterly* 22 (1969): 629-636.

[64]C. Herman Pritchett, *The Roosevelt Court, A Study in Judicial Politics and Values, 1937-47* (New York: Macmillan, 1948).

some facets of the internal politics of the Supreme Court as a small group but the function of fairly durable interpersonal alliances on the Court. These studies, if they do nothing more, take a long step away from the old concept of judges "finding the law and applying it."[65]

Theoretically, those who have followed the small-group approach have brought about a modest number of refinements in the study of judicial behavior. Sidney Ulmer, for example, looks at individual role orientations as the determinant of cliques of judges.[66] Theodore Becker, in a survey of Hawaiian judges, finds consistency between judges' orientations toward precedent and their conceptions of how decisions should be reached regarding "objective" and "subjective" criteria.[67] Unfortunately, Becker does not go on to provide any independent evidence of whether the self-descriptions provided by his questionnaires predict actual decision-making behavior. The small-group orientation, placed in the larger social context, has led Pritchett to argue that the Supreme Court serves as much as a molder as it does a reflector of public opinion.[68]

This emphasis upon the social role of the Court as a small group directs attention to the intracourt leadership structure. The effectiveness of chief justices in obtaining unanimity from their colleagues has been studied by David Danelski,[69] enabling him to compare the persuasive powers of different chief justices. Ulmer has been able to describe the success with which certain members of the Michigan Supreme Court obtain the assent of their colleagues.[70] Although these

[65]See, for example, S. Sidney Ulmer, "The Analysis of Behavior Patterns on the United States Supreme Court," *Journal of Politics* 22 (1960): 633-640.

[66]Ibid.

[67]Theodore L. Becker, "A Survey Study of Hawaiian Judges: The Effect on Decisions of Judicial Role Variations," *American Political Science Review* 60 (1966): 677-683.

[68]C. Herman Pritchett, "Equal Protection and the Urban Majority," *American Political Science Review* 63 (1964): 809-815.

[69]David J. Danelski, "The Influence of the Chief Justice in the Decisional Process," in *Courts, Judges, and Politics,* ed. Walter H. Murphy and C. Herman Pritchett (New York: Random House, 1961), pp. 497-508.

[70]S. Sidney Ulmer, "Leadership in the Michigan Supreme Court," in *Judicial Decision-Making,* ed. Glendon Schubert (New York: The Free Press of Glencoe, 1963).

studies do not lend themselves to broad generalizations on the nature of the policy process, they do provide the basis for a systematic audit of interpersonal behavior on the Michigan court. This research certainly qualifies as sound pre-theory if not as a corpus of explanatory statements.

Reflecting the studies on the social background of legislators and the consequences of the personal and political characteristics of legislatures, students of the political socialization of judges have compiled a modestly impressive body of findings. Inquiry into the social inheritance of judges was begun by John Schmidthauser in his massive study of the socioeconomic backgrounds of Supreme Court justices.[71] Schmidthauser describes in detail the overwhelmingly upper-class, white representation on the Court; clearly, judges of the Supreme Court are not drawn from a representative sample of the populace. In terms of the consequences of such characteristics, Stuart Nagel has attempted, in a study of state appellate judges, to test the effects of a judge's personal background upon his decisions.[72] He finds some evidence to indicate that Republican judges and judges with Anglo-Saxon, Protestant backgrounds tend to be somewhat more conservative than are their Democratic, foreign stock, Catholic colleagues. His findings are confirmed by Ulmer's studies of the Michigan court.[73] The number of studies that relate background characteristics—including mode of appointment and legal experience—to decisions, however, is substantially out of proportion to those that attempt to identify causal connections.[74]

[71] John Schmidthauser, "The Justices of the Supreme Court: A Collective Portrait," *Midwest Journal of Political Science* 3 (1959): 1-57.

[72] Stuart Nagel, "Political Party Affiliation and Judges' Decisions," *American Political Science Review* 55 (1961): 843-850. See also his "Judicial Backgrounds and Criminal Cases," *Journal of Criminal Law, Criminology, and Police Science 53* (1962): 333-339, and "Ethnic Affiliations and Judicial Propensities," *Journal of Politics* 24 (1962): 92-100.

[73] S. Sidney Ulmer, "The Political Party Variable in the Michigan Supreme Court," *Journal of Public Law* 11 (1962): 352-362.

[74] Joel Grossman, for example, argues strongly against the sufficiency of background research as an approach to the explanation of judicial behavior. Grossman, "Social Backgrounds and Judicial Decision-Making," *Harvard Law Review* 79 (1966): 1551-1579.

The study of judicial attitudes has been the objective of the most prolific member of the judicial behavior fraternity—Schubert. In a number of studies, Schubert has employed several sophisticated techniques for identifying attitudinal orientations through the decisions of justices.[75] Guttman scaling and such powerful statistical devices as factor analysis have been used by Schubert and others to identify attitudinal blocs on courts at various levels. This work has been inspired by psychology rather than by sociology. Consistent with the findings of small-group studies, the attitudinal studies do demonstrate the presence of stable, evidently predictable, orientations on the part of individual justices.[76]

If past decisions can be taken as indicators of attitudinal orientations, then attitudes certainly help to explain, or at least predict, the voting patterns of judges. Stable patterns of voting orientation have been identified by Schubert and others in such substantive areas as labor-management relations, civil liberties, and race relations. By far the most disputation within the fraternity of scholars studying judicial attitudes has centered around the conceptualization, measurement, and adequacy of attitudinal research for explanations of judicial behavior. This argument has been vigorous and on occasion virulent. It points up the difficult task and serious problems faced by students of judicial behavior.

Not a little of the difficulty has been induced by the predominant focus of attention on the Supreme Court. Thousands of other courts operate in America, yet no one has demonstrated any major field of public policy in which differences between jurisdictions are caused by differences in judicial personnel, structure, or attitudes. At most, the systematic and empirical studies of the recent past have shown how particular characteristics—political, socioeconomic, or attitudinal—of judges have structured their orientation toward certain selected types of cases. No area of widespread public services—housing, welfare, highways, conservation, utilities, and so forth—has been demonstrated to vary systematically with judicial

[75]Schubert, "Behavioral Research in Public Law," pp. 433-445, especially, 442-445.
[76]Schubert, "The 1960-61 Term of the Supreme Court: A Psychological Analysis," *American Political Science Review* 56 (1962): 90-107.

characteristics. Racial relations might be cited as a contrasting example. Yet even there, no systematic differences in general public policy have been attributed to correlative differences in judiciaries. To the extent that we find systematic differences in judicial behavior from one jurisdiction to another on racial decisions, the same forces that are operative in other institutional settings are operative here—namely, the North-South difference between the states.[77]

It may well be that sufficient variance does not exist in judicial characteristics to generate visible policy differences. If that is true, then comparative analysis is neither possible nor necessary. General statements of scientific interest cannot and need not be made about the judiciary as a determinative part of the political system. All that is required is not a scientific generalization but merely a mechanical description of what courts have done and are doing as a part of the conduit through which policy flows. In fact, most studies—both traditional and modern—of judicial activity in America are mechanical descriptions. Little effort has been made to compare judicial systems. The best we have are comparisons of jurists.[78] And Supreme Court justices have received the lion's share of attention—at least until very recently.

Comparative analysis of judicial activity is possible, however, over time, and it is through the time element that we must identify what varies within the Supreme Court in order to account for variance in its decisions. Schubert argues that the changing substantive values of justices explain policy changes over time.[79] And it is to these values that we must look to *explain*—rather than merely *describe*—the impact of the judiciary on policy. Presumably, the change from a concern over nation-building to the problems of industrialization to the problems of citizenship in the modern world is a result of changing judicial attitudes.[80] The question that remains,

[77]Kenneth N. Vines, "Federal District Judges and Race Relations Cases in the South," *Journal of Politics* 26 (1964): 337-357.

[78]Nagel has made some comparisons and attempted to identify the consequences of differential systems of appointment; however, no apparent relationship exists between mode of appointment and patterns of decisions. Nagel, "Political Party Affiliation."

[79]Schubert, *Judicial Policy Making*, p. 135

[80]Ibid.

however, is whether—at a reasonably interesting level of abstraction
—we are satisfied to stop with "attitudes." Does it happen by accident that attitudes "occur" or change, collectively or individually? Is
this line of reasoning not simply a variant on the "Great Man" theory
of history? I would argue that we could return to Schubert's list of
environmental factors and find clues to explanations that, in a sense,
lie beneath or precede the attitudinal factors. We must look to attributes of the socioeconomic context in which judges live and work.
Was Marshall's nationalism a cause of the period of nation-building?
Was the laissez-faire orientation of the Court during the 1920s a
cause of industrial capitalism? Was the economic liberalism of the
1940s and later a cause of the New Deal?

Basic canons of scientific inference would force us to answer
each of these questions in the negative. The adjustment of judicial
attitudes, in every major period, *followed* the corresponding sociopolitical events. An effect cannot, logically or empirically, precede a
cause. Mr. Dooley observed that the "Supreme Coort follows the
iliction returns." I am arguing that it also follows the broader
course of economic and political history. The time lag may be
caused by a few structural attributes of the judiciary, compared with
the Congress or the president; judges serve longer terms, for example,
and they are not as immediately exposed to socioeconomic dislocations. These, however, are short-term structural differences. The
general cause-and-effect, event-and-attitude explanation still holds.
Was it only an "attitudinal" change, however, that opened the "flood
gates" of a "whole series of pro-business" decisions in the years
after 1895.[81] Surely some connection exists between this pattern of
judicial behavior and the election of William McKinley by a coalition
of labor and management. The unleashing of capitalist energy manifested by these policy-relevant phenomena has its counterpart in other
industrial nations, and it did not occur because of some autonomous
value adjustment on the part of jurists. The reason this unleashing
occurred is buried much more deeply in the socioeconomic forces
from which values are but one visible outcrop. And the attitudes that
constitute the data of judicial analysts are themselves the conse-

[81]Ibid., p. 142.

quences of broader social changes. This thesis, however, may have to be amended for the Warren Court.

The landmark decisions of the 1950s and '60s are not as neatly tied to observable social and political changes as were those of preceding judicial periods. Civil rights and civil liberties are not orderly reflections of macrosocial phenomena in the way that the regulation of commerce or labor was during the industrializing period. Nevertheless, a good deal of the rising aspirations of black people in America can be attributed to the broadened horizons provided by experiences during World War II. Further, Schubert himself provides what sounds very much like a "conventional" or "group-interaction" explanation for the behavior of the Warren Court:

> It was not until the Democratic party mobilized the Negro vote in the big cities of the Northeast and the Midwest, not until the demographic changes that accompanied and followed World War II (including the migration of millions of Negroes from the South to the big cities elsewhere in the country), not until the general educational upgrading of the populace that accompanied the affluence of the war and post-war period, and not until many other basic changes had occurred in the structure of American political society (mainly within the past three decades) that there was anything like a national political majority in favor of racially integrated public schools.[82]

Surely by this time the reader may wonder why there should be any argument about such chicken-and-egg propositions. The field of judicial research is strange in many ways in the context of contemporary political science. There are perhaps more categories and self-applied labels for "schools of scholarship" in the judicial-research field than in any other in American political science. And one reason for this surfeit of categories and labels is because so many of those doing judicial research are former law students. No other field of the discipline has so many members who were trained in another profession before entering political science. Several of the leading students of the judiciary attended law schools before gaining their Ph.D.'s in political science. Historically, the academic study of law has wandered in and about moral philosophy. Philosophers seem

[82]Ibid., p. 152.

universally to have a taxonomic bent. Self-designed appellations for this and that approach abound: "analytical," "sociological," "realist," "political-jurisprudence," "traditionalist," "conventionalist," "behavioralist," "historical," "legalist." Unfortunately, as much printed space seems to have been used in arguing over categorical identity and purity as in recording research. The ratio of vitriol to tested hypotheses is greater in the field of judicial research than in any other I know of—including such highly personal fields as political philosophy. This acrimony reaches its peak in the writing of a scholar who has actually responded in print to a substantive statement by one of his peers with the comment: "And perhaps (one is tempted to add) there really is a Santa Claus, Virginia."[83] Ad hominum argumentation appears to be the final retreat of those who argue most vociferously for value-free objective science of judicial politics. Much of Schubert's comment on his colleague's comments reads like Lenin on the Renegade Trotsky.[84]

Part of this acerbity may simply be attributed to the rhetorical preferences and personalities of a few individuals in the field. But part of it may also be attributed to a lack of agreement on the research objective, which boils down to a question of the unit of analysis being employed. Is the objective to study judges? If so, then the disaggregated approach of attitudinal studies seems warranted. We do find the opinions of judges reflecting stable attitudinal structures over a set of only minimally related cases. Regrettably, we do not have much to tell us *why* certain judges have some attitudes and others have different ones. Party and ethnicity are relevant, but scant testing of the causal factors of attitudinal differences has been done.

If the unit of analysis is the whole court, then the analysis of group inputs, facts of cases, and the overall evolution of outputs seems most appropriate. Moreover, we would want to compare courts with other agencies of policy-making to see if particular types

[83]Ibid., p. 168.

[84]See, for additional examples, Wallace Mendelson, "The Neo-Behavioral Approach to the Judicial Process: A Critique," *American Political Science Review* 57 (1963): 593-603, and the communications in response to Mendelson in the same issue, pp. 948-953.

of conflicts enter the courts while others are fought out in the
bureaucracy, the legislature, or the electoral process.

It may be that the appropriate unit of analysis is the judicial
decision. If so, studies of leadership, roles, and the confluence of
group claims are appropriate. Such factors may well explain why
one particular option of several is chosen by the court as a collectivity. Much of the theory employed in the explanation of collective
decision-making in other contexts would be applicable to the judicial
decision-making process if judicial decisions were accepted as the
appropriate orientation.

If the unit of analysis for political science is the political system,
however, then courts, judges, and their decisions are included along
with the other participants and forces operative in the policy process.
Different sectors and characteristics of institutions can be measured
in terms of their differential effects in the production of policies
measured as outcomes of total systems, the parts of which jointly
and collectively convert particular inputs into policy products. The
systems approach, however, suggests a conceptualization of the policy
process that looks upon whole systems as the units of analysis rather
than upon particular institutional arenas. It is to the development
and application of the systems approach to the explanation of public
policy that Chapters IV to VIII are devoted.

In addition to the study of legislators, executives, and judges,
another subject of inquiry, one that reaches a bit beyond the exclusive focus on holders of formal office, is in order: the nongovernmental policy-makers. Studies of governmental versus nongovernmental policy-makers have been pursued in a fairly systematic
manner. The approach still falls within the study of policy-*makers*
rather than *policy* itself, and is therefore consistent with the theme
of this chapter.

Nongovernmental Policy-Makers

The assumption of political scientists in America prior to World War
II was that those who occupy posts in government are those who
govern. The subsequent concentration of attention upon those occupying formal posts is in large part due to this assumption. If legislators,

presidents, or judges do not "govern"—that is, if they do not form and enforce policy—why should political scientists study them, no matter how rigorous and "scientific" their observational methods? Justification does exist for starting inquiry into the policy process with governmental personnel. As I said earlier, they make the clearest tracks. But other and appealing arguments also suggest that formal officeholders may be mere front men or, at best, partners with less legitimate, informal influencers. The transformations of legitimate authority from the voters into the power of public officials may be diverted and badly warped by the impact of certain "power elites."

From the time of Marx to the present, many social critics abroad and at home have seen as grossly naïve the widespread acceptance of the simple Jacksonian tenets of popular control in this country. Thomas Nast, the nineteenth-century cartoonist, pictured the United States Congress as a group of lackeys responding to the whim and caprice of pot-bellied, cigar-smoking, diamond-studded robber barons. The muckrakers of the Progressive era saw private power and the avarice bred by it as enveloping and defiling democratic procedures. More recently, the late C. Wright Mills portrayed a structure of control by a "power elite" that is

> . . . in command of the major hierarchies and organizations of modern society. They rule the big corporations. They run the machinery of the state and claim its prerogatives. They direct the military establishment. They occupy the strategic command posts of the social structure, in which are now centered the effective means of the power and wealth and the celebrity which they enjoy.[85]

Although the average workingman might say that "the big shots run things," until fairly recent years most studies of politics in this country have concentrated on the electoral process and the holders of public office. One exception to this line of study is the early work of those political scientists who shared in the concern of the Progressives; they saw the partnership between business and government as a function of the dominance of business. Another,

[85]C. Wright Mills, *The Power Elite* (New York: Oxford University Press, 1956), p. 4.

somewhat short-lived exception is found in some early studies of the impact of interest groups in attaining certain self-centered objectives in the legislative process.[86] However, even the students of interest groups came to a position that denied the concentration and mobilization of private power for purposes fundamentally adverse to the public interest.[87] It was left to a group of sociologists, beginning their work in the 1920s, to raise significant challenges to the acceptance by political scientists of the operative quality of the democratic premise.[88]

American sociologists as early as the 1920s and '30s were impressed with the arguments put forth by several European scholars to the effect that complex organizations, including governments, were somehow inexorably bound to be controlled by, and in the interests of, a small, unified group of economic leaders. Marx, to be sure, offers the most comprehensive argument relating the structure of power to the form of the modern industrial economy. Two Italian sociologists, Gaetano Mosca and Roberto Michels extended and refined Marx's arguments to apply to any large organization at any place in time. Michels' "iron law of oligarchy" posits an irrevocable process in which large organizations necessarily develop specialized leadership, controlled communications, and the institutionalization of elite self-interest.[89] Apparent verification of these ominous hypotheses is contained in numerous community studies conducted by American sociologists. The Lynds' studies of Muncie, Indiana, found economic, religious, political, and educational life to revolve about and conform to the interests of the "X family."[90] W. Lloyd Warner

---

[86]E. E. Schattschneider, *Politics, Pressures, and the Tariff* (Englewood Cliffs, N. J.: Prentice-Hall, 1935).

[87]David B. Truman, *The Governmental Process* (New York: Alfred A. Knopf, 1951).

[88]The watershed of this line of research is Robert and Helen Lynd's *Middletown* (New York: Harcourt, Brace and Co., 1929).

[89]Roberto Michels, *Political Parties: A Sociological Study of the Oligarchical Tendencies of Modern Democracie*s, trans. Eden and Cedar Paul (London: Jarrolo and Sons, 1915); Gaetano Mosca, *The Ruling Class,* trans. Hannah D. Kahn (New York: Macmillan, 1939).

[90]Robert and Helen Lynd, *Middletown in Transition* (New York: Harcourt, Brace and Co., 1937).

and Paul Lunt, as well as August Hollingshead, seemed to discover similar concentrations of authority—outside legitimate political channels—in their studies of small towns.[91]

All these earlier community studies are marred by methodological imprecision. The Lynds have been criticized for not specifying the techniques by which they found and identified the role of the "X family" in Muncie.[92] The same criticism may be directed at the Hollingshead and Warner studies. It could even be argued that their orientations toward inquiry predetermined their results. If one starts with the assumption that those who control the major economic instrumentalities of a community are at the center of all community activities, the hypothesis can become self-fulfilling in the absence of fairly precise research techniques. The same argument applies to the power-elite hypothesis. If it is assumed that someone "behind the scenes" controls the key decisions in the community, then no matter how much one may demonstrate the existence of decision-making authority by legitimate—for example, governmental—officials, one can always argue that those who appear to be making decisions are doing so, in fact, on the orders of someone else. And if this influential "someone else" is exposed, it is always possible to continue regressing the defense, maintaining that there is yet another still further "behind the scenes" in the murky recesses of illegitimate power. Such a nonfalsifiable hypothesis has no scientific credibility, but it can, nevertheless, have considerable intellectual appeal.[93]

A serious attempt was made by Floyd Hunter, in the early 1950s, to deal with the problem of methodological imprecision in community studies.[94] The clarity with which Hunter articulated portions of his research technology sparked a series of cumulative and rigorous studies of the power structure in a large number of com-

[91]W. Lloyd Warner and Paul S. Lunt, *The Social Life of a Modern Community* (New Haven: Yale University Press, 1941); August Hollingshead, *Elmtown's Youth* (New York: John Wiley and Sons, 1949).

[92]Peter Rossi, "Community Decision-Making," *Administrative Science Quarterly* 1 (1947): 415-443.

[93]Robert A. Dahl, "A Critique of the Ruling Elite Model," *American Political Science Review* 52 (1958): 463-469.

[94]Floyd Hunter, *Community Power Structure* (Chapel Hill: University of North Carolina Press, 1953; and New York: Doubleday Anchor Books, 1963).

munities.[95] But methodological precision invites methodological criticism, and it is perhaps the very exactness with which the Hunter-inspired studies were carried out that has led to a sharpening and clarification of alternative theories of the structure of power in American communities. A brief discussion of these studies, followed by a comment on the technology of research they employed, will both illuminate the intellectual conflicts over power structures as well as lead to an evaluation of where we currently are in the study of power structures in the policy process.

The power-elite model is summarized in the quotation from Mills. It asserts the presence of a power structure whose influence extends over most matters of public (or national) consequence. The power structure is comprised of a small group of people who are unified in the furtherance of their own definition of the public interest. Power is based primarily on control of economic resources and secondarily, but almost synonymously, on social status. Public officials, to the extent that they are not identical with the power elite, act either in response to or in anticipation of the desires of those who control economic resources.

Contrasted with the elite model is the "pluralist" interpretation of political life. Where E. E. Schattschneider saw interest groups manipulating public policy to selfish ends, David Truman saw a multitude of competing, compromising groups in which overlapping memberships lead to accommodation, legitimacy, and stability.[96] Pluralists see not one pyramid of power but a polynuclear structure. Different groups of "influentials" occupy different and competing structures of interest. The groups, however, often share a sizable portion of their supporters. Who is influential within the group depends on the particular issue being considered. The pluralists view political life as a multiplicity of functionally specialized centers of influence competing for and appealing to several publics and their elected officials. The resolution of conflicts between groups, to the

[95]See the review essay by Charles M. Bonjean and David M. Olson, "Community Leadership: Directions of Research," *Administrative Science Quarterly* 4 (1964): 278-300.
[96]Schattschneider, *Politics, Pressures, and Tariff;* Truman, *Governmental Process.*

extent that the conflicts are of public consequence, tends to be brought about by legitimate decision-makers in the exercise of their officially derived authority. Where Michels inspires the elitist model, Madison orients the pluralists.[97]

Each model has developed complementary research strategies and a sizable corpus of studies. Elite theorists have leaned toward the "reputational" approach, while most pluralists have used the "decisional" approach to identify structures of political influence.[98]

Reputational Studies

Although the reputational approach has several variations, Hunter's *Community Power Structure* still provides the simplest and clearest example of this strategy. In his study of "Regional City" (Atlanta, Georgia), Hunter identified members of the power structure by asking selected judges who the "influentials" were in community affairs. The names suggested were then arrayed according to the number of times they were chosen. These top leaders were then interviewed to ascertain the extent of their agreement with the ordering of influentials and the nature of their interactions with one another.

Hunter's inquiry led him to conclude that power in Regional City was in the hands of a few men. Their position was based upon their incumbency at the apex of the community's economic life. Beneath these key leaders were various "crowds" of lower-strata people who executed the desires of the leaders. In this second echelon were major public officials, attorneys, bank vice-presidents, and so forth. Virtually absent from positions near the top were labor-union officials, ethnic leaders, and public officials. Hunter's inquiry seems to confirm the more impressionistic findings of the earlier community studies by the Lynds, Warner, and Hollingshead.

[97]Robert A. Dahl, *Preface to Democratic Theory* (Chicago: University of Chicago Press, 1956).

[98]The outstanding example of a reputational study is Hunter's *Community Power Structure*. Robert A. Dahl's *Who Governs?* (New Haven: Yale University Press, 1961) and Edward Banfield's *Political Influence* (New York: The Free Press of Glencoe, 1961) stand out as major decisional studies.

Delbert Miller suggests that the centrality of holders of economic power in the overall power structure of a community may not be universal, but rather a function of national value structures.[99] In his comparison of Seattle, Washington, with Birmingham, England, Miller found that the occupants of the power structures in the two countries—these structures being identified reputationally—had different characteristics. The English power structures have a higher proportion of intellectuals and public officials compared with the disproportionate representation of businessmen in Seattle's ruling group. Miller attributes this difference to the relatively different values placed upon business activity as opposed to academic and political activity in the two nations. Consistent with the early sociological theorists, he does not deny the inexorability of concentrations of power; he does, however, suggest that those who emerge on top may have culturally different characteristics.

In addition to studying national cultural values, other sociologists have looked at the effect of the local economic structure upon the patterns of influence in communities. Several studies have noted that power has a tendency to be more concentrated and more business oriented in communities where the predominant economic activity is in home-based manufacturing.[100] In communities increasingly dominated by absentee-owned establishments, the power structure becomes somewhat more open, heterogeneous, and fluid. The possibilities for managers of absentee-owned plants to enter the power structure may be great, but they are invariably preoccupied with company activities. Their career aspirations permit them to take little account of the community in which they momentarily reside. As a consequence of their abdication from leadership, middle-

[99]Delbert C. Miller, "Industry and Community Power Structure: A Comparative Study of an American and an English City," *American Sociological Review* 24 (1959): 804-814.

[100]Robert O. Schultze, "The Bifurcation of Power in a Satellite City," in *Community Political Systems,* ed. Morris Janowitz (Glencoe, Ill.: The Free Press, 1961), pp. 19-80; Oliver P. Williams and Charles R. Adrian, *Four Cities* (Philadelphia: University of Pennsylvania Press, 1963); Robert E. Agger et al., *Rulers and the Ruled: Political Power and Impotence in American Communities* (New York: John Wiley and Sons, 1964).

class professional, small-business, and local political leaders are likely to fill the vacuum.

Several authors argue against an equation of control over the execution of policy and control over the invention or initiation of policy alternatives. Peter Clark distinguishes between the role of the expert in defining alternative solutions to particular situations and the role of the power-structure member in commanding the execution of options once identified.[101] M. Kent Jennings points to a pattern of shared and complementary influence between bureaucratic experts from local organizations and the members of the more clearly defined economic power structure.[102]

Oliver Williams and his associates have found certain long-term patterns of change in membership of reputationally identified power structures in Michigan communities. According to Williams there seems to be an increasing frequency with which community leaders seek to occupy governmental office directly rather than exercise influence from behind the scenes. Furthermore, the movement of population to the suburbs has created internal tension and fissions within power groups, leading to conflicts and the possibility for entrance into the centers of leadership by people formerly excluded.

A number of criticisms have been leveled at the reputational techniques employed by Hunter and his followers.[103] Several scholars express concern over the mode of Hunter's questions. To ask, "Who has influence?" may lead to confusion over consequential participation in policy-making and a popular conception of social status. Given

[101]Peter B. Clark, "Civic Leadership: The Symbols of Legitimacy" (Paper delivered at the 1960 Annual Meeting of the American Political Science Association, New York, September, 1960).
[102]M. Kent Jennings, "Public Administrators and Community Decision-Making," *Administrative Science Quarterly* 8 (1963): 18-43.
[103]Bonjean and Olson, "Community Leadership"; Thomas J. Anton, "Power, Pluralism, and Local Politics," *Administrative Science Quarterly* 7 (1963): 425-457; Lawrence Herson, "In the Footsteps of Community Power," *American Political Science Review* 55 (1961): 817-831; Herbert Kaufman and Victor Jones, "The Mystery of Power," *Public Administration Review* 14 (1954): 205-212; Nelson W. Polsby, *Community Power and Political Theory* (New Haven: Yale University Press, 1963); Rossi, "Community Decision-Making."

the extent with which most people accept an elitist model, regardless of its empirical reality, the likelihood of blurred responses is high.[104] Hunter's respondents were not asked whether there was a power structure, nor were they asked to describe its shape. Rather, they were asked to tell who was on top of a predetermined monolithic structure. They were asked, in effect, to fill in the blanks of a pyramidal chart.[105] Thus, the reputational technique does not measure *leadership* as such, but the *reputation* for leadership.[106] Power roles are so vaguely described that what is elicited from the informant is not a report on reality but a test of his attitudes toward the social system.

The reputational approach has been criticized further for its assumptions about the processes and nature of group life in policy-making activities. The technique does indeed produce a list of prominent people, and on-the-spot checks always confirm that these people are conspicuous in the community's affairs. But it is not clear whether the reputational technique has discovered an integrated structure of influence or merely an aggregation of political leaders. Reputational studies assume both frequent contact and a high degree of common orientation within the "elite." What is assumed to be a group *process,* however, may be either a set of isolated individuals or, indeed, a list of competing actors.[107]

[104]Thomas R. Dye, "Popular Images of Decision-Making," *Sociology and Social Research* 47 (1962): 75-83.

[105]Nelson W. Polsby, "Sociology of Community Power: A Reassessment," *Social Forces* 37 (1959): 232-236.

[106]Raymond Wolfinger, "Reputation and Reality in the Study of Community Power," *American Sociological Review* 25 (1960): 636-644.

[107]Nelson W. Polsby, "Three Problems in the Analysis of Community Power," *American Sociological Review* 24 (1959): 796-803; Banfield, *Political Influence.* Some attempts have been made to test the extent of interaction among members of the power structure. See Charles M. Bonjean, "Community Leadership: A Conceptual Refinment and Comparative Analysis" (Ph.D. diss., University of North Carolina, 1963); William V. d'Antonio and Eugene C. Erickson, "Further Notes on the Study of Community Power," *American Sociological Review* 27 (1962): 848-854. The techniques employed, however, are still not wholly convincing to most critics.

Decisional Analysis

The import of the pluralist criticism of reputational studies is that the method assumes what it is designed to prove. In contrast, most pluralists support an alternative theory and an alternative technique of inquiry. This theory draws its inspiration from the group-interaction approach to politics, mentioned in our discussion of judicial research, and it maintains that policy is the product of group interactions in which a stable, generally salutary balance among group interests is approximated. Activity is in response to a fairly open, competitive bargaining process. The pluralist alternative does not argue that classical democracy is a fact of life in modern technological societies. Small numbers of people still do most of the governing.[108] But there is considerable functional specialization by issue area—highways, education, sanitary-sewer systems—and considerable competition within issue areas. The competitive situation forces participating groups to be dependent upon legitimate arbitrators—public officials. Thus, resolution of major conflicts is referred to and frequently guided by men elected in accordance with legal and visible means. These men, in turn, must be sensitive not only to the balance of active group interests, but also to the less articulated interests that can manifest themselves in mass response and have election-day consequences.

The research strategy that complements this theoretical orientation is called "decisional analysis."[109] To avoid the status-influence or reputation-reality problem, this approach seeks to discover influence by investigation of specific issues or policy events. The actions and relationships of specific actors are traced retrospectively or on the spot in regard to concrete circumstances. Interviews, public records, direct observation, official reports, and so forth are employed to yield a multisource data base.

[108]Dahl, *Who Governs?*
[109]Banfield, *Political Influence;* Dahl, *Who Governs?;* Warner Bloomberg, Jr., and Morris Sunshine, *Suburban Power Structures in Public Education* (Syracuse: Syracuse University Press, 1963); Roscoe C. Martin et al., *Decisions in Syracuse* (Bloomington: Indiana University Press, 1961); Aaron Wildavsky, *Leadership in a Small Town* (Ottawa: Bedminster Press, 1964).

Robert Dahl's *Who Governs?* is one of the principal decisional studies. Dahl examined sixteen major decisions in New Haven concerning urban development, political nominations, and public education. He discovered very little overlap of key participants in these different issue areas. The pattern of influence and interaction differed from one issue to another and altered with time. Many individuals moved into and out of the centers of decision-making and from one issue area to another. Similar results were obtained by Banfield in his study of major policy decisions in Chicago.[110] Both Dahl and Banfield found the mayor in their respective communities to be the only person occupying a key role in several issue areas. Mayor Richard Lee at New Haven acted as a vigorous participant in the generation and execution of policy. Mayor Richard Daley of Chicago opted for a pattern of conflict resolution and benevolent mediation. The clear implication from both studies, however, is that the stance taken by each mayor was a matter of choice rather than a role dictated either by inexorable forces or the preferences of a group of unofficial power wielders. Neither mayor sat at the top of a pyramid. Rather, each moved in and out of several intersecting circles of influence. Wildavsky's study of Oberlin, Ohio, disclosed a similar pattern.[111]

In the pluralist's model—and apparently verified by their data—interest in public affairs and a willingness to engage in policy-making activity seems to be more important as determinants of influence than either economic resources or status connections. As Dye puts it, "Competition, fluidity, access, and equality characterize community politics."[112] Banfield attributes this openness of the system to the resources and structure of groups in the policy process. Consistent with Clark's assertion on the sources of policy options, Banfield argues that initiative is taken in response to the "maintenance and enhancement needs of large formal organizations." That the leaders of these private and public organizations do not constitute a power elite is a function of their resources and structure. The lead-

[110]Banfield, *Political Influence.*

[111]Wildavsky, *Leadership in Small Town.*

[112]Thomas R. Dye, *Politics in States and Communities* (Englewood Cliffs, N.J.: Prentice-Hall, 1969), p. 332.

ers of large organizations are rarely in accord on the priorities and value of particular policy options. Further, they lack the means for communicating among themselves or for coordinating policy activity. This absence of unified, coordinated, mobilized organizational activity explains the multiple choices available to formal officeholders. In sum, the pluralists argue that the appropriate question for students of policy-making is not so much, "How many people are involved in the policy process?" but, "What interests are served?" and, "How legitimate are the decision-makers?"

Pluralists and decisional studies have come in for their own share of criticism. For instance, how does one select a case? No rules determine the typicality of policy issues. Also, once an issue is picked for study, where does the investigator start? Can he be sure that what he observes is not a charade for decisions already taken "behind the scenes"? Because decisional inquiry is so expensive, it is unlikely that large numbers of examples can be accumulated from several settings. The research strategy adopted most often by pluralist scholars, therefore, suffers all the problems of any case study. (See discussion in Chapter III.)

A more telling criticism of decisional analysis involves the problem of setting the agenda, or what have been called "nondecisions."[113] Critics of decisional analysis object to a form of inquiry that studies the agenda of policy deliberation as it is found; they argue that decisional inquiry is unable to determine the rules by which particular issues find their way into the process of deliberation. It is reasonable to argue that the most consequential decision is not how to dispose of a particular alternative, once it has been articulated; the appropriate question in the long run concerns the capacity of and means by which the total political system discovers and filters the needs and desires that are to be considered in the policy process. The problem is basically this: once a set of decisions is placed on the agenda for

[113]Peter Bachrach and Morton S. Baratz, "Decisions and Non-Decisions: An Analytic Framework," *American Political Science Review* 57 (1963): 632-642; idem, "Two Faces of Power," *American Political Science Review* 56 (1962): 947-953. A comprehensive critique is given by Richard M. Merelman, "On the Neo-Elitist Critique of Community Power," *American Political Science Review* 62 (1968): 451-460.

policy deliberation, it is theoretically quite easy, as demonstrated by Dahl, Banfield, and others, to discover the relevant actors and to offer some explanation for their actions. But there may well be a "mobilization of bias" in the system that prevents the articulation of particular types of issues and the interests they embody.[114] Out of the nearly infinite range of issues in a particular substantive area that could be considered during a period of time, a political system or set of systems actively considers but a tiny proportion. Elite theorists could argue that certain forces suppress, either deliberately or by omission, particular types of issues. The potential beneficiaries of a policy decision may never see that issue on the schedule for deliberation. Arthur Vidich and Joseph Bensman's *Small Town in Mass Society* is the best-known effort to examine the processes of nondecision-making.[115]

One of the problems, of course, in trying to assess the relative merits of reputational versus decisional studies is determining whether the different findings are a function of the methods employed or of the communities studied. No doubt the extent of elite control versus openness differs from one community to another in this country.[116] Unfortunately, because of the enormous investment of research resources required by either approach, the chances for large-scale comparative community studies are fairly slim. A few projects, however, have sought to test both the relative merits of reputational versus decisional inquiry and the extent to which community differences rather than methodological differences account for variations in findings. Robert Agger, Daniel Goldrich, and Bert Swanson conducted an intensive study of influence in four communities over a fifteen-year period. Their study presents a typology of power structures that accommodates not only the degree of citizen participation and influence but the degree of competition and conflict among

[114]E. E. Schattschneider's phrase, quoted by Bachrach and Baratz, "Two Faces of Power," p. 949.
[115]Arthur J. Vidich and Joseph Bensman, *Small Town in Mass Society* (Princeton: Princeton University Press, 1958).
[116]See Williams and Adrian, *Four Cities;* Agger et al., *Rulers and the Ruled;* and Robert Presthus, *Men at the Top; A Study in Community Power* (New York: Oxford University Press, 1964).

political leaders.[117] Agger and his colleagues found that the different methods of inquiry do indeed yield somewhat different results, and that the type of power structure a community has is also a function of its own cultural and economic structure. Similar findings have been reported by Robert Presthus.[118] Presthus points out that reputational and decisional strategies tend to complement and expand on each another. Each produces a common set of individual political leaders, but each also suggests participants in the policy-making process that the other method has omitted.

The number of community studies being done by political scientists has declined significantly in recent years. In no small degree this decline is the result of problems involved in the alternative approaches. The assumptions of both reputational and decisional analysis have been revealed and found to be serious. Pluralists have come in for much criticism as defenders of the status quo. To the extent that they find the policy process open and amenable to democratic influence, pluralists do provide a rejoinder to those who see "the capitalist system" as corrupt and exploitative. The problem, as viewed particularly by left and radical critics, is that the desires of major portions of the population may somehow be "left out." The means may not be present within the political structure for aggregation and satisfaction of the interests of, for example, the poor and the black. One can see some merit to the argument without getting embroiled in the polemics and emotion of radical versus liberal conflicts. The means for setting the agenda of public policy is a legitimate object of inquiry and need not be accepted as given. Neither the reputational nor the decisional approach, however, is

<hr/>

[117]Agger et al. develop a four-cell typology of power structures: (1) "consensual mass," in which there is a broad distribution of political power and minimal conflict among political leaders; (2) "competitive mass," a broad distribution of power and competition among leaders; (3) "consensual elite," a narrow distribution of power among the citizenry and little competition among political leaders; and (4) "competitive elite," a narrow participation—but competition nonetheless—among political leaders. In effect, the archetypical pluralist model is the equivalent of the "competitive mass" type and archetypical elitist model is the "consensual elite" type.

[118]Presthus, *Men at the Top*.

adequate for discovering the means by which alternative policy options are perceived and scheduled.

Conclusion

The inability to specify the agenda-setting rules for elites, whether governmental or nongovernmental, is endemic to the study of policy-*makers* as opposed to studies of policy-*making*. Social scientists have come a long way in their understanding of the motivations and interaction of legislators, executives, judges, and nongovernmental decision-makers; as individual actors involved with one another and the public, they have been in the scholarly spotlight. But this inquiry, as a body, has a certain circularity. Especially in the study of legislators, political scientists have learned more and more about a limited sector of the policy process without making any basic advances in the explanation of the larger process. Although we have refined techniques for tracing out the interrelationships between legislators or judges or community elites, the literature examined so far offers no comparably systematic technology for assessing the importance of legislators or judges or community elites in any larger policy process. Nor does this literature tell us what, in the larger process, sets the ground rules for the behavior of these policy-makers. Scholars have assumed that these actors are part of the policy process. Either their formal title or their manifest behavior has been used to warrant the assumption that their behavior or changes in their behavior are of consequence to policy.

How to go beyond institutional settings has been a major quandary for political inquiry. One way to delimit the political universe in a manageable way is to look intensively at a few instances of policy-making. An impressive body of case material has developed out of this particular orientation.

chapter III

Case Studies and
the Dynamics
of Policy-Making

Types and Purposes of Case Studies

Most of the books and articles written about the policy process are case studies. A case study is an in-depth examination of a particular instance of something. This is in contrast to an aggregation of characteristics of many instances. A case study tells a story. In social science, it enriches our understanding by putting flesh on the skeletal generalizations about society. Some scientific enterprises, such as psychoanalytic research, rely almost exclusively upon case studies for their basic data.

Case analysis, therefore, should not be confused with journalism. The journalist selects and reports his material to communicate facts and, quite often, to entertain the reader. The adage about the man biting the dog, while not the exclusive journalistic guidepost, is nevertheless operative in journalism. Journalism is inclined to be reportorial, though often critical. Social science, on the other hand, aims to explore and illuminate the typical rather than the atypical. Facts are conveyed, but not for their own sake. Facts are employed by the social scientist in order to reveal and to test generalizations. A case study by a social scientist should present a detailed rendition of a particular dynamic instance that is, in some essential respect, an example of general social behavior.

Case studies of the policy process have many forms and focuses. They may be divided and subclassified in several ways. We could classify case studies in three ways: according to the types of policies studied, according to the set of actors upon whom the analyst focuses, or according to the purposes for which the inquiry is undertaken. The present discussion concentrates primarily on case studies that aim to shed light upon the *process* of policy-making rather than the substance or the success of the policies themselves. Some mention should be made first, however, of the large body of literature of a case nature that is chiefly concerned with the aims and accomplishments of particular public policies. As with journalism, much of what is considered policy analysis qualifies as a form of social criticism.

Policy Cases and Social Criticism

Certain obvious gray areas lie between journalism and social science. Much of what is written by political scientists on public policy can, without any pejorative connotation, be characterized as mainly journalistic. It may be sophisticated journalism in that in addition to reporting circumstances, as seen by the observer, it also aims to offer reasoned arguments for change and reform either of policies or of the processes by which policies are made. The goals sought by the political scientist are those he deems valuable, rather than those identified by some sort of "objective" inquiry. The tone is critical. The degree of objectivity or subjectivity of such studies is quite variable. It is also possible for students of policy to take as given the stated aims of the policy-makers themselves and to assess, by fairly rigorous and objective techniques of inquiry, the success with which enacted policies have attained these stated aims.[1]

Critics and evaluators of the success of policy, however, need not necessarily accept the stated aims of policy-makers. It is not

---

[1]See, for example, James R. Davis, Jr., and Kenneth Dolbeare, *Little Groups of Neighbors: The Selective Service System* (Chicago: Markham Publishing Co., 1968); Gilbert Steiner, *Social Insecurity* (Chicago: Rand McNally, 1960); Edward Banfield, *The Unheavenly City* (Boston: Little, Brown and Co., 1968). See also those books and articles cited in the discussion of executive decision-making in chap. II.

uncommon for sensitive and insightful students of politics to criticize the ends sought by policy-makers as well as the means employed for their attainment.[2]

The unifying characteristic of what I am here calling social criticism by policy-case analysts is the attempt to measure the match between policy objectives and policy effects, the objectives being those of either the policy-makers or the policy analysts. The results of such inquiry are often negative criticisms either of the substance of policy or the mechanisms by which policies are formulated. Given the fact that we are discussing the writings of *political scientists,* it is not uncommon for students of the political process to see faults and shortcomings in policy as the result of "defects" in the mechanisms by which policies are formulated. The irrationalities of law and practice are often traced back to apparent irrationalities in the mechanisms by which laws are formed and practices defined.[3] What the man on the street or the newspaper reporter may attribute to the ignorance or self-interest of policy-makers, the political scientist often blames upon the inefficient or inappropriate mechanisms of governance.

The political scientist's relationship, in his professional capacity, to the policy-maker has been a matter of self-conscious concern for many years.[4] Recently, coincident with the increase in radical political activity on college campuses, concern has emerged within the profession that the search for "scientific rigor" or "value-free political science" has led to an abdication of social responsibility on the part of the political-science community.[5] It is argued by many socially

[2]See Leonard Freeman, *Public Housing: The Politics of Poverty* (New York: Holt, Rinehart and Winston, 1969); Duane Lockard, *Toward Equal Opportunity* (New York: Macmillan, 1968).

[3]See James MacGregor Burns, *Deadlock of Democracy* (Englewood Cliffs, N. J.: Prentice-Hall, 1963), chap. 14; Alan F. Campbell, ed., *The States and the Urban Crisis* (Englewood Cliffs, N. J.: Prentice-Hall, 1970).

[4]See Austin Ranney, *Political Science and Public Policy* (Chicago: Markham Publishing Co., 1968).

[5]See Christian Bay, "Politics and Pseudopolitics: A Critical Evaluation of Some Behavioral Literature," *American Political Science Review* 59 (1965): 39-51; for a descriptive treatment of this movement, see David Easton, "The New Revolution in Political Science," *American Political Science Review* 63 (1969): 1051-1061.

conscious members of the profession, both young and old, that the political scientist's obsession with methodological exactness and quantitative inquiry has rendered him not only less critical, but made him a tool of established power interests in the society.[6] This argument was encountered in the last chapter with regard to the criticism of "pluralist" studies of community power structures. One answer offered in rebuttal is that political scientists have been engaging in critical studies of public policy for many years, that they have seldom cast their information in a wholly unbiased mode, and that they have frequently made their services and expertise available to agencies and formulators of policies designed to improve the lot of the citizenry.[7] The dialogue between prescribing participators and objective outsiders, however, is likely to continue and to intensify for many years to come.

Neither those who urge a more active role for political scientists nor those who urge the role of disinterested observer deny the necessity for doing a better job of explaining politics. No one makes the argument that ignorance is a virtue either for the scientist or the activist. Fortunately, ample case material is available to the student of policy-making, whether he is mainly interested in political change or political explanation. Much of this case material has been prepared and organized to aid in the understanding and explanation of how policies get to be the way they are. Such case studies help to obtain and increase a level of rigor and objectivity in the methods by which analysis proceeds. What is done with such information is up to the reader.

Explanatory Case Studies

What I am here calling explanatory studies pertains to both the processes of policy-making and the substance of policy itself. The objective, however, is not an assessment of aims and accomplishments, but an illumination of the way in which specific processes work or in which particular policies get formulated. Explanatory case

[6]See Christian Bay, "The Cheerful Science of Dismal Politics," in *The Dissenting Academy*, ed. Theodore Roszak (New York: Pantheon, 1967).
[7]Easton, "New Revolution."

studies of policy-making can take almost as many forms as there are patterns to the curiosity of observers of the policy process. Several objectives fit the case mode and many different emphases fit the same objectives. The most common studies, and probably the most useful for explanation, are those that take up a central observation post and catalog the passing traffic at a selected institutional junction. In many instances we have the benefit of observations by persons who have been participants themselves in the policy-making process or were on-the-spot analysts.* The traffic one observes, nonetheless, is a function both of keen eyesight and of the junction at which one happens to be located. While a generally accepted framework is used in most systematic, explanatory case studies, continuing and nagging problems of inclusion and selection of information are also in evidence. How much information is necessary to fulfill the explanatory goals of a case study? What are the standards by which the relevance of information is determined? The goal of most political scientists' case studies is to tell us why a particular result occurred and how the process that produced it worked. But how much and what kind of information is needed to provide this explanation? Despite these problems, numerous case studies have become standard references because of their insight and obvious relevance in assisting toward an understanding of the policy process.

Explanatory studies have a fairly common format. First, a single public-policy decision—such as an executive order or a statute—or a set of closely related policy decisions is isolated for investigation. Second, the case analyst gives a history of the development of policy in the particular area. Thus, Raymond Bauer, Ithiel Pool, and Lewis Dexter, in their joint, detailed, and penetrating study of foreign-

*See, for example, Stephen K. Bailey, *Congress Makes a Law* (New York: Columbia University Press, 1950); Daniel M. Berman, *A Bill Becomes a Law* (New York: Macmillan, 1962); Thomas Anton, *The Politics of State Expenditures in Illinois* (Urbana: University of Illinois Press, 1966). One of the most extensive and best known programs for stimulating and publishing case studies of the policy process—many of which were prepared by participant observers—is the Inter-university Case Program. A collection that illustrates the fruits of the program is Edwin A. Bach and Allan K. Campbell's *Case Studies in American Government* (Englewood Cliffs, N. J.: Prentice-Hall, 1962), copyrighted by the Inter-university Case Program.

trade policy provide a concise and yet comprehensive history of foreign-trade legislation from early American experience to 1962.[9] Stephen K. Bailey in his study of the Full Employment Act of 1946 presents a similar history of governmental activity in the regulation of the economy.[10]

Most case studies focus upon political conflict. The investigators attempt to identify the interests and individuals involved in hammering out a policy product. Certain issues are selected because they seem, by some standard or other, to embody "representative" combatants in the policy process. Affected interest groups are identified and an effort is made to assess the impact of their activities.

Finally, the last step that most case studies have in common is to reconstruct, within the context of a bargaining model, the attitudes of participants and the actions they pursued. The various components that are perceived to have been operative in the policy-making process are weighed and their relative effect on the output is gauged and assessed.

Most explanatory case studies lay heavy emphasis on the personalities and individual preferences of conspicuous actors in the policy process. The case student's creed is summarized by Bailey: "The birth of a public policy is, after all, the result of the impact of seminal ideas on strategic persons and propitious times."[11] Case studies, partly because of their narrative mode, stress the actions, hopes, and expectations of individuals; it is one of their strengths that they bring to the curious student a sense of the human dimension in the policy-making process. If the impact of impersonal historical and socioeconomic forces is somehow played down and given inadequate attention in such a framework, it is probably balanced by the richness of detail with which individual participant phenomena are portrayed, at least in the more literate and sensitive case studies.

A summary of a few examples of outstanding case analyses will serve both to illustrate their central features and to give some idea of what they can teach us about the policy-making process.

[9]Raymond A. Bauer, Ithiel de Sola Pool, and Lewis Anthony Dexter, *American Business and Public Policy* (New York: Aldine-Atherton, Inc., 1963).

[10]Bailey, *Congress Makes a Law.*

[11]Ibid., p. 38.

Dozens of outstanding explanatory case studies have been written by political scientists. It is no easy task to select a few for critical examination. Each has its own focus, strengths, and shortcomings. Each has its own scale of priorities on matters of central attention and on matters of peripheral concern. Case studies vary in length from brief essays to extended volumes. Their vantage points differ. Some concentrate on the legislative process, others on the judiciary, and still others on execution and administration. High quality case studies have been conducted on policy-making at all levels of government. The Inter-university Case Program has supported the publication of short case studies on most facets of the policy process.[12] Each year several doctoral dissertations are produced that qualify in one way or another as case studies of the policy process. Over time certain case studies are relegated to the shelf and gather dust, while others find their way into the standard repertory of practicing students of politics. Two that clearly serve the long-range interests of systematic political science are Bailey's *Congress Makes a Law* and Bauer, Pool, and Dexter's *American Business and Public Policy*.[13] The authors of these volumes, published respectively in 1950 and 1963, received the American Political Science Association's Woodrow Wilson Award, given annually to the most significant book in the discipline; it is a credit to the value of case analyses of the policy process that the profession should seek so to honor two such studies. A third volume that I shall examine is A. Lee Fritschler's *Smoking and Politics*.[14] This small book does not have the original insight, the comprehensive detail, and the methodological self-consciousness of the other two studies. It does convey in clear detail, however, some aspects of the policy process not revealed by either the Bailey or the Bauer studies. By his close attentiveness to the rule-making activity of a federal regulatory commission in a particularly controversial area of policy, Fritschler provides a vivid and

[12]See Bach and Campbell, *Case Studies.*
[13]The quotations in the following summary from *Congress Makes a Law* are reprinted by permission of the Columbia University Press; those from *American Business and Public Policy* are reprinted by permission of Aldine-Atherton, Inc.
[14]A. Lee Fritschler, *Smoking and Politics* (New York: Appleton-Century-Crofts, 1969).

discerning picture of the interplay between professional bureaucrats, private interests, and the United States Congress.

Bailey: The Congressional Obstacle Course

It is indeed a tribute to Bailey's study that, more than two decades after it was originally published, it is still cited frequently by students of Congress. Although political science has been transformed dramatically in this period, Bailey's volume continues to inform and influence students of legislative behavior. What follows in the next few pages is a summary and evaluation of his study. That which is not obviously my evaluation is a summary of Bailey's presentation.

The Political Setting

On January 22, 1945, the following bill was introduced in the Senate:

A BILL

To establish a national policy and program for assuring continuing full employment in a free competitive economy, through the concerted efforts of industry, agriculture, labor, State and local governments, and the Federal Government.

Be it enacted by the Senate and House of Representatives of the United States of America in Congress assembled.

SECTION 1. This Act may be cited as the "Full Employment Act of 1945."

DECLARATION OF POLICY

SECTION 2. The Congress hereby declares that—

(a) It is the policy of the United States to foster free competitive enterprise and the investment of private capital in trade and commerce and in the development of the natural resources of the United States;

(b) All Americans able to work and seeking work have the right to useful, remunerative, regular, and full-time employment, and it is the policy of the United States to assure the existence at all times of sufficient employment opportunities to enable all Americans who have finished their schooling and who do not have full-time housekeeping responsibilities freely to exercise this right; . . ."[15]

On February 20, 1946, this bill became law—the Employment Act of 1946—with the signature of President Truman. The law read in part as follows:

AN ACT

TO DECLARE a national policy ON EMPLOYMENT, PRO-DUCTION, AND PURCHASING POWER *AND FOR OTHER PURPOSES.*

Be it enacted by the Senate and House of Representatives of the United States of America in Congress assembled.

SECTION 1.   This Act may be cited as the *"EMPLOY-MENT ACT OF 1946."*

DECLARATION OF POLICY

SECTION 2.   The Congress hereby declares that it is the CONTINUING policy *AND responsibility of the Federal Government TO USE ALL PRACTICABLE MEANS consistent with its needs and obligations and other essential considerations of* national policy *WITH THE ASSISTANCE AND COOPERATION OF* industry, agriculture, labor, and State and local governments, *TO COORDINATE AND UTILIZE ALL ITS PLANS, FUNCTIONS, AND RESOURCES FOR THE PURPOSE OF CREATING AND MAINTAINING, IN A MANNER CALCULATED* to foster AND PROMOTE free competitive enterprise and the general welfare, *CONDITIONS UNDER WHICH* THERE WILL BE AFFORDED *useful employment, FOR THOSE* able, *WILLING,* and seeking to work, *AND* TO PROMOTE *MAXIMUM* EMPLOYMENT, PRODUCTION, AND PURCHASING POWER.[16]

In the year between the introduction of the Full Employment Bill and the signing of the Employment Act of 1946, the American public witnessed many political dramas. President Franklin D. Roosevelt, having served in the White House longer than any other man, sud-

[15]Bailey, *Congress Makes a Law,* p. 243.
[16]Ibid., p. 228.

denly died. A little-known vice president moved into the White
House. The second great war of the century came to a close with the
opening of the Atomic Age. Problems of reconversion to a civilian
economy, which had been talked about in the abstract during the
war, became a reality as raised voices called for the boys to be
brought back home.

Policy in 1945, however, was not being made solely in response
to the occurrences in that year. Many events had transpired in the
previous two decades to alter significantly the direction and scope of
public policy in America. The most devastating economic crisis of
our history had created incredible rates of unemployment. New Deal
administrators had responded to this crisis with a range of experiments and emergency measures that were innovative in form and
unprecedented in scope. The ideology of limited government and
the primacy of private enterprise had been tested and found wanting.
But the experimental phase of the Great Depression and the New
Deal was cut short before a complete audit of public policies could
be conducted. World War II injected a new dimension into public
policy and shelved, for the time being, any comprehensive evaluation of the programs enacted to combat the Depression. Throughout
the war, however, an uneasiness and an awareness concerning the
abortive nature of the New Deal experiment persisted. Considerable
fear existed that, with war contracts canceled, business would not be
able to switch over to a peacetime operation without a period of
serious economic adjustment and that millions of returning GIs
would have a hard time finding work. Counterbalanced against these
potential depressants was a substantial amount of deferred private
spending, though no accurate predictions of its effect as an economic
stimulant could be computed. In the universities and in the councils
of government, a backlog of untried experiments and ideas, only
partially used during the New Deal, also offered hope. Keynesian
principles of economic regulation had had a marked impact, but
their full implementation and the consequent test of their effectiveness had been postponed.

John Maynard Keynes, however, was not the only source upon
which policy planners and those who worried about economic matters
had to draw.

> The Full Employment Bill of 1945 was the product of a long
> history. Any comprehensive attempt to describe the bill's family
> tree would lead the genealogist back through devious and dis-
> mal paths of history to the earliest human crimes against eco-
> nomic insecurity. In the broadest perspective of time, the mod-
> ern concern about full employment is but the last version
> of man's age-old petition, "Give us this day our daily bread."
> If attention is now addressed to Washington or London or
> Moscow rather than to heaven, it is only because man has
> changed his mind about the relative competence of God and
> government in dealing with pressing economic issues.[17]

Though Bailey's opening paragraph, quoted above, is somewhat
grand and imprecise, it does point out that an active role for government in the economy was not an invention of those sponsoring
the Full Employment Bill. But American governmental economic
policy had been directed mostly at business promotion rather than
job security. Hamilton's financial plan in the early years of the Republic was a controversial adventure, yet in many ways it was based
upon colonial precedents. Land and railroad policies of the federal
government in the nineteenth century were typical of national practices; they were designed to accelerate the expansion of a dynamic,
capitalistic economy. States and localities also were not noted for
laissez-faire, even when that philosophy appeared for a short period
to be dominant at the national level. In terms of national policy, however, more recent history must be consulted to find the beginnings of
an orientation that sees individual job security as a central public goal.

> ... the Great Depression of the 1930s was the first occasion
> in our nation's history when the federal government took active
> and positive steps to alleviate widespread economic suffering,
> and undertook to use its offices to harness destructive economic
> forces and to establish institutional mechanisms for protecting
> the individual against economic disaster.[18]

The despair of the Depression generated new attitudes. The
"trickle-down" theory was no longer credible. Changed attitudes
create changed expectations. Changed expectations lead to changed

[17]Ibid., p. 3.
[18]Ibid., p. 5.

demands. "Without this change there would have been no Full Employment Bill of 1945."[19]

Despite extensive experimentation with devices aimed at relieving the plight of the jobless during the New Deal, nine million workers were still unemployed in 1939. "It was the war that 'killed' the unemployment problem."[20] The specter of a replay after the war lurked in the minds of policy planners—both within and outside governmental circles, and polls showed public opinion approving some form of employment guarantee by the federal government.

In addition to changed attitudes, significant developments had taken place within the federal structure to provide programmatic and administrative mechanisms for the type of planning and social auditing envisioned by those advocating a vigorous federal role in assuring high levels of employment. In 1937 Roosevelt had established the National Emergency Council to coordinate relief programs. Extensive reorganization of the presidential office had brought modern administrative services to the chief executive. The Bureau of the Budget, even in its early years, had shown a potential for program coordination. The Office of War Mobilization and Reconversion had monitored and highlighted the problems at hand. The National Resources Planning Board had legitimized the concept and practice of coordinated federal economic surveillance.

Depression and war—historical forces beyond the deliberate control of policy-makers in the mid-1940s—left their mark on the institutions and programs of the federal government. But history is not inexorable. It is filtered through the attitudes and purposeful actions of individual men and women. "If the Great Depression and the war set the stage for the legislative drama of the Full Employment Bill, they did not write the script. Necessity is the mother of invention, but it is not the invention."[21] Social needs become public policy only when linked by the ideas and institutions of people in positions of governmental authority.

From the standpoint of ideological influence, the pivotal figure is clearly Lord Keynes. His ideas of purposeful regulation of the econ-

[19]Ibid., p. 7.
[20]Ibid., p. 20.
[21]Ibid., p. 13.

omy by political means were readily grasped as alternatives to the remnants of classical economics that had been tattered by the Depression. The Brain Trusters of the New Deal, while hardly a group of unified ideologues, were sufficiently receptive to Keynes to create an atmosphere favoring experimentation. The "intellectual middlemen" between the advent of Keynes and the advent of the Full Employment Bill worked through both public and private channels. Most notable were the National Planning Association, the National Farmers Union, the fiscal division of the Bureau of the Budget, and the National Resources Planning Board. Bailey reviews the manner in which each of these organizations served as an incubator for new economic ideas and as a generator of stimuli for change. These and other groups produced proposals leading up to the introduction of the Full Employment Bill.

Despite these multiple stimuli, however, most of Bailey's attention is given to congressional actors—both members and staff.

> What we have seen so far is sufficient to indicate that the background of the Full Employment Bill was composed of a national, even world-wide, economic experience; of popular wartime fears about the postwar world; and of the impact of particular economic ideas, especially those of Lord Keynes, upon certain public and private planners in this country. Most of this picture has been snapped at a considerable height and has revealed only the broadest contours. We must now dive close to the ground and photograph the United States Congress at work on postwar problems during the late war years. In these close-ups, we will find the legislative origins of the Full Employment Bill of 1945.[22]

The Policy-Makers

The balance of Bailey's study describes and assesses actions within and around the Congress. His view of the process is that of one stationed on the floor, in the lobbies, and in the committee rooms of Congress.

Interestingly enough, the president is scarcely visible throughout Bailey's study. The presidential role is compounded historically, of

[22]Ibid., pp. 27-28.

course, by Roosevelt's death and Truman's accession in the very midst of the struggle over the Full Employment Bill. But little weight is attached by Bailey to the role of the president in the gestation period of the bill, except insofar as the New Deal created fertile soil for its introduction and insofar as FDR was the chief architect of the New Deal. The role of the president as pictured by Bailey appears minor indeed from the vantage of the 1970s.

This deviation from present-day patterns of the presidential office is hard to evaluate. Did FDR and Truman care what was happening? Was the presidency of the 1940s simply not yet the chief legislative office it was to become? Or did Bailey's vista on Capitol Hill fail to encompass much that was done in and around the White House? Bailey does record a few executive inputs. For example, he notes that FDR gave strong support in the 1944 campaign to the principle of federally guaranteed full employment. But Bailey lists Roosevelt's death as only one in a string of events that diverted congressional attention in 1945, and Truman's role at the time of the hearings on the bill gets half a paragraph. Despite Truman's importuning of key congressmen and his radio appeal for popular support, executive-related factors are mentioned but once in a list of nine forces affecting the bill as passed by the House of Representatives. Was the legislative process of 1945 fundamentally different from that of the 1970s? Or was the Full Employment Bill not a typical piece of major legislation? Or is Bailey's report distorted? We cannot tell from the material offered in his case study.

Bailey gives credit for much of the success in steering the bill through Congress to Senator James Murray, chairman of the War Contracts Subcommittee of the Military Affairs Committee. The formal rationale for the committee assignment of the bill rested on the committee's responsibility for war-contract termination. The committee naturally considered the economic problems that reconversion was likely to create. In fact, the committee assignment of the bill was itself a minor battle in its legislative history. Assignment apparently rested on the personal interest and special competence of Murray and his subcommittee staff, especially its director, Bertram Gross. Gross, himself a political scientist and friend of Bailey's, was the chief tactician of the entire struggle over the Full Employment Act. His role as a planner, drafter, and political operative is given careful attention and heavy emphasis by Bailey.

Much of the activity of congressional staff members and lobbying groups is treated by Bailey in terms of their relationship with staff director Gross. Presaging the more extensively documented findings of Bauer, Pool, and Dexter, Bailey sees lobbying groups, at least those supporting the legislation, as responsive rather than innovative. Gross aroused, prodded, and coordinated the public activities of several private groups, and he choreographed their contacts with key congressmen. Most of the lobbying activities of liberal and labor groups, the "Lib-Lab lobby," as Bailey puts it, served to reinforce rather than to convert congressional predispositions.

> ... it would be difficult to prove that the direct pressures of the Lib-Lab lobby changed a single Congressional mind. By and large, the members of Congress who listened with any semblance of receptivity were friends of the liberal cause to begin with. Most of those against S.380 had little or nothing to fear from the Lib-Lab lobbyists, whose power was largely confined to the urban-industrial centers of America.[23]

In examining the role of opposition groups, Bailey catalogs statements and activities of such organizations as the National Association of Manufacturers and the United States Chamber of Commerce. He identifies spokesmen, reports on their mailings and describes their publications. Several paragraphs are devoted to such items as the virulently anti-Communist literature of the Committee for Constitutional Government. Bailey does not attempt to assess the influence of this material on the legislator; to do so is perhaps impossible. He sees the telling effects of opposition activity as indirect.

> Many legislators vote their own conscience and would be affronted by attempts of conservative organizations to exert direct influence on their votes. What they fail to recognize is that their consciences have been previously conditioned by the climate of values assiduously cultivated by these same conservative pressures. It is there, not in campaign contributions, direct lobbying, and letter campaigns, that the real and enormous power of the conservative lobby rests.[24]

[23]Ibid., p. 97.
[24]Ibid., pp. 148-149.

Analysis of the Process

From Bailey's case study, therefore, we are given a generalization about the formation of congressional attitudes and the determination of congressional behavior. We are told not to expect direct
and measurable effects from overt efforts to form congressional opinion or to influence behavior with regard to particular issues. Rather,
we are guided to look to much more indirect, formative influences
on the overall orientations of the minds and preferences of policy-
makers.[25] Bailey assumes, as do most students of policy-making, that
the action of congressmen and other participants in the policy process
is determined by various factors. Personal background is one. Political
experience is another. The climate of public opinion is still another.
So, too, are constituent preferences.

The intensity and direction of public opinion toward the Full
Employment Bill and related issues, as measured by Gallup polls
during the period involved, are reported in detail by Bailey. Here he
follows other students of legislative behavior in their concern with
the representative function. He finds a public more sympathetic to
the proposed legislation (in principle, though ignorant of the facts of
the specific bill) than the Congress itself. Bailey uses this disjuncture
as a springboard to critique the unevenness of representation between
rural and urban constituencies in the positions of power within the
House of Representatives.

Congressional structures and formal practices—such as the
seniority rule—still are not to be considered less important in the
policy process than the individuals making the decisions. "Congressmen are people," asserts Bailey. Their preferences and prejudices
are molded by many influences in their life situations and personal
histories. On the basis of this belief, Bailey presents a series of
fascinating vignettes encompassing items from the personal and
political experiences of representatives and senators serving on the
Conference Committee—the joint committee charged with recon-
ciling the House and Senate versions of the Full Employment Bill.

[25]In the years following Bailey's study, a considerable amount of inquiry was
made into the social matrix and personal histories of decision-makers. Typical
of these is Donald Matthews, *The Social Background of Political Decision-
Makers* (Garden City, N. Y.: Doubleday, 1955).

We are told of Senator Robert Taft's schooling and his family; we are given a picture of Representative Clare Hoffman as a curmudgeon; we learn of Senator Charles Tobey's love for his New Hampshire farm; and we are told of Representative George Bender's boyhood admiration for Theodore Roosevelt. The problem for both Bailey and his readers, of course, is to know how important this information is in explaining the legislation produced by the institutions of which the congressmen were a part. Does background information rank in importance with public opinion, the Lib-Lab lobby, or Gross in explaining the Employment Act? This question is typical of those facing case-study analysts of the policy process. Nonetheless, the contextual richness and vitality given to the narrative by such material can, if presented as well as Bailey presents it, outweigh the dubiousness of its contribution to generalizations about the policy process. Good literature can be as intellectually satisfying as good social science—even for the social scientist.

Bailey not only offers personal histories and details of group efforts, he also illuminates the conflict points—both substantive and symbolic—in the history of the Employment Act. In a manner seldom approached by alternative modes of inquiry, the ably presented case study can show the importance of political symbols in the policy process. Conflicts in policy-making are as often over how something is said as over what is done by means of law. A good deal of the battle in this instance was over the inclusion of the phrases "full employment" and "right to work" in the bill's declaration of intent.[26] "Once agreement had been reached on the Declaration of Policy," Bailey said of the fight in the Conference Committee, "the rest of the discussion went rapidly."[27] The final act did assert that henceforth it was to be the policy and responsibility of the federal government to "use all practicable means consistent with the needs and obligations" to foster and promote conditions affording useful employment to all willing and able to work. The language adopted was considerably less neat and clearly less liberal than the

---

[26]The phrase "right to work" in the context here should not be confused with the term used in reference to state laws whose purpose was to limit the closed shop. Here it is a declaration of a universal right to employment by all who are able and willing to work.

[27]Bailey, *Congress Makes a Law,* p. 226.

original version supported by Murray, Gross, and their allies. Even so, the planning mechanisms were not very much unlike those originally envisioned by the sponsors of the legislation. The final version called for the president to make an annual economic report; it established a Council of Economic Advisers, appointed by the president and confirmed by the Senate; and it set up a Joint Committee on the Economic Report in Congress.

Bailey, however, joins the supporters of the legislation in regarding the final outcome as but a shadow of the original objective. His disappointment seems to emanate from the same source as that of the bill's sponsors—namely, the watering down of the Declaration of Policy, that is, the symbolic rhetoric of intent.

Bailey concludes his study with a chapter entitled "Conclusion and Hypotheses." He does not offer a series of hypotheses constructed for subsequent testing, however; instead, he provides a rendition of concerns typical of those held by political scientists in the 1950s.[28] Why can't "rational policies" get through Congress? Because the legislature is balkanized into a number of power centers. How can we get "better policies"? By strengthening "Presidential capacity for leadership" and "by strengthening party cohesion in Congress." The roots of rationality in policy-making, in other words, are to be found in the form of the institutions in which action takes place.

Bauer, Pool, and Dexter: Patterns of Influence and Communication

The formal concerns of Bauer and his colleagues are not fundamentally different from Bailey's. They seek to identify the forces that, by impinging upon policy-makers, produce special kinds of outputs. Their concern is with a series of legislative acts involving foreign-trade policy. Further, they are interested as much in the structure and actions of particular types of persons and groups outside the halls of Congress as in the actions and attitudes of Congressmen themselves. Nonetheless, their model, like Bailey's, looks at

[28]See, for example, James MacGregor Burns, *Congress on Trial* (New York: Harper and Row, 1949).

the policy process from the vantage of individual actors and seeks to unravel the connections between pressure, attitudes, and action. Specifically, Bauer, Pool, and Dexter emphasize the flow of communications to and between those groups and individuals involved in making foreign-trade policy. They concentrate their attention on the network of communications among the public, the business community, and the Congress. Each of these sectors is perceived as generating and consuming different degrees and forms of policy-relevant communication.

This study reflects the changes that occurred within political science in the years between 1950 and 1963. The work of the three analysts is oriented much more than earlier studies toward producing general statements and explaining particular situations in terms of usual patterns. Around the set of specific incidents examined, they systematically collect a body of data for the purpose of testing individual, theoretically interrelated hypotheses. They have sought to catalog and measure a host of subtle and indirect forces that might be expected ultimately to converge in affecting the behavior of actors in the policy process. The actions studied by them are those taken between 1953 and 1963 regarding United States foreign-trade policy.[29]

Historical Background

From 1789 to 1910, revenue from customs duties exceeded internal revenues in all but eleven years.[30] Although today we may think of tariffs principally as instruments of economic and foreign policy, through our history their main purpose has been to raise revenue for the federal government. Even in the early years, however, the intricate and manifold implications of tariff policies were widely realized. Hamilton's financial plan included a conscious effort to protect the new nation's "infant industries." Later attempts to protect northern industries were a major cause of disaffection within the

[29]As in my discussion of Bailey's study, what follows is a report and evaluation of the Bauer, Pool, and Dexter book. Evaluations as such will be obvious in the discussion.

[30]U. S. Bureau of the Census, *Historical Statistics of the United States, Colonial Times to 1957* (Washington, D. C., 1960), p. 712.

cotton-exporting southern states. That the customs-duty device was primarily for revenue did not prevent the growth of an elaborate network of lobbies seeking special tariff considerations for their particular commodities.[31] The stereotypical image of the selfish, corrupt, and corrupting lobbyist drew its inspiration from the tariff lobbyists of the nineteenth century.

In the post-Civil War era especially, a marked dividing point between the political parties was their stand on the tariff. Tariff policy formed the hub around which electoral coalitions were formed, and Bauer, Pool, and Dexter imply that party history may well have perpetuated different attitudes toward the tariff long after their economic rationale disappeared. Despite the growth in the South of textile manufacturing and other activities that could benefit from protection, southern congressmen were slow to abandon their anti-protectionist position.

The central international role gained by the United States after World War I added a new dimension to foreign-trade policy. More became at stake than the health of the federal treasury or the "infant industries" of America. United States tariffs often had critical effects upon foreign economies. The acme of protectionism was reached in 1930 with the Smoot-Hawley tariff.[32] Though designed to protect American products in times of economic distress, it "precipitated widespread foreign protest and retaliation and was itself undoubtedly a cause of prolongation and intensification of the worldwide collapse of trade. It was one of the ways in which America contributed to the export of depression."[33]

Perhaps circumstances have to get very bad before they can get better.

> The passage of the Reciprocal Trade Act in 1934 marked a turning point in American foreign-trade policy. For the first time, the leading role in tariff-setting passed from Congress to the Executive. Also, the act reversed a long-range trend of increasing American tariffs. This trend, which ran from the first Congress in 1789 to the passage of the Smoot-Hawley

[31]E. E. Schattschneider, *Politics, Pressures, and the Tariff* (Englewood Cliffs, N. J.: Prentice-Hall, 1935); cited in Bauer et al., *American Business*, p. 25.
[32]Bauer et al., *American Business*, chap. 1.
[33]Ibid., p. 25.

tariff in 1930, was interrupted by only two periods of lowered tariffs; from 1832 to the beginning of the Civil War and from 1913 to 1922.[34]

The Reciprocal Trade Act—in fact, an amendment of Smoot-Hawley —gave the president power to negotiate tariff cuts of up to 50 per cent in the 1930 rates. The act expired in three years, but its general form was retained through renewal and moderate liberalization until the passage of the Trade Expansion Act in 1963. The latter allowed the president wide discretion in negotiating multilateral agreements for broad categories of goods instead of by item as had been the procedure under the several Reciprocal Trade Acts. The Trade Expansion Act was advocated by President Kennedy as a necessary step to accommodate the United States to the new international trade conditions brought about by the growing strength of the European Common Market.

The period from 1934 to 1963 saw not only the notable shift of prime responsibility from the Congress to the president in setting trade policy, but also major alterations in the support bases for tariff protection and liberalization. Increased foreign trade and foreign manufacturing operations by United States firms had somewhat obscured the point at just where the self-interest of American businessmen lay. Moreover, industrialization in the South had so altered the economy of that region that some southern congressmen were encouraged to take a protectionist stance. And perhaps most dramatic politically, a Republican, Eisenhower, entered office as a strong supporter of the New Deal Democrats' approach to executive flexibility in tariff negotiations.

Attitudes and Activities

Bauer, Pool, and Dexter concentrated their analysis upon the decisions in the 1950s and early 1960s to renew and liberalize the Reciprocal Trade Acts and on the changes brought about by the Trade Expansion Act of 1963. A wide array of data was employed to illuminate the patterns of preference, communication, and influences upon policy-makers involved in foreign-trade legislation. Polls

[34]Ibid., p. 11.

of popular attitudes were consulted. Hundreds of interviews were conducted by the authors and their associates to gauge the attitudes and activities of congressmen, congressional staff members, business leaders, national administrators, journalists, and lobbyists. Their inquiry into the centers of policy activity was backed up by exploring the influence brought to bear upon certain congressmen by their home constituencies.

As Bailey found with the Full Employment Bill, Bauer and his colleagues discovered a low level of awareness of specific legislative alternatives on the part of most of the public.

> American foreign-trade policy has not been a burning issue in the minds of the American people for the past two decades. Even at the height of the controversy over the Reciprocal Trade Act of 1955, a bare half of the adult voters were aware of what was going on. On the whole, those Americans who are interested, aware, and have an opinion of the subject, have switched from a protectionist doctrine to what appears to be a predominate support for a liberal position.[35]

In the mid-1950s, the better educated, wealthier, and more politically active segments of the population tended to support liberalization of trade policy. On the basis of these findings, one would assume a growing constituency for freer trade. The balance of public opinion against protectionism is offset, however, by little direct involvement by the public in the issue. As with many other important issues, the attitude of a majority of the public is counterbalanced by the public's lack of intensity over the issue and by the activities of smaller but more highly motivated opposition groups with specific stakes in a policy controversy.

Following this hypothesis, therefore, Bauer, Pool, and Dexter report on their investigation of businessmen's attitudes and activities regarding foreign-trade policy. Their findings are quite at variance with some common stereotypes. They quote and take issue with the statement of an economist: "Tell me what a businessman manufactures and I will tell you where he stands on foreign trade."[36]

Few businessmen thought that tariffs or foreign competition

[35]Ibid., p. 103.
[36]Ibid., p. 3.

was as vital to their operation as taxes, wages, or even foreign political stability. Interest in tariff legislation was somewhat greater among businessmen from smaller than from larger firms. For the most part, however, the businessmen of the 1950s were antiprotectionist— reflecting, apparently, an increasing awareness of the place of postwar United States vis-à-vis the rest of the world. "Much of the appeal of the liberal trade policy was that such a policy was seen as strengthening the Free World economically and politically in the fight against Communism."[37]

The political activities of businessmen hardly constitute a single pattern. Opponents of trade liberalization were more inclined than supporters to communicate their preferences to Congress. Those with an interest in free trade were less active than the smaller, but more vociferous groups who had products needing protection. The larger the company a businessman worked for, the larger his clerical staff, the better his education, and the wider his travels, the more often he wrote members of Congress on foreign trade.

> If a congressman were looking to opinion-poll data to tell him how the business community as a whole wanted him to vote, he would have concluded weakly that it favored his voting in favor of liberal-trade policies. However, though the situation may have been otherwise in specific Congressional districts, he could usually have voted as he pleased without arousing either the support or opposition of the business community as a whole.
>
> If the congressman looked not at the polls but at the communications activity of the business community, the tables would be somewhat turned. In the 1950's he would have found more messages suggesting he vote for protection than for freer trade.[38]

The personal inclinations of individual businessmen were a product of many factors. As noted above, economic self-interest had become more and more difficult to define, largely because of the expanding foreign activities of American business. Yet even where a reasonably objective determination of economic self-interest on trade policy could be made for a group of businessmen, their business ac-

[37]Ibid., p. 153.
[38]Ibid., p. 227.

tivity was a feeble predictor of their attitudes or actions on policy. Personal ideology, formulated independently of particular policy stances, filtered attitudes toward protection. Isolationists leaned toward protection and internationalists toward liberalization, often regardless of business interests. Foreign travel, exposure to national media, and, especially, verbal communication with others about the issue all had independent effects upon the attitudes of businessmen regarding foreign-trade policy. All of Bauer, Pool, and Dexter's findings demonstrate the complex nature of influences upon policy attitudes and discourage a single, "self-interest" explanation. As a consequence, a congressman is not apt to find communications reaching him from the business community especially unsettling—unless he is seeking national support for his own position. Congressmen do not represent national constituencies, and national unity on foreign-trade policy is not the norm among businessmen.

In the critical literature on Congress, much is made of the consequences of regionalism and special influences brought about by the unrepresentativeness—in a national sense—of a particular district's claims. The congressman is often pictured as a man bound body and soul to the parochialisms inherent in the socioeconomic structure of his constituency. In order to identify the passage of communication and pressure between specific congressmen and economic groups in the district, Bauer and his co-workers studied eight communities in depth. In their attempt to capture a range of political and social types of communities, they included in their study Detroit, Delaware, and Wall Street as well as a poor Appalachian town, a New England textile community, and a congressional district with no apparent stakes in foreign-trade legislation.

The community studies led them to formulate two opposing models of political communications: the vertical and the horizontal.

> There could be a situation in which tariff issues were discussed vertically within industries, but not at all horizontally between industries in the same communities. That would tend to happen if, for example, businessmen viewed the tariff as a purely business question on which they took their stand in terms of their own balance sheet with no reference to ideology, national interest, or the world's needs. Communications about trade and tariff matters, if viewed in that light, would be thought of

as appropriate for referral to higher echelons and central offices within the company and from them to trade association executives, attorneys, and legislative agents.[39]

In this pattern, the businessman takes little cognizance of the community as a significant part of his business-oriented political activity. He probably does not even consider, in more than a casual manner, the relevance of his interests to the local congressman.

> The other, or horizontal, extreme type of communication network is that which is favored by the constitutional structure of the House of Representatives. It would exist in pure form if each congressman believed that his sole business were representing the interests of his district, irrespective of national interest. In that case, or if people who cared about tariffs thought that the only effective way to organize was by precinct work or local meetings, all communications would flow first from citizen to citizen within local communities for the purpose of mobilizing local opinion and then from the community to the congressman. The practice obviously lies somewhere between the two extremes.[40]

Usually, however, it is the vertical, more cosmopolitan pattern that characterizes business activity regarding foreign-trade legislation—because of the national structure of modern business and because of the national nature of the issue. Tariffs have differential effects, depending upon the commodities in question, the foreign interests of companies, and so forth. But it is unlikely for firms in a congressional district to have a unified tariff policy.

The community studies suggest several other observations on the role of big business in policy-making. Detroit is as good an example of a one-industry town as can be found for a city that large. In the popular image, Delaware is owned by du Pont. The evidence found by Bauer, Pool, and Dexter suggests an interesting configuration of orientations. Businesses such as these have long-range, continuing relationships with the federal government. But the realization of de-

[39]Ibid., pp. 247-248.
[40]Ibid., p. 248.

pendence upon government, rather than uniting and invigorating their policy positions, seems to inhibit their efforts to influence policy. Big corporations are sensitive about their image. They know they are big. They know their bigness invites hostility and suspicion. "Power is often illusory. In a democracy, those who have influence, wealth, and power may not be free to use it. The price of holding power may be self-denial. The penalty for using power may be to be stripped of it."[41]

Beyond revealing the paradoxes of size and power characteristic of large corporations, the authors were unable, in most of the communities studied, to discover a distinct sense of business identification with a particular policy. Unity on foreign trade, they found, is by far the exception rather than the rule. From the standpoint of the congressman trying to gain a reading of preferences, the local community does not prove to be much help.

> In general, the community studies reinforced the conclusion suggested by our survey of businessmen and our study of Congress—that men tended to communicate with those they think not opposed to their position. Rather than concentrate on changing the opinions of antagonists, they try to convince the neutral or activate the already-convinced. Only when Congressmen received conflicting communications in substantial volume or impressive character did they feel constrained to explore seriously the nature of their constituency's interest; and then the questioning usually concentrated only on those groups which were already communicating with Congress. Seldom did the congressman ask how these interests fit in with the community as a whole.[42]

Since the three analysts ascertained the vertical model of political communication to be more appropriate than the horizontal, they directed their attention to the activities of national lobbying groups. Here again, they feel compelled by their evidence to dispel some common caricatures of the policy process. "Historically, the tariff has been a favorite concern of lobbies. Its story has more than once

[41]Ibid., p. 264.
[42]Ibid., p. 316.

been written as a history of lobbying tricks, stratagems, and propaganda devices."[43]

Two elements of lobbying, however, require a critical amendment of this picture. Most interest groups, first of all, are understaffed, poorly financed, and badly managed. They are ". . . at best only marginally effective in supporting tendencies and measures which already had behind them considerable Congressional impetus from other sources."[44] Trade-association leaders are less initiators of policy than they are mediators among conflicting forces within their own organizations. Most funds available to them are consumed by internal organizational expenses, with little left for propagandizing and coordinating assaults on the policy process. As reported by Bailey regarding Gross's relations with interest groups, Bauer, Pool, and Dexter conclude that the lobbyist is ". . . in effect a service bureau for those congressmen already agreeing with him, rather than an agent of direct persuasion."[45] This observation prompted their second major conclusion respecting lobbying activities: lobbyists work almost exclusively with those congressmen who they are fairly certain agree with them. Little or no activity is directed toward converting the opposition. Activation rather than conversion is the objective.

The analysts argue that too much is made of lobbying as a direct activity of interest groups and not enough is made of the communication and mobilizing function. While lobbying organizations play a relatively minor role in the immediate processes of legislation, their organizational activity often does bring about an awareness and sensitivity among their constituents. "[A] pressure group's function is frequently to define the interests of its partisans."[46]

We are left, at this point in Bauer, Pool, and Dexter's treatment, with several qualifications on how policies are made. The "business community" is a misnomer. "District interests" are ill-defined and rarely articulated. And "pressure groups" do not pressure. What, then, in the life situation of the policy-maker is of consequence for his actions?

[43]Ibid., p. 323.
[44]Ibid., p. 324.
[45]Ibid., p. 353.
[46]Ibid., p. 398.

Options and Constraints

In their style of professional life and in their choices on particular issues, most congressmen come out of Bauer, Pool, and Dexter's examination looking like remarkably free men. The authors list twelve different aspects of a congressman's job, any one of which could serve as the primary focus for his time and energy,[47] and forty-three legislative issues up for consideration between 1953 and 1955, all of which were of sufficient consequence to have consumed a majority of his time.[48] Understandably, these job options and the multitude of tasks faced by a congressman are severely constraining. Certainly, congressmen are very busy. Time for recreation and reflection is rare. Yet these myriad, competing claims on a congressman's personal resources also constitute a set of options from which he can choose and fashion his own style of action.

Congressmen determine what they will do and also what they will hear. Their own perceptions and preferences filter the communications they receive. And the public stand they take automatically suppresses many contrary stimuli. "One implication of the fact that the congressman makes his own job and hears what he chooses to hear is that he can be a relatively free man, not the unwilling captive of interest groups or parties."[49]

With respect to foreign-trade legislation, this theme propounded by Bauer, Pool, and Dexter is somewhat paradoxical. Perhaps more obviously than in most policy fields, a shift of initiative has occurred from the Congress to the president. The authors make much of this transfer. Admittedly, the issues in question in their study deal with the aspect of foreign-trade policy over which Congress still retains some control—that is, the *structure* of decision-making on tariffs. The president has the power to negotiate and set rates because Congress has established and reaffirmed that way of doing things. But it is still reasonable to assume that the influence of the president and his executive personnel seriously cramp the apparent "freedom of choice" enjoyed by members of Congress—even though the incidence of calls from the White House is low. Direct importunings, threats, or

[47]Ibid., p. 409.
[48]Ibid., p. 410.
[49]Ibid., p. 421.

temptations from presidential emissaries are exceptional, the analysts found. A few key votes were obtained in 1953 to 1955 by executive pleading, but ordinarily the influence exerted by the president, and party leadership, was subtle rather than direct. "Over the two years which we studied most intensively, the overwhelming majority of Congressmen would have felt no more pressure toward conformity to party or administration views than that which they generated within themselves from reading the newspapers and knowing what the President and party leaders were saying."[50]

Executive influence, in this setting at least, was much more consequential in structuring the policy-making agenda than in determining the vote of individual congressmen. In the larger picture, control over the agenda is of far more consequence in the direction and scope of policy than is the power to muster or convert key votes on short-term issues. If any broad criticism is to be made of Bauer, Pool, and Dexter's study, it is that they did not give more attention to the external forces that structure the agenda of policy-makers. Here, however, one may ask to what extent the agenda is deliberately controlled at all. Eisenhower was seeking renewal of an act in existence for nineteen years; he certainly did not control his foreign-policy agenda in that regard. And Roosevelt, who brought about the most consequential change of the long span of tariff policy, had a major historical crisis working for him. Thus, even though it can be effectively argued that Congress responds to executive inputs rather than initiates its own options, the constraining effect of established policy or external socioeconomic and historical forces should not be underplayed.

Case studies are not well adapted for the examination of any phenomenon in a long-term setting. Case analysis is necessarily bound somewhat to the terms and specifics of limited time references. As a result, attention is transferred from macro- to micro-considerations —from historical and developmental factors to the behavior of individuals. For the individual legislator, Bauer, Pool, and Dexter conclude that, in the long run "the sanction that counts more than party or executive leadership in the congressional picture is that of re-

---

[50]Ibid., p. 422.

election by the voters of one's district. But in that regard, too, the congressman is quite free."[51]

The long-term explanation of the fate of a particular set of issues cannot ignore either external social constraints or prior policy experience. In a comparable manner, within the legislative situation, we must bear in mind the continuous nature of relationships between members. A legislature is itself a kind of social system within which no individual exists in isolation from the rest of the collective institutional life.

> ... action on any one bill affects action on other bills, too. The single enduring issue that complicates the consideration of all individual issues is the necessity for the congressman to maintain effective working relationships with other congressmen. In the words of Speaker Sam Rayburn, you have to "go along" to "get along."[52]

Considerations of ongoing working relationships often mean that operational connections obtain between issues that, on their face, appear to have no relation whatever to one another.

The heavy schedules of congressmen limit their detailed awareness of all but a modest portion of the business collectively considered. Mutual reliance for guidance on issues at the periphery of individual concern is an operative fact. Moreover, friendships and relations of mutual assistance are normally made in terms of political compatibility. The result of acting on collegial advice is, therefore, much the same as acting on "rational" assessments of how to be consistent with one's own preferences.[53] It is in this context of a durable social structure that one must explain policy-making activity. As Bauer, Pool, and Dexter point out, "the appropriate general model is not one of linear causality, but a transactional one, which views all the actors in the situation as exerting continuous influence on each other. All the actors are to some extent in a situation of mutual influence and interdependence; A's influence on B is to some extent a result of B's prior influence on A."[54] It was the "structures that controlled

[51]Ibid., p. 423.
[52]Ibid., p. 426.
[53]Ibid., p. 437.
[54]Ibid., pp. 456-457.

attention and the capacity for action determined, as much as the communications received, the interests of which Congress could become conscious and to which it could respond."[55]

Issues, therefore, are not considered seriatim but in terms of structured processes. The products of the congressional milieu reflect this in another way. Seldom is finis written to an issue. The defeat, passage, or amendment of a bill does not constitute a statement of finality. Congress is aware of its continuing life. Policy is not *made*; it is guided. A legislative enactment

> . . . is normally a verbal formula which the majority of congressmen find adequate as a basis for their continuing a policy struggle. It sets up new ground rules within which the issue may be fought out. The ground rules will reflect the balance of forces, but the minority is seldom so weak on a major issue that it has to accept a once-and-for-all decision.[56]

Perhaps Bailey would have been less upset with the amendments to the Full Employment Bill had he considered the continuous nature of the policy process. Case studies must be read with Bauer, Pool, and Dexter's conclusion in mind: "Congress is not a temporary convocation. It is an ongoing social system which must preserve itself intact and which deals with problems on a long-run, rather than a one-shot, basis."[57]

To understand the resolution of particular issues, therefore, one must look to the social nature of policy-making institutions. But it is also important to understand the impact of the environment within which these institutions are formed and in response to which they continue to operate.

Fritschler: Administrative Policy-Making

Both studies discussed above concentrate upon the legislative arena. But each is also careful to examine extralegislative influences. Bauer,

[55]Ibid., p. 458.
[56]Ibid., pp. 426-427
[57]Ibid., p. 427.

Pool, and Dexter give most of their attention to an exploration and
analysis of the political activities of nonlegislative groups that might
be involved in the shaping of foreign-trade policy. Even so, their
focus is still upon the legislative scene, viewing as they do all other
aspects of the policy-making process as inputs into the legislative
situation. Most case studies written by political scientists follow this
pattern. Another book, though, has analyzed an interesting instance
of quasi-autonomous administrative policy-making. A. Lee Fritschler's *Smoking and Politics* describes a rather dramatic move by an
independent regulatory commission to change the pattern of public
policy in a controversial area. Specifically, he examines the attempt
by the Federal Trade Commission to require tobacco companies to
print the health warning on cigarette packages and in advertisements.

Fritschler's study is not so comprehensive or so technically ele-
and their operation in the policy process. As with those who have
studied legislative situations, he views the administrative structure
as being in a "whirlpool" of policy-making activity. An administrative unit is one among many consequential instruments in the policy
process, participating in an elaborate pattern of interdependencies
and reactive situations.

Fritschler's study is not so comprehensive or so technically elegant as Bauer, Pool, and Dexter's, nor does it profit from the observational advantages enjoyed by Bailey. It is a fairly straightforward
effort to tell the story of a single agency in a specific policy-making
situation, and to explore the kinds of problems and circumstances
with which that agency and its personnel had to cope. To guide his
inquiry, Fritschler works with the idea of a policy "subsystem."

> The term 'subsystem' describes a structure dependent upon a
> larger political entity but one which functions with a high
> degree of autonomy. A committee of Congress could be called
> a subsystem of the larger legislative system just as an agency
> might be referred to as a subsystem of the bureaucracy. The
> tobacco subsystem is different from these in that it is a more
> encompassing policy subsystem. It cuts across institutional
> lines and includes within it all groups and individuals who are
> making and influencing in government decisions concerning
> cigarettes and tobacco.[58]

[58]Fritschler, *Smoking and Politics,* pp. 2-3.

The concept of "subsystem" allows us to perceive actors in a particular setting in terms of their being interdependent with other actors for whom the setting may not be of immediate consequence. In this sense, Fritschler's treatment of the "tobacco subsystem" can be viewed in relation to the discussion by Bauer and his co-workers on the legislature as a social system. In other words, that which takes place within a policy subsystem necessarily is affected not only by the ongoing social nature of the policy process, but also by other policy subsystems coterminous with the one of primary interest. The facts of life for the legislator have obvious counterparts in the administrative structure as well.

Development of the Issue

Fritschler's study concerns the political response to the fierce controversy over the aftereffects of tobacco consumption. He offers a brief and entertaining summary of the history of tobacco use from the time of its introduction into Europe by explorers who borrowed it from the American Indians. Tobacco's "marvelous curative powers" were touted to the European continent by the French ambassador to Portugal, Jean Nicot, in 1560. His missionary activities in favor of what was later to be considered by James I as a "vile weed" accounted for Nicot's name becoming the genus of the plant, *Nicotiana*. From the time tobacco was first used widely, contention surrounded the practice of smoking and the legal response to it. Prohibition groups had secured anticigarette laws in nine southern and western states by 1913. Antismoking legislation receded, however, and by 1921 no state prohibitions remained on the books. Cigarette sales grew apace with mass advertising through the 1930s, '40s and '50s.

The first phase of contemporary public concern over smoking occurred in 1953 with the publication of a report linking smoking to lung cancer. Sales dropped slightly, but after a two-year lag returned to their former ratio of increase. Sales increases were not to be interrupted until the publication of the United States surgeon general's report, *Smoking and Health,* in 1964. Yet despite the convincing nature of the evidence and the prestige of the report, sales dropped only a little the following year, and the number of smokers continued to rise until 1968. In that year, however, the results of governmental and private group antismoking activity began to appear; cigarette sales again began to level off and then to decline slightly.

Various policy options have been pursued with regard to tobacco consumption. Cigarettes and tobacco products have long been taxed by state and federal agencies. The effect of taxation, however, has been to produce revenue—not, in any recognizable way, to alter consumption patterns. Policy options have included variations on the package warning label, regulation and possible abolition of broadcast advertising, and liability for cases of disease induced by smoking. Up to the time of Fritschler's study, little of the initiative for vigorous antismoking policies was taken by Congress.

> Because the tobacco interests exerted considerable influence within the traditional legislative system through congressmen serving on committees or subcommittees immediately involved in tobacco politics, there was little hope for the successful initiation of new policy within Congress. To effect a change in public policy, other avenues of policymaking had to be used. Through the collaboration of a few members of Congress and two agencies of the bureaucracy which were not part of the tobacco subsystem, a new coalition was formed to combat the tobacco interests.[59]

Actions and Reactions

Initiative is necessary to change policy. In this instance, the Federal Trade Commission (FTC) became the most visible initiator, and the congressional agenda was forced to include alternative regulations of the tobacco industry. The regulatory agencies constitute a peculiar instrument of governance. They are legislative, in that they have the power to promulgate certain rules within their congressional mandate. They are judicial, in that they supervise the activities of special boards that review the activity of regulated groups, determine the presence of violations, and specify the punishments required. Despite their legislative and judicial functions, their regulations can, of course, be appealed to other policy channels. Agency rules can be chal-

[59]Ibid., p. 9.

lenged in the courts as to their propriety within the statutory mandate of the regulatory agency. There are also established and routine methods by which the quasi-judicial determinations of an agency can be appealed through the court system as to their reflection of the law. And appeals can be made to Congress to countermand specific rules or to modify the nature of the rule-making authority.

The requirement for a health warning on cigarette packages and in advertising was promulgated by the FTC. In the face of obvious congressional inactivity, the FTC issued the first rule requiring a health warning on cigarette packages. The extent to which the Commission was at odds with the prevailing congressional climate then became apparent in fairly short order. The rule was subjected to considerable congressional counterattack. "The Commission rule called for a warning in advertising and on packages. Congress wanted neither, but the Commission's action forced Congress to accept half the ruling."[60] The label on packages stood the test of congressional review, but the advertising requirement was repealed.[61] Much of Fritschler's case study deals with the tugging and hauling that took place between the FTC and Congress over the labeling rule. To illuminate the battle, Fritschler spent a good portion of his study examining the background, interests, and activities of the combatants.

The "enemy" of the "public interest" is identified by Fritschler in rather definitive terms: it is the tobacco industry. In spite of the statistical association demonstrated repeatedly in studies published by various medical journals, spokesmen for the tobacco industry consistently disputed the causal inference drawn from the correlations between smoking and respiratory or cardiovascular diseases. The general line of the industry's argument was that such correlations may well be spurious. Persons prone to the relevant forms of physical debilitation may also have some psychological or psychosomatic reason for smoking. Therefore, the diseases attributed to smoking may in fact be the result of some prior psychological or physical

---

[60]Ibid., p. 11.

[61]Congressional action after Fritschler's book was published contradicts his prediction of continued congressional inactivity. By virture of a congressionally enacted requirement, public advertising of cigarettes through the broadcast media ceased as of January, 1971.

precondition—a precondition that "causes" smoking as well as the maladies being attributed to smoking.

The tobacco industry, however, did not confine itself to arguments and counterarguments. It also organized for political action. After the first studies linking smoking to lung cancer were made known, spokesmen for the cause of the industry founded the Tobacco Industry Research Committee, later called the Council for Tobacco Research. Between 1954 and 1967, it spent $11 million for research on smoking and health. A lobbying and public-relations organization, the Tobacco Institute, Inc., was set up in 1958 to produce publications and journals aimed at spreading the gospel and improving the image of the tobacco industry. Selected for executive director of the institute was Earle C. Clements, a former United States Senator from Kentucky and close associate and strong supporter of onetime colleague Lyndon B. Johnson.

To be sure, the strength of the tobacco cause does not and did not rest primarily on interpersonal influence. Tobacco has been big business for a long time. In 1963, $7 billion was spent for cigarettes. In that year six hundred thousand families relied upon tobacco farming as their main source of income. Thirty-four thousand employees worked in cigarette factories. And national, state, and local governments received $3.2 billion in cigarette taxes. Eight per cent of total television advertising revenue was from cigarette promotion. One-half of the total farm income in North Carolina was from tobacco; tobacco was responsible for smaller but still impressive proportions in Kentucky, South Carolina, Georgia, Tennessee, and Virginia.

Notwithstanding the continuous efforts of a few members devoted to the antismoking cause, Congress had not considered seriously any of the fifteen bills introduced between 1962 and 1964 to restrict sales or alert the public to the health hazards of smoking. To a certain extent, the antismoking contingent was made up of members, like Senator Warren Magnuson, who were active in other areas of consumer-protection legislation. But the leading lights were members with a keen interest in the dangers of smoking. Senator Maurine Neuberger was the widow of the late Senator Richard Neuberger, a victim of lung cancer. Utah's Senator Frank Moss was a devout Mormon who came to his antismoking position with considerable moral energy.

Although several scattered attacks against the tobacco industry were launched within and outside Congress, no specific antismoking policies (aside from taxes) had been implemented prior to the FTC labeling rule. Individual damage suits against the companies had failed to withstand appeal. The Department of Agriculture's policies were designed to protect and nurture the economic well-being of tobacco farmers.[62] In 1965, at the time of congressional debate over the health-warning label, the department officially opposed the legislation. Except for the surgeon general's proposal, others within the Department of Health, Education and Welfare have ranged from lukewarm to negative regarding antismoking legislation. Similar reluctance was found in the Food and Drug Administration. The FDA had been in an unfavorable limelight following the drug investigations under Senator Estes Kefauver in the early 1960s. Just as other regulatory agencies have been charged,[63] the Kefauver hearings revealed that considerable influence was being exercised within the FDA by the industry ostensibly being regulated.

The different degrees of concern and orientations by federal agencies toward the smoking issue exposes a key attribute of the policy process. The issue demonstrates the difficulty of advancing a policy that does not occupy top priority within any one agency or group, although it may clearly be "in the public interest." Pressure for action on other issues and the inertia of mechanisms for policy innovation thwart efforts to obtain positive actions. No single agency or group had antismoking legislation at the head of its list of policy priorities or clientele interests. Thus, peculiar circumstances were necessary to catalyze action. The amount of consumer-protection legislation enacted by Congress has increased recently, but this type of legislative policy, more than most, still appears to need the impact of spectacular events or key individuals.

At certain times in consumer history a dramatic event or the work of a single individual has provided the impetus necessary

[62]Price supports for tobacco have continued alongside the federally sponsored antismoking campaign. Perhaps the rationale is to keep the price of tobacco up and thereby discourage its consumption.

[63]See Theodore Lowi, *The End of Liberalism* (New York: W. W. Norton, 1969); Grant McConnell, *Private Power and American Democracy* (New York: Alfred A. Knopf, 1966).

to stimulate a change in policy. Upton Sinclair in his book, *The Jungle,* on the stenches of the meat packing industry at the turn of the century, and Ralph Nader's recent forceful volume, *Unsafe at Any Speed,* accusing the automobile industry of irresponsibility in the safety field, are examples of this. The Kefauver drug control legislation was floundering until Frances Kelsey, M.D., shook the conscience of the government with data demonstrating that a sleep-inducing drug called Thalidomide, when taken by pregnant women, caused severe, ghastly deformities in babies. Air travel safety systems were expanded and improved after two commercial airplanes collided over the Grand Canyon killing several persons.[64]

In the antismoking controversy, the events that catalyzed action were not so dramatic as an airplane crash or Nader's public activities.[65] Nevertheless, a series of fortuitous circumstances, which would not have been easy to predict, were necessary before regulatory action could proceed. The 1964 report *Smoking and Health,* issued with considerable publicity by the surgeon general, was the contemporary counterpart of *The Jungle.* Surgeon General Luther Terry, however, did not arrive at his famous press conference entirely on his own initiative.

As mentioned above, Senator Neuberger and others had urged direct action on a number of occasions. In 1962, she had introduced a Senate joint resolution seeking the establishment of a presidential commission on tobacco and health. President Kennedy had then been asked a question regarding the suggested presidential commission at one of his news conferences. In a manner uncommon in his press conferences, Kennedy was caught unprepared and responded ambiguously, indicating he would have more information on the question in a week. The press conference, Fritschler concludes, moved the issue from the Congress squarely into the office of the president. The president was suddenly committed to some kind of public response. Following the press conference, Kennedy asked the Public Health Service to report on what it had been doing in the field of smoking and health. The Public Health Service had compiled considerable evidence from

[64]Fritschler, *Smoking and Politics,* p. 36.
[65]See Mark Nadel, *The Unorganized Interests* (Ph.D. diss., Johns Hopkins University, 1970).

various medical studies, and unlike other agencies, it had taken a fairly vigorous position, expressing its anxiety about the deleterious effects of tobacco consumption. Two weeks after the press conference, the Advisory Committee on Smoking and Health was announced by the surgeon general. It appears to have been an alternative posed in readiness for proper conditions.

Fritschler discusses the alternative forms and uses of advisory commissions. The "expert" advisory commission, which was the kind set up by the surgeon general at President Kennedy's instigation, serves primarily to provide an agency with special kinds of information that it could not garner from its own staff. These bodies are also created to build support in a wider constituency by the force of reasoning and prestige brought into play through its respected membership. Contrasted with the expert advisory commission, is the "representative" advisory committee; it is composed of spokesmen for various interests. Representative committees do not supply expert information; they provide a mechanism for bringing into visibility a broad range of points of view and possible reactions to proposals that agencies may have on tap.

In the case of the Advisory Committee on Smoking and Health, the surgeon general picked its membership with considerable care. Although selecting his appointees primarily on the basis of competence, he did invite suggestions and pass the names of nominees made by such organizations as the American Cancer Society, the American Medical Association, the Tobacco Institute, and the National Tuberculosis Association. In this manner he guaranteed the acceptability of his group prior to their final appointment. He even went so far as to avoid appointing persons who had taken a visible public position one way or the other in the smoking controversy.

The advisory committee, comprised of ten experts—eight of whom were M.D.'s—made an early determination not to sponsor original research but to collect, review, and evaluate all existing evidence on the relationship between smoking and health. A skilled staff was assembled by assigning to the committee persons already in the employ of the Public Health Service. Secrecy of their meetings and proceedings was protected during the period of work between November, 1962, and the publication of the report in 1964. The effect of the surgeon general's report, plus the manner of its handling, was to alter the priority attached to public policies dealing with tobacco consumption.

The release of the report on Saturday, January 11, 1964, was well staged. Fritschler speculates that Saturday was selected not only to dramatize the report, but also to minimize its impact on prices of tobacco shares on the stock market. The committee's findings strongly linked smoking to a variety of health problems, and they were stated in clear, succinct, and disturbing language. The issue of causation, as distinct from correlation, was not resolved in the text of the report. Nevertheless, the conclusions of this expert advisory committee, as well as those of the surgeon general himself, were set forth unequivocally in terms that few could misinterpret. Although no specific legislation was recommended in the report, it is clear by hindsight that one of the objectives sought by the surgeon general and his committee was to spur legislative action.

It was a regulatory agency, however, not Congress, that took up the antismoking cause. The Federal Trade Commission was established by Congress in 1914 to define and adjudicate rules promulgated in accordance with the provisions of the Clayton Antitrust Act. The FTC was charged with preventing "unfair trade practices." In its early years, the breadth of FTC regulatory power was considerably restricted by a series of court decisions. Its jurisdiction over unfair trade practices was limited to cases where the injured party was a business in competition with the offending company. Consumers were not regarded as eligible for the protective umbrella of the FTC's authority. In 1938, however, Congress expanded the power of the commission to deal with "unfair or deceptive acts or practices in commerce." It specifically gave the FTC authority over the false advertising of drugs, foods, and other commodities. Following this expansion in authority, the antitrust activities of the FTC began to fade in comparison with its more consumer-oriented activities, especially those involving the regulation of deceptive advertising.

Regarding cigarette consumption, the FTC became increasingly troubled over the nature and consequences of cigarette advertising. During the 1950s, the rapid increase in television viewing and the form of television advertisements for cigarettes was a source of uneasiness to the commissioners. The portrayal of cigarette smoking as a key to social status and popularity found a critical audience in the FTC. Problems of regulation, though, were far greater than merely recognizing that regulation was desirable. "The Commission was attempting to regulate cigarette advertising on a case-by-case basis. Each time the Commission ruled a particular advertisement deceptive, the industry came up with a variation which could squeak by under the rule of the previous case. This was proving to be an endless and fruitless process."[66]

The FTC became fully aware that general rules were needed and some alternative to the case method had to be devised. In 1963, therefore, the commission had devised procedures for issuing regulations covering not specific cases but whole categories of industries, and it was this procedure that was to be employed in the cigarette labeling rule. Customarily, the FTC works out solutions to regulatory problems informally—through the opinions of advisers and conferences with the parties to a dispute. General rule-making, of course, is a much more authoritative and powerful device. Yet it had been used only with reluctance by the commission. Given the difficulties of handling cigarette advertising on a case-by-case basis, however, many were convinced at the time of the surgeon general's report that the health claims and subtleties of television advertisements could not be counteracted except by requiring a positive health warning in the content of advertisements. Quasi-legislative rather than quasi-judicial authority would have to be employed if the FTC was to have an effect upon mass smoking habits. As Fritschler says:

> The Surgeon General's report gave the Commission the impetus and the substantive information it needed to use its new rulemaking procedure in the field of cigarette advertising. This new procedure was set into motion one week after the Surgeon General released his report on smoking and health.[67]

Paul Rand Dixon became chairman of the FTC in 1961, and began an immediate investigation of the possibility of devising general rule-making powers to be used in just such problem cases as the one involving cigarette advertising. In April, 1962, he was approached by Senator Neuberger who urged that the FTC require a health warning

[66]Fritschler, *Smoking and Politics,* p. 65.
[67]Ibid.

on cigarette packages. The commission announced the adoption of general rule-making procedures in June, 1962. Fritschler suggests that it may well have been adopted in anticipation of the specific issue to be raised by the surgeon general's report a year and a half later. Prior to the health-warning regulation, a few others had been issued regarding certain products and the claims made for them. But Fritschler suggests that the FTC may have been merely flexing its muscles in preparation for the big controversy. The FTC appointed a liaison man who attended many of the open meetings of the surgeon general's advisory committee. Two months after the surgeon general's report was made public, the FTC began hearings on two different drafts of a proposed warning:

a. CAUTION—CIGARETTE SMOKING IS A HEALTH HAZARD: The Surgeon General's Advisory Committee has found that "cigarette smoking contributes to mortality from specific diseases and to the overall death rate."
b. CAUTION: Cigarette smoking is dangerous to health. It may cause death from cancer and other diseases.[68]

During three days of hearings, virtually all views and interests on the smoking controversy were heard by the FTC. The commission delayed decision and maintained an open official record for a period of two months after the formal hearings closed in order that additional statements could be filed. In the rule it did adopt, however, neither of the original drafts of the health warning was used. The wording of the health warning was left up to the cigarette companies, and the language that was eventually written into congressional legislation, and that was used on cigarette packages for a time, was considerably weaker than the commission's proposals.[69] The rule issued by the FTC also required a health warning to be contained in all advertising. The twofold ruling was to take effect on January 1, 1965.

Interest-group and congressional activity in the period between the publication of the rule and its effective date was swift and intensive. The industry created a voluntary code of self-regulation, and ap-

[68]Ibid., pp. 82-83.
[69]"Caution: Cigarette smoking may be hazardous to your health." This warning was subsequently strengthened to read, "Warning: The Surgeon General has determined that cigarette smoking is dangerous to your health."

pointed former New Jersey Governor Meyner as code administrator. Although the effect of this self-regulation has been difficult to assess, the chief purpose of the Cigarette Advertising Code and Meyner's direction was to curtail television advertisements that were likely to appeal to children and young people and to supervise the type of entertainment sponsored by tobacco companies.

Congressional response was aimed directly at reducing the severity of the FTC ruling and at easing the pressures on the tobacco industry. Fritschler points out that it is not uncommon for a bill to be introduced with the intent of abrogating a decision of an administrative agency, though the rate of success for such bills, is quite small. In this instance, however, the specificity of the bill was unusual in its citing the language of a particular regulation. Eventually, Congress was to annul the FTC's rule-making authority with respect to the tobacco industry and to remove the possibility of state and local legislation in this field. The health warning on cigarette packages was retained, but the requirement for warning in advertising was eliminated. Fritschler outlines the interesting and sometimes dramatic events that transpired between the promulgation of the rule and the passage of the legislation that, in effect, set it aside.

One should bear in mind the fierceness of interest-group activity, which was being pursued simultaneously with the legislative activity. In the legislative arena, Congressman Oren Harris, chairman of the House Interstate and Foreign Commerce Committee asked Dixon to delay implementation of the ruling. Dixon, aware of the dependency of his agency on Congress and the extent to which it was obviously in jeopardy of losing significant congressional support, agreed to delay the effective date, pending congressional action.

Fritschler claims that the final outcome of the legislative process was a distinct victory for the tobacco interests. He makes the claim even though the legislation distinctly identified tobacco as a potential hazard and alerted the public to the dangers of smoking. To be sure, the ruling of the FTC had been set aside and its net effect in specific terms had been minimized. But the long-range importance of legitimizing regulation of the tobacco industry as a matter of public and governmental prerogative should not be underestimated. Fritschler tends to do just that.

One may wonder, nonetheless, how, in the face of such over-whelming medical evidence and concern, the Congress could be so bold as to "capitulate" to the blatant self-interest of the tobacco indus-try. In the background we must realize, as has been noted, that more was at stake than the profits of a few plantation owners. Tobacco is big business in America. It is a major revenue base, and it is the cor-nerstone to the economic health of several states. The "public enemy" is not so personal and distinct as we might at first imagine.

Other circumstances seemed to have had a catalytic effect in this struggle. Certainly Senator Clements' experience on Capitol Hill, plus his close association with the Democratic leadership and with Pres-ident Johnson, had unquestionable weight in bringing about a legis-lative response favorable to the Tobacco Institute. Though little evi-dence exists that the White House interfered in the legislative process at this point, there is also little evidence that the White House opposed the legislation curtailing the FTC rule. Harris, chairman of the com-mittee that considered the ruling, represented a rural section in Arkan-sas; seven of the thirty-three committee members were from tobacco regions. Then, too, health groups could not mount any concerted po-litical drive to prevent Congress from changing the FTC rule. And Chairman Dixon, as already mentioned, had no desire to jeopardize further the shaky support he and his commission enjoyed in the Con-gress. On January 27, 1965, the president signed the Cigarette Label-ing Act into law—not a total victory for any of the sides involved: the tobacco industry, the government, or the public.

Fritschler does concede that the FTC action and the subsequent legislative response legitimized governmental attacks on the tobacco industry and virtually guaranteed continuance of tobacco use on the policy agenda. He notes: "Although things around the Federal Trade Commission grew quieter, the cigarette controversy continued. The non-smoking genie was out of the bottle and it began to appear and reappear in other, often unexpected places."[70] A skirmish only may have been won, but the battle has continued. Indeed, the appendix to Fritschler's book, published in 1969, presents a chronology of events succeeding the 1965 act; it lists such vigorous steps as the Federal Communications Commission's proposed rule to ban all

[70]Fritschler, *Smoking and Politics,* p. 129.

cigarette advertising from radio and television; the request by Secretary of Health, Education, and Welfare Wilbur Cohen to extend health warnings to advertising (part of the original FTC rule); and the continued FTC activity to make the language of the health warning on cigarette packages and in advertising more forceful. Fritschler, however, predicted that the Congress would not move to ban radio and television advertising. It is to his credit that a political scientist has the courage to make such a forecast. That it was proved wrong in no way detracts from the quality of this kind of analysis.

Smoking and Politics, in a manner not revealed by the other two case studies we have examined, shows the nature of conflict between professional bureaucracies, defined private interests, and the pluralist nature of legislative interests. Fritschler's study, like Bailey's and Bauer, Pool, and Dexter's, focuses primarily upon the attributes of a policy-making situation and the activities of the individuals involved in it. Although his study is much briefer and, as a consequence, much less useful in formulating durable generalizations about the legislative process, it reveals another dimension to the policy process—namely, the potential for initiative that rests with highly professionalized administrative agencies, in this case the offices of the surgeon general and of the Federal Trade Commission.

Case Studies of the Policy Process: Summary and Conclusions

These three studies are not by any means representative of all "case studies" of the policy process. They are illustrative, however, of that type of case study I call "explanatory," as opposed to "evaluative." Although these studies articulate, in varying degrees of explicitness, some of their authors' own preferences and estimates of the accomplishments of particular policies, the objective of each is to illuminate the processes by which policies are formed and the forces operating on the behavior of policy-makers. Toward this end, they suggest a number of useful generalizations.

Historical circumstances set the stage and provide the range of options available to policy-makers. The Depression and World War II signaled the necessities for a new federal employment policy in the late 1940s. Worldwide patterns of industrialization and the United States's role in world trade provided the setting for foreign-trade policy. And the progress of medical science, almost entirely independent of conscious governmental activity, generated the conditions for controversy over the proper government stance on the consumption of tobacco.

While historical and economic "inexorables"—considered as such by any set of governmental actors contending with changing circumstances—always create some critical aspects of the occasion for decision, the speed with which issues get politicized, the form of the options, and the manner of their disposition are decisively dependent upon individual perceptions, preferences, and leadership skills. Had Senator Murray or Bertram Gross not been on the scene, or had they taken a different course of action, or had they been less adept in political maneuvering, the Employment Act of 1946 would undoubtedly have proceeded at a different pace down a different path. Had President Eisenhower not run the risk of "me-tooism" on reciprocal trade, and had he instead followed the urgings of many protectionist Republicans, the course of foreign-trade policy in the postwar years would have been significantly altered. Had Senator Neuberger not kept attacking the "vile weed," and had not Chairman Dixon been willing to jeopardize some of his commission's political security, regulation of the tobacco industry might have taken a number of years longer than it has. Long-range economic, ideological, and institutional changes set the climate for policy innovation, amendment, and continuance. But particular men dispose—for a time—of particular items in particular settings. How individual decision-makers respond to the larger environment within which they work is, to some indeterminate extent, a function of their relationship to the groups that serve as the human reflections of socioeconomic and historical forces.

The three cases I have described give us some interesting contrasts and insights into the role of interest groups in the policy process. Interest groups are hardly the omnipotent, venal creations of man's collective greed and individual avarice that we may have once thought, the tobacco industry not excepted. Private groups, more often than not, act as service bureaus and publicizers at the behest of those officially in the policy process. Likes attract and opposites repel. Lobbyists do not seek out their opponents. Rather, they seek out—

and are sought out by—their allies. Their operating norm is to mobilize a potentially sympathetic response, not to convert opponents. And the lobbying group is more often the object of mobilization by policymakers than it is itself a mobilizing force.

The official policy-maker is aware of organized groups as but one of a multitude of environmental factors with which he interacts. His party (at home and in the Capital), the press, his constituents, and his colleagues all constitute sources of intersecting, complementing, and, sometimes, conflicting claims. Bailey and Bauer, Pool, and Dexter leave us with the impression that, more often than not, the resolution of role conflict is in response to the dictates of the institutional social system within the policy-making arena. The extent to which this applies outside legislative settings is not made clear by these studies. Fritschler's brief study does not provide a full picture of the regulatory agency or bureaucratic structure as a social system. However, other studies of the executive and of bureaucratic behavior would support the analogy of a social system.[71] Continuous interactions within the legislative structure maximize the relevance of collegial relationships and minimize the impact of more episodic, conflicting claims from without.

The public, whether on a national or congressional-district scale, allows the decision-maker considerable latitude. The image of congressmen hog-tied by "pressures back home" is a badly drawn caricature. As a rule, public opinion is a bit more "liberal" than most of the articulate interest groups. But public activity and public familiarity with legislative circumstances are low compared with the vigor and awareness of well-organized groups with definite interests at stake on specific issues. Just how clearly an interest group perceives the threats and benefits of a policy proposal often explains the success or failure of its claim.

Neither the automobile nor the chemical industry presented a united front on tariff policy. One might have expected to find rock-ribbed protectionists, girded for battle, bribes in hand. Instead, research disclosed an aggregation—not even a "group"—of people with mixed perceptions of self and national interest, a low level of

[71]See Richard Neustadt, *Presidential Power: The Politics of Leadership* (New York: John Wiley and Sons, 1960).

involvement, and a sense of insecurity about the proper bounds of corporate influence in the policy process.

The tobacco industry presented a different picture. Certainly no one could claim on the basis of available evidence that it is inhibited or self-conscious about the exercise of its influence. Nor could one claim that the industry is confused about where its interests lie with respect to the effects of certain policy options upon its profits. The cigar and pipe tobacco subsidiaries might stand to gain by a reduction in cigarette consumption, but to draw an analogy from this to the foreign operations of the auto and chemical industries would strain credibility. Therefore, despite the evidence of experts on the health consequences of smoking, and despite the likely popular support for tighter federal regulations on labeling and advertisement, the tobacco lobby could move with single-mindedness of purpose and apparent legislative effect in a way that protectionist interests could not.

How much effect upon the perceived targets of policy—smokers, importers, manufacturers, employers, laborers—policy pronouncements have, or could be anticipated to have, seems to be a peripheral matter in many policy disputes. As often as not, the symbols of policy are as important or more important than the substantive effects on social behavior. Symbolic phrases in the Declaration of Purpose were a chief concern for those engaged in the battle over the Full Employment Bill. Perceptions of foreign and domestic producers mattered as much as the balance of payments in calculations on foreign-trade legislation. And the health warning on cigarette packages was seen as a blow by the tobacco industry and a coup by the protagonists of the policy, whether or not cigarette smoking was reduced as a result of the label.

These observations, to the extent that they are drawn from a reliable set of examples, are of obvious value in explaining how the policy process operates. How central they are to the process, or what difference it would make to policy if they were not true, is unknown at this point. Writing about politics is necessarily colored by what the writer thinks politics *is*. And most writers about public policy seem to think that what politics *is* is what politicians *do,* and little else. This is especially true of case-study analysts.

Activity by individuals and the conflict of groups in the governmental sphere is what political scientists and popular opinion alike regard as "politics." Politics is interpersonal and inter-group conflict, bargaining, campaigning.

The prospect of nonconflictual "politics" does not enter most models. Most case analysts view the policy process in terms of potential winners and potential losers. It is not hard to imagine policy-making situations, however, in which conflict is of little consequence. Disaster relief after a tornado would be an example; the need for public action is not in dispute, and the goals are tangible. Conflicts in means, no doubt, would exist. Yet the bulk of activity in disaster relief would involve administrative coordination and implementation—both vital parts of the policy process. Nonetheless, if a typical political scientist were to set out to study programs of disaster relief, the odds are he would concentrate upon conflict situations—even though policies can be produced by factors other than interpersonal antagonisms, competing group aspirations, and so forth. But politics from the vantage of most case studies is seen as group conflict and individual bargaining, set within or close to the arenas of formal government. The prospect of nonpersonal or nonconflictual "politics," or both, is often ignored.

In the cases reviewed, the pattern of the bargaining process is observable. We see the conflict model at work. Even so, in seeking the roots—the generative forces—of policy, we are led by each case in different directions. Bailey points to the work of a few dedicated legislators and their staffs, while at the time alerting us to the historical and ideological climate that acted as a backdrop for individual leadership. Similar environmental influences are found by Bauer, Pool, and Dexter with respect to trade policy, though they give much more prominence to executive leadership and to cumulative results of foreign-trade policies. Little significance, in either instance, is attached to the initiative of private or nongovernmental groups, and agency pressures and bureaucratic aspirations are seen to have a minimal effect.

Fritschler reports the activity of a few dedicated legislators, mainly to emphasize the futility of their actions. Considerable credit for innovation must be laid to the concerns of professionals within and without the government—the surgeon general and some sectors of the medical community respectively. Implicitly, Fritschler's case study reveals the agenda-setting results of intragovernmental conflict. Policy is delayed, shaped, and advanced much in terms of an interplay between agency initiative, legislative perception of priorities, and private-group activities. Fritschler's picture of the interest group is quite at odds with that painted by Bailey or by Bauer and his colleagues. He does not attempt to persuade or to dissuade the reader regarding the typicality of the tobacco industry as a political group. However, the other cases would raise doubts as to the generality of the phenomena Fritschler observes.

All three studies, individually and collectively, illustrate both the strengths and the weaknesses of the case approach to an analysis of the public-policy processes. The primary virtue of the case approach is the richness of detail and the lucidity it can offer in illuminating the dynamics of policy-making. Further, the case approach has occasioned a number of important hypotheses that can be tested individually in many contexts.[72]

One of the possible fruits of the contextual richness provided by well-written case studies is an appreciation of the psychological dimensions and symbolic implications of policy-making activity. As noted previously, this is one of the major contributions of *Congress Makes a Law*. There is no other mode of analysis that conveys so well the consequentiality of symbols in the policy process.[73]

[72]See, for example, L. Harmon Zeigler and Michael Baer's *Lobbying* (Belmont, Calif.: Wadsworth, 1969) and their efforts to test in a comparative context many of Bauer, Pool, and Dexter's hypotheses.

[73]We might even develop a fairly elaborate theory that takes as its mainstay the hypothesis that the major function of legislative bodies in modern policy systems is to accommodate policy to socioeconomic necessity by means of symbols of legitimacy. This hypothesis is similar to, but divergent from, Murray Edelman's discussion of symbols in *The Symbolic Uses of Politics* (Urbana: University of Illinois Press, 1964). Edelman sees symbols as almost always substitutes for substantive change. On the contrary, it may be that in certain cases, such as the Employment Act of 1946, that the legislature blocks the use of symbols of innovation in order to provide a façade of continuity, while the policy in question is actually an innovative step that, if characterized as such, would antagonize established interests and power centers. The symbolic role of Congress is underscored in the area of foreign policy by James Robinson's inquiry, *Congress and Foreign Policy Making* (Homewood, Ill.: Dorsey Press, 1962). What, for example, did the Gulf of Tonkin Resolution or its equivalent change?

The weaknesses of case studies are revealed in their normal format. To review briefly, this format presents the historical background of an issue, isolates a decision or set of decisions on a policy, identifies interests and central actors, and reconstructs participants' attitudes and actions as they affected the outcome. Aside from the problem of how one decides whether or not a particular case is representative of the policy process, each of these steps has its own pitfalls.

"History" is an empty box into which the historian puts items from the past that he feels are relevant to his object of study. The Industrial Revolution, World War II, and the Great Depression were all relevant in some degree to domestic employment and foreign trade in the 1940s and 1950s. But so were certain geographic and climatic considerations—for example, those that made it feasible for the South to grow and export cotton. Had there been no war, would our current employment or trade policies be different? Had the Tobacco Institute not hired Earle Clements, would Congress indeed have been less churlish toward the FTC?

Picking one's historical facts is no more difficult than picking one's "decision." The points raised in Chapter II regarding decision studies of executive behavior are equally relevant here. Bauer, Pool, and Dexter make this point in discussing the interim nature of policy decisions. The case study gives a snapshot when a movie would be more appropriate. Perhaps it is unjust to argue that a study covering a few years (Bailey and Fritschler) or a decade (Bauer, Pool, and Dexter) is static. Yet the authors themselves emphasize the developmental nature of the issues they examine. Where are the cutoff points? When does a continuous process produce a "decision"? New York liberalizes its abortion laws, and within hours potential amendments are being discussed. The president signs an increase in social-security benefits, and immediately the next raise or modification in the program surfaces as an issue-to-be.

Identification of interests and participants is only a little less arduous than the filtration of historical background or the isolation of a "decision." As Bauer and his fellow analysts point out—much to the surprise of many observers of the policy process—those one would expect to have an interest and to articulate it forcefully may not perceive their role that way at all. The criticisms of "decisional" studies of community power also apply here. How do we know we have uncovered all those who might be "behind the scenes"? And, conversely, how can we be sure that persons and groups appearing to engage in policy-relevant activity are having any consequential impact?

These are problems of both the context and the content of decisions in the policy process. Not all of them have been solved by alternative modes of inquiry. Not all of them can be solved, given current research technology. However, the evolution and application of comparative methods have made some significant inroads toward their solution and have added a new dimension to policy analysis. The development of comparative policy studies is the subject of the remaining chapters.

chapter IV

Comparing Sociopolitical Environments of the Policy System

Introduction: The Progress of Inquiry

Policy-makers often choose from among mutually exclusive options. This process is usually a collective one. The mechanisms by which the collectivity is assembled and persists are institutionalized. One of the more prominent institutions is called government. Both the people and the institutions that constitute a government work, for the most part, with found material. They are enriched and encouraged or deprived and depressed in their policy-making activities by the resources and constraints of the sociopolitical environment.

The sociopolitical environment has not yet been accommodated systematically in the types of policy studies I have so far discussed. A relatively recent line of inquiry, however, has sought to make just such an accommodation. By systematic, comparative analyses of the relation between environment and politics, several studies have opened the gate on this exciting terrain of inquiry. These comparative studies —to be discussed in the succeeding chapters—do not start with the behavior of people whose role in the policy process is defined institutionally. Nor do they look at only a single case or small set of cases. Rather, they compare numerous systems in terms of their social and

political similarities and differences. In the American context, this has
meant that in comparative studies considerable attention has been
given to the policy activities of state and local governments.

Comparison precedes explanation. You cannot say *why* some circumstances are different from others until you know *how* they differ.
To compare we must be able to classify and measure the attributes
being compared. "Social structure" and "political systems" are concepts that, if they are to be used in comparative inquiry, must be dis-
tinguished and measured in terms of real-world components and
indicators that depict these components. How we sort the political
world and how we measure the pieces depends a great deal on our
theories of how politics works. In recent years some gains in theory—
with implications for measurement and comparison—have been made
in the study of public policy.

As noted above, much of the innovation in the comparative analysis of public policy has taken place in studies at the state and local
levels. The study of "state and local government" was transformed in
the 1960s about as dramatically as any other in political science.
Developments in the state and local government fields of inquiry parallel those of the entire discipline of political science. From an emphasis in the early decades of the century on formal structures of
government and the nuances of constitutional terminology, the study
of subnational governments in America has become an arena for
vigorous empirical political inquiry. It has moved from a legalistic
orientation through a period of single-state case studies to a fairly
high level of technical sophistication and theoretically suggestive
comparative analysis. A common frame of reference is becoming
accepted in the field, and a rudimentary *systems model* has been employed in most of the recent comparative inquiry.[1]

The systems model, in its most simplified form, treats the political system as a dynamic interplay between inputs (demands and
supports) from the environment, which are transformed by political
processes into some kind of outputs (policies, symbols, and services),

[1]See David Easton, *The Political System* (New York: Alfred A. Knopf, 1953);
or Thomas R. Dye, *Politics, Economics, and the Public: Policy Outcomes in
American States* (Chicago: Rand McNally, 1966); Richard E. Dawson and
James A. Robinson, "Inter-Party Competition, Economic Variables, and Welfare Policies in the American States," *Journal of Politics* 25 (1963): 265-289.

which themselves have subsequent consequences (feedback) for inputs and the political process. The sequence is frequently discussed in terms of three boxes connected by arrows. (Figure IV-1) Demands and supports enter the political system from one side of the paradigm. The political system accommodates and converts these demands and supports into outputs, customarily termed "policy."[2]

Although no self-conscious attempt has been made to take cognizance of the most elaborate extensions of the systems model,[3] in the comparative state and local government field one can find a deliberate effort to identify patterns of input, conversion, and output of political systems in a comparative setting.

The landmark publication in this field appeared in 1963 with the report of research conducted by Richard Dawson and James Robinson. Dawson and Robinson ran a series of correlations between certain aspects of state wealth and social structure, indicators of party

Figure IV-1

MODEL OF THE POLICY SYSTEM

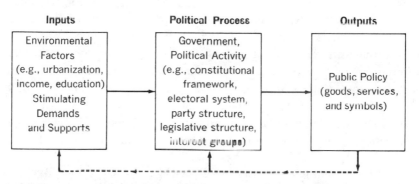

Adapted from Thomas R. Dye, *Politics, Economics, and the Public* (Chicago: Rand McNally, 1966), p. 4. See also, John G. Grumm, "The Effects of Legislative Structure on Legislative Performance," in *State and Urban Politics*, ed. Richard I. Hofferbert and Ira Sharkansky (Boston: Little, Brown and Co., 1971), p. 300.

[2]See Dye, *Politics, Economics, and Public*, chap. 1 for an elaboration of the model.

[3]See, for example, David Easton, *A Systems Analysis of Political Life* (New York: John Wiley and Sons, 1965).

systems, and expenditures for a variety of welfare-related programs. The socioeconomic variables were conceived as rough cognates of the demands and supports posited in the systems model. The indicators of party competition were conceived by Dawson and Robinson as at least one part of the conversion or "political" sector of the model. And the indicators of expenditure were used to reflect system outputs. In the process of their inquiry, Dawson and Robinson were able to question the relevance of interparty competitiveness to public expenditures. We shall return to this question later. Their contribution to the study of public policy, of course, went beyond this simple iconoclastic finding. The Dawson and Robinson article had at least three significant consequences.

First of all, Dawson and Robinson encouraged a form of inquiry that had been often advocated but seldom practiced. They demonstrated more conclusively and dramatically than most of their predecessors the potential for systematic, comparative study of policy in the states.[4]

Dawson and Robinson's second contribution was to cast doubt on the relevance of many political characteristics that most scholars had valued for their ability to explain public policy. In particular, the co-authors demonstrated—admittedly with limited data and with narrowly defined indicators—that no apparent systematic relationship exists between interparty competitiveness and the welfare orientation of state and local public policies. This finding has been subjected to a variety of tests and has been qualified somewhat, but it is still sufficiently credible to introduce an element of concern and reaction among more traditional students of state politics.[5] Dawson

[4]A few economists had used comparative state data to examine some hypotheses about fiscal policy, but these studies failed to stimulate a general response by political scientists. See, for example, Soloman Fabricant, *The Trend of Government Activity in the United States Since 1900* (New York: Bureau of Economic Research, 1952).

[5]Duane Lockard, "State Party Systems and Policy Outputs," in *Political Research and Political Theory,* ed. Oliver Garceau (Cambridge, Mass.: Harvard University Press, 1968), pp. 190-215; John H. Fenton and Donald W. Chamberlayne, "The Literature Dealing with the Relationships Between Political Processes, Socioeconomic Conditions and Public Policies in the American States: A Bibliographical Essay," *Polity* (1969): 388-404.

and Robinson, therefore, motivated policy analysts to challenge the wisdom of trying to explain public policy by means of either formal structures of government or the party systems of the states.

Analysts of American politics, especially those concerned with electoral politics, have long instructed us that two-party competition has a direct bearing upon the decisions of a policy-maker within the states. V. O. Key, Jr., and Duane Lockard have argued rather convincingly that a close balance between two parties will lead each of them to make appeals to the have-not sectors of the electorate.[6] Furthermore, the continuous threat of a viable opposition party will force the incumbents to carry out at least a significant portion of these promises. Dawson and Robinson indeed found high correlations between interparty competition and levels of state and local expenditures in certain welfare related policies. But when they controlled for levels of urbanization, income, and industrialization, the competitiveness-spending correlation disappeared. Evidently, opposition from a threatening minority party is not a marked inducement for policy-makers to heed the needs of have-nots through state governmental means. The Dawson and Robinson article has served as the watershed for much comparative policy analysis since 1963, despite subsequent qualifications of their rather uncommon assertions.

In his *Politics, Economics, and the Public,* Thomas R. Dye refined the technology and expanded the scope of inquiry to a much longer list of policy variables. His findings demonstrate the utility of the reasoning stimulated by Dawson and Robinson. Party and structural variables—including legislative apportionment, political control, competition, and voter turnout—have no systematic, independent effect upon most of the quantitative indicators of policy studied by Dye. Other scholars have examined the impact of different institutional characteristics—for example, legislative professionalism or partisan divisions between houses and governmental branches—and several objective indicators of policy output. The usual finding is that the independent relationship is very low.[7]

[6]V. O. Key, Jr., *Southern Politics in State and Nation* (Alfred A. Knopf, 1951), pp. 298-314; Duane Lockard, *New England State Politics* (Princeton: Princeton University Press, 1959), pp. 320-340.

[7]John Grumm, "Structure and Policy in the Legislature" (Paper presented at the 1967 annual meeting of the Southwest Social Science Association, Dallas,

The implications of this line of research for our conceptions of how governments work could indeed be disturbing to many a thoughtful advocate of the democratic process. If these findings were to stand without challenge, they would say that within the range of variation that exists in the United States the form of government one has does not make a great deal of difference. This, of course, harks back to Alexander Pope's couplet, "For forms of government let fools contest/whate'er is best administer'd is best." The aristocratic implications of Pope's dictum were always ill-received by confirmed democrats. And yet much current research in public policy indicates that those who seek to explain variations in policy by means of the "democraticness" of governments—again, at least within the range found in America—are apt to be quite disappointed. Fortunately for the peace of mind of such democrats, subsequent inquiry has indeed qualified much of the initially heretical findings of this research.[8] These qualifications in no way detract, however, from the long-range contributions, both methodological and theoretical, made by these earlier suggestive inquiries.

The third consequence of the Dawson-Robinson article (and its successors) has been to increase the attention given to socioeconomic structures. I would argue that this is probably the most consequential long-run contribution, even if the specific findings do not stand up under more detailed scrutiny. In particular, Dawson and Robinson demonstrated the possibility of constructing clear measures of socioeconomic development within the states. They also showed the applicability of these measures to the task of explaining patterns of public policy.

Although it is a pretty loosely formulated prescription, the message and method that emerges from these studies assert the need and means for looking at historical and socioeconomic environments in

---

March, 1967); Richard I. Hofferbert, "The Relation Between Public Policy and Some Structural and Environmental Variables in the American States," *American Political Science Review* 60 (1966): 73-82.

[8]John Grumm, "The Effects of Legislative Structure on Legislative Performance," in *State and Urban Politics,* ed. Richard I. Hofferbert and Ira Sharkansky (Boston: Little, Brown and Co., 1971), pp. 248-322; Ira Sharkansky and Richard I. Hofferbert, "Dimensions of State Politics, Economics, and Public Policy," *American Political Science Review* 63 (1969): 867-880.

order to explain levels of variation in policy patterns. When the characteristics suggested by inquiry into electoral politics or institutional structure are the only ones employed to explain policy, misleading and disappointing results are likely to be obtained; we simply must look at more than the party structure and the legal apparatuses of the political system if we are to understand why policies come out the way they do. Further, we have seen the difficulties involved in trying to explain differences in policy by looking at the behavior of legislators, governors, judges, or community leaders. A necessity for opening theoretical boundaries to include some facets of social and economic development has been demonstrated. Case studies cannot do so because they lack firm standards for choosing environmental features for analysis.

The lesson provided by Dawson and Robinson at the state level has not gone unheeded by students of comparative local politics. The comparative mode, the focus on policy, and the concern for social structure have been adopted in a variety of urban research projects.[9] Local inquiry has included a slightly different set of structural considerations and, more than the state studies, has been directly concerned with the specific reform measures instituted in American cities during the Progressive era. The model most commonly employed in the local studies, however, is the same as that used in the state-level research.

The model posits the three-part structure we have been considering: socioeconomic environment, political processes, and policy outputs. The correspondence between this simple structure of inquiry and the variations on systems analysis that have been adopted in different settings needs no elaboration. Numerous studies in recent years have examined the hypotheses suggested by this model and have developed conceptualizations of its component parts. Each

---

[9] These projects are summarized up to 1967 by Lewis A. Froman, Jr., "An Analysis of Public Policies in Cities," *Journal of Politics* 29 (1967): 94-108. See also Robert L. Lineberry and Edmund P. Fowler, "Reformism and Public Policies in American Cities," *American Political Science Review* 61 (1967): 701-716; Richard I. Hofferbert, "State and Community Policy Studies: A Review of Comparative Input-Output Analyses," in *Political Science Annual,* vol. III, ed. James A. Robinson (Indianapolis: Bobbs-Merrill, 1972).

component is complicated, conceptually and in reality. Each is difficult to define and to measure. Much scholarly inquiry has been spent defining and measuring "socioeconomic structure" in such a way as to be useful to the policy analyst.

Socioeconomic Structures
in Comparative Perspective

It would be very nearsighted for any group of contemporary scholars to lay claim to having themselves discovered the relevance of social structure to the operation of political systems. Since classical times, the intersection of society and politics has consistently drawn the attention of political philosophers. Aristotle demonstrated this interest in his oft-quoted statement: ". . . the state is a creation of nature, and man is by nature a political animal."

By classifying polities in terms of social structures, Aristotle sought to derive the most suitable form of government. Political philosophers from then to now have looked at the structure of society to discover the mainsprings of political activity. Fortunately for contemporary inquiry, a considerable amount of technological expertise and scientific rigor is now being incorporated into what used to be a purely metaphysical and normative exercise. Aristotle's concern was to ascertain the "best" form of government, given certain social conditions. The contemporary concern is to discover what modes of political activity empirically seem to be determined by particular levels and forms of social structure. But how do we perceive and measure "social structure" so that several policy systems can be compared? We need measures that allow us to see how different social structures influence corresponding differences in policies.

Cross-National Examples

Some of the roots of contemporary policy analysis lie in cross-national studies. In the late 1950s, a few political scientists did start the systematic, comparative analysis of sociopolitical relationships at the cross-national level. The most frequently cited essay is Seymour

Martin Lipset's "Some Social Requisites of Democracy."[10] Lipset's was the first in a series of studies examining the relationships between levels of economic development and democratic attributes of national regimes.[11] Lipset found a modest relationship between a host of economic development indicators—for instance, the number of doctors, telephones, and radios—and the democratic stability of non-Communist regimes. Comparable findings have been reported by Lyle Shannon in relating "capacity for self-government" to various indicators of development.[12] In both Lipset's and Shannon's studies, however, ranges within categories of "democraticness" are sufficiently elastic to allow for many deviant cases—developed nondemocratic systems or less developed but still democratic polities.

Other scholars have moved from Lipset's suggestions and have increased the precision with which both the social and the political variables are measured. One 1963 article concludes: "Knowledge of the level of development of the communications system accounts for 65 percent of the variation in scores around the mean of the political development index."[13] Of several facets of national development, communications systems seem to be most important politically.

Paralleling many of the state and community studies of recent years, Phillips Cutright also examined the relationship between political structure, economic development, and social-security programs at the national level.[14] Using as his dependent variable scores based upon several social-security programs, Cutright determined that structures of representation—that is, the "democraticness" of popular

[10]Seymour Martin Lipset, "Some Social Requisites of Democracy. Economic Development and Political Legitimacy," *American Political Science Review* 53 (1959): 69-105.

[11]Phillips Cutright, "National Political Development: Measurement and Analysis," *American Sociological Review* 28 (1963): 253-264; Deane E. Neubauer, "Some Conditions of Democracy," *American Political Science Review* 61 (1967): 1002-1009; Arthur K. Smith, "Socio-Economic Development and Political Democracy: A Causal Analysis," *Midwest Journal of Political Science* 12 (1969): 95-125.

[12]Lyle W. Shannon, "Socioeconomic Development and Demographic Variables as Predictors of Political Change," *Sociological Quarterly* 3 (1962): 27-43.

[13]Cutright, "National Political Development," p. 64.

[14]Phillips Cutright, "Political Structure, Economic Development, and National Social Security Programs," *American Journal of Sociology* 60 (1965): 537-550.

representation—are of minimal impact upon policy outputs at the national level. Much more important are the level of development and the prior colonial status. Countries with high levels of economic resources have more generous welfare programs regardless of the apparent democratic or nondemocratic structures of the governmental institutions.

Many problems have plagued inquiry at both the cross-national and the comparative subnational level. Some are technical. But most of them stem from the dilemmas relating to how one conceptualizes "social structure." Are indicators of the number of television sets or the number of doctors or the number of highways or the number of factories in a nation adequate to give a precise and useful picture of the total structure of that society? Or does the choice of such indicators reveal a conceptualization of social structure that is unduly and narrowly oriented toward the example of social change provided by the United States and a few other Western countries?

Conceptualization of "Social Structure"

Each of the studies in both the cross-state and the cross-national fields has used a somewhat different list of socioeconomic characteristics. Whether or not these characteristics relate in such a way as to constitute a picture of "social structure" is rarely explored. The reader must simply share each author's assumption that the variables included tap aspects of society that are important for politics.

"Social structure" is a term involving troublesome processes and concepts—"modernization," "development," "mobilization," "transition," "differentiation," "cleavage," and so forth. Even a summary discussion of the problems that have been encountered by scholars attempting to use these concepts would more than fill this volume. But a few of the problems have a direct and immediate bearing on assessing and reviewing comparative policy studies. Two key problems are linearity and dimensionality; they reveal themselves in questions about social and political change.

Whenever people talk about economic development, modernization, or any other dynamic social process, terms implying change are central to the discussion. It is reasonable to ask, however, whether there is a process of change common to the societies, political systems, or both, included in one's view. Have all the nations or states moved from a condition called "traditional" to one called "modern?"[15] Also, are the aspects subject to change—for example, industrialization, urbanization, democratic development—all changing in a common direction? Or are there multiple and perhaps independent patterns of change both between and within countries? Certainly during the past generation, the course of the many experiments in democratization in new nations illustrates that the Western pattern is anything but universal or inexorable. And some very "modern" regimes, like Weimar Germany and Fourth Republic France, have "decayed."

Neither Lipset's nor Cutright's cross-sectional analysis, conducted in one point in time, confronts the question of linearity at the level of nation-states. Nor is the question confronted in the earlier comparative state-politics studies that examine the relevance of social development to policy, though some effort has been made to demonstrate the uniformity of socioeconomic change among the American states.[16] Ample evidence is contained in these explorations to show that the American states are indeed changing in common directions. The evidence further suggests that the patterns of interrelationship between aspects of social structure have been fairly constant over a long period.[17]

Even if the question of common directions of socioeconomic change is resolved in the affirmative, however, the problem of the dimensionality remains. Much of the early literature from development economics assumes that socioeconomic change is unidimensional—that one central form of social change is most salient within all societies.[18] Reinhard Bendix argues that industrialization and the

[15]Reinhard Bendix, "Tradition and Modernity Reconsidered," *Comparative Studies in Society and History* 9 (1967): 292-346.

[16]Richard I. Hofferbert, "Ecological Development and Policy Change in the American States," *Midwest Journal of Political Science* 10 (1966): 464-483; Hofferbert, "Socioeconomic Dimensions of the American States: 1890-1960," *Midwest Journal of Political Science* 12 (1968): 401-418.

[17]Hofferbert, "Socioeconomic Dimensions."

[18]See, for example, Walt W. Rostow, *The Stages of Economic Growth: A Non-Communist Manifesto* (London: Cambridge University Press, 1964); Daniel Lerner, *The Passing of Traditional Society: Modernization in the Middle East* (Glencoe, Ill.: The Free Press, 1958).

patterns of interaction that go with it neither require nor necessarily imply the abandonment or the declining relevance of "traditional" structures within a society.[19] It is possible—indeed likely—that many features of "pre-modern" society will persist virtually unaffected by massive changes in, for example, modes of production, status aspirations, and governmental activity.[20]

Measuring Multidimensionality

The American states can be viewed in terms of more than one "dimension" of socioeconomic differentiation.[21] In order to examine and measure this multidimensionality, however, some unavoidable statistical discussion is called for.[22] In attempting to measure attributes of any complex process, such as social structure or political participation, a strong correlation between sets of indicators is frequently demonstrated. If we are to refer to a *process* or a *structure,* we are indeed assuming the presence of functional connections—something more than the simple presence of discrete attributes. Certain things occur together and depend on one another's presence. If some conditions remain the same, then others also hold. In an effort to exclude those things that are independent and to weigh the interdependence of those that are connected, Ira Sharkansky and I analyzed a large array of state social and political characteristics.[23] Our objective was to explore and measure the "dimensions" of state social structures and political processes. We sought to analyze sufficiently distinct aspects of these state structures and processes so that the interrelationships between social and political phenomena could be revealed and would yield indices more comprehensive in scope than any of the specific items formerly used in sociopolitical analysis of state politics.

[19]Bendix, "Tradition and Modernity."

[20]See Lloyd and Susanne Rudolph, *The Modernity of Tradition: Political Development in India* (Chicago: University of Chicago Press, 1967).

[21]Hofferbert, "Socioeconomic Dimensions."

[22]The reader is advised that the techniques to be discussed here will be employed fairly regularly in the balance of the book. A succinct and lucid discussion of factor analysis is contained in Rudolph Rummel, "Understanding Factor Analysis," *Journal of Conflict Resolution* 11 (1967): 444-480.

[23]Sharkansky and Hofferbert, "Dimensions of State Politics," pp. 867-880.

In any situation where one seeks to pin numbers on a concept, a wise stratagem is to employ several measures in the hope that they will, in a sense, triangulate on the conceptual target more accurately than any single item.[24] Multiple measurement, however, still leaves one guessing about what is the common element of the many variables used. Averaging scores or ranks and constructing composite indices of unweighted items run the risk of making several unwarranted and unnecessary assumptions. Averaging allows for no indication of the relative impact of the items included. Multiple regression analysis—pyramiding correlation coefficients, in effect—runs a similar risk. A strong case can be made for a lengthy list of indicators of any concept used in research, but one also needs a mechanism for sorting out that which is common and that which is not. Two-party balance may be part of a system of political participation; it may closely relate to voter turnout and several other elements. But some facets of competition or turnout may have nothing whatever to do with the "process" one is seeking to index. If used with some sensitivity, factor analysis serves this need.

The technique of factor analysis starts from the basic assumption that interrelations among separate variables signal the existence of underlying traits—or "factors"—that the variables share in common. We may not be sure ahead of time exactly what the precise relationship is between the variables and the common trait, but we have good reason to suspect some mutuality of relevance. A factor analysis manipulates a collection of variables in order to discern the patterns of relationships among them. The groups of variables that relate closely to one another—but only loosely or not at all to variables in other groups—are extracted as the principal factors. The individual variables that show the strongest relationships with other members of their factor have, in the language of factor analysis, the highest *loadings*. A variable's loading is like a coefficient of correlation between that variable and the underlying factor.[25] By knowing the

[24]For an enlightening critique of single-indicator analysis and a discussion of the methodological justification for multiple indicators, see Eugene J. Webb, Donald T. Campbell, Richard D. Schwartz, and Lee Sechrest, *Unobtrusive Measures: Nonreactive Research in the Social Sciences* (Chicago: Rand McNally, 1966).

[25]See Rummel, "Understanding Factor Analysis," p. 463.

variables with the highest loadings on each factor, it is possible to infer something about the underlying traits that the factor represents. The variables with the highest loadings come closest to representing the underlying trait, although it is unlikely that any single variable represents that trait perfectly. The technique examines the correlation matrix of the individual variables and extracts factors whose members show maximum correlations among themselves and minimum correlations with the members of other factors.

Some writers have been critical of certain uses to which factor analysis has been put—particularly in view of the increased availability of pre-packaged computer programs and sophisticated computing facilities. Two major criticisms are relevant in the present context. First, it is charged that factor analysis has been used in lieu of theory.[26] If one simply plugs into the machine all the data at his command, some kind of factors will emerge. Factor analysis is not a substitute for theory. There must be some prior rationale that justifies the particular variables fed into the computer. Secondly, the technique has been criticized because the factors that emerge often seem to make little sense in terms of the theory with which one is working.[27] Theory is then juggled to accommodate the machinery.

This is not the appropriate context in which to explore the intricacies of factor analysis. But Sharkansky and I did recognize the necessity to account for some of the major criticisms and to point out how we tried to minimize the difficulties in our inquiry. We attempted to avoid these pitfalls in two ways. First, the variables we included were used because of their widespread currency in analyses by other scholars and because of the appealing theoretical rationale these analysts offered. Secondly, as will be apparent, the factors we obtained make sense, and we employed a number of checks to insure that the sense they make is not an artifact of the technique. In order to use the results of factor analysis to test relationships among dimensions of politics, economics, and public policy, we derived "factor

[26]J. Scott Armstrong, "Derivation of Theory of Means of Factor Analysis, or Tom Swift and His Electric Factor Analysis Machine," *American Statistician* (1967): 17-21.

[27]See, for example, John E. Mueller, "Some Comments on Russett's 'Discovering Voting Groups in the United Nations,'" *American Political Science Review* 61 (1967): 146-148.

scores" for each state from the combination of its values—in real property, for example, in farmland, in manufacturing—on the individual variables and the loading of each variable on each factor.

Socioeconomic Dimensions of the States

Table IV-1 presents the factors and factor loading for the variables analyzed to construct indices of state socioeconomic structure. Table IV-2 presents the factor scores for particular states. The analysis reveals two dimensions labeled "industrialization" and "affluence." Industrialization is characterized by a high degree of manufacturing employment as opposed to a large amount of agricultural activity. It is an eminently modern phenomenon, it accounts for the gravitation of most of the foreign born to manufacturing areas, and it distinguishes, for example, New Jersey from Wyoming. The other dimension of social structure—affluence—taps those differences between the states most commonly seen in the North-South distinction. We can view the states in terms of wealth and high levels of educational attainment, a view that will indicate the affluence of certain states— those that do not have many nonwhites, considerable tenant farming, and low property values. Mississippi and Arkansas are among the least affluent states; Nevada and Connecticut are among the most.

The affluence dimension subtly identifies attributes of pre-industrial American society. The differences that separate Connecticut from Georgia date back to the early periods of white settlement on the North American Continent. Yet this difference, as well as the differences in industrialization, has extremely important effects on the patterns of policy the states follow today.

A bit of reflection on the economic history of the states will underscore the value of separate indices of socioeconomic structure. Economically, large sections of the South have always been poorer than the rest of America. In this respect, the late-nineteenth-century South was similar to plantation economies in some of today's less-developed nations.[28] To the extent that the South has industrialized, it

[28]Richard I. Hofferbert and Ira Sharkansky, "Socioeconomic Structure and Politics in Subnational Systems: A Comparison in Four Nations," in *Legislatures in Comparative Perspective*, ed. Allan Kornberg (New York: David McKay, 1971).

Table IV-1 Loadings of Socioeconomic Variables on Two Principal Factors: 1960

Industrialization Loading		Affluence Loading	
Value added by manufacture per capita	+.91	Median school years completed	+.91
Percentage employed in manufacturing	.88	Estimated value of real property per capita	.79
Value per acre of farmland and buildings	.83	Personal income per capita	.73
Population per square mile	.78	Motor vehicle registration per 1,000 population	.70
Per cent foreign	.70	Telephones per 1,000 population	.68
Total population	.67	Per cent increase in population	.55
Per cent urban	.66	Per cent urban	.52
Telephones per 1,000 population	.65	Acreage per farm	.49
Average number of employees per manufacturing establishment	.64	Divorce rate	.43
Personal income per capita	.57	Per cent failures business + comm. establishments	.29
Per cent failures business + commercial establishments	.42	Per cent housing owner occupied	.24
Estimated value real property per capita	.13	Per cent foreign	.23
Per cent black	.07	Total population	.04
Per cent illiterate	.04	Value per acre of farmland and buildings	.02
Per cent increase in population	.01	Value added by manufacture per capita	.01
Median school years completed	.03	Population per square mile	.01
Per cent farms operated by tenants	.27	Percentage employed in manufacturing	.13
Per cent housing owner occupied	.32	Average number of employees per manufacturing establishment	.35
Divorce rate	.32	Per cent farms operated by tenants	.47
Acreage per farm	.50	Per cent illiterate	.74
Motor vehicle registration per 1,000 population	−.57	Per cent black	−.75
Per cent of total variance	32.4	Per cent of total variance	25.3

Source: Hofferbert, "Socioeconomic Dimensions of the American States, 1890-1960," *Midwest Journal of Political Science* 12 (1968): 405-409.

Table IV-2   Socioeconomic Factor Scores for the States: 1960*

State	Industrialization Factor Score	State	Affluence Factor Score
New Jersey	2.1	Nevada	2.3
Illinois	2.0	California	1.5
Connecticut	1.9	Wyoming	1.3
New York	1.9	Colorado	1.2
Massachusetts	1.6	Oregon	1.0
Delaware	1.2	Washington	1.0
Pennsylvania	1.2	Montana	0.9
Rhode Island	1.2	Kansas	0.8
Ohio	1.1	Nebraska	0.8
California	1.0	Connecticut	0.7
Michigan	0.9	Utah	0.7
Indiana	0.8	Delaware	0.6
Maryland	0.8	Idaho	0.6
Wisconsin	0.5	Florida	0.5
Missouri	0.4	Arizona	0.4
New Hampshire	0.3	Iowa	0.4
Washington	0.0	Massachusetts	0.4
Minnesota	−0.1	Minnesota	0.4
North Carolina	−0.1	New Jersey	0.4
Tennessee	−0.1	New York	0.4
Virginia	−0.1	Illinois	0.3
Georgia	−0.1	Michigan	0.2
Iowa	−0.2	New Mexico	0.2
Louisiana	−0.2	Ohio	0.2
Maine	−0.2	South Dakota	0.2
South Carolina	−0.2	Oklahoma	0.1
Texas	−0.2	Indiana	0.0
West Virginia	−0.2	Maryland	0.0
Oregon	0.3	New Hampshire	0.0
Alabama	0.4	North Dakota	0.0
Florida	−0.4	Texas	0.0
Kentucky	−0.4	Wisconsin	0.0
Vermont	−0.4	Pennsylvania	−0.1
Colorado	−0.5	Missouri	−0.2
Kansas	−0.5	Rhode Island	0.2
Utah	−0.6	Vermont	−0.2
Nebraska	−0.7	Maine	−0.3
Arkansas	−0.8	Virginia	−0.8
Mississippi	0.8	Kentucky	−1.3
Oklahoma	−0.8	West Virginia	−1.3
Arizona	−1.0	Arkansas	−1.4
Idaho	−1.2	Georgia	−1.4
Nevada	−1.2	Louisiana	−1.4
New Mexico	−1.3	Tennessee	−1.4
Montana	−1.3	Alabama	−1.5
South Dakota	−1.4	North Carolina	−1.6
North Dakota	−1.5	South Carolina	−2.0
Wyoming	−1.5	Mississippi	−2.2

*Alaska and Hawaii are excluded from this and subsequent analyses because they were granted statehood late in the period covered by much of the state policy research.

has done so late. But it is not the absence of industrialization alone that explains the relative poverty or low affluence of the region. Several southern states were low in industrialization in 1890 and have subsequently moved into the ranks of the more industrialized states. North Carolina, while becoming relatively no more affluent, was in the bottom third in industrialization in 1890; it has now moved into the top third in terms of industrial activity per capita. Conversely, Montana is relatively less industrial today than in 1890, yet in such terms as per capita income and education levels it has remained among the most affluent states.[29] By comparison with New Jersey, Michigan, or Illinois, the states of the Plains and Rocky Mountains are not industrialized. Nonetheless, Nevada has one of the highest levels of income and education in the country. Wyoming, too, cannot be described as economically "underdeveloped," despite the absence of factories. The agrarian regions of the Plains and the West are not industrialized, but neither are they poor in the way that so many of the areas of the South are poor—often in spite of considerable industrialization. To equate Idaho with Arkansas merely because both have few factories is apt to cause many problems of analysis and to conceal some differences that are critical in understanding each state's political process.

If we reflect upon the style and economic role of southern agriculture and compare it with the agriculture of either the Midwest or the Plains, the differences become obvious. And when one tries to relate socioeconomic differences to political behavior or policy, indiscriminate categorization can cause severe distortions. Arkansas has one of the lowest levels of political competition and turnouts in the country, Idaho one of the highest. This difference can, at least in part, be related to differences in their social structure having nothing to do with industrialization. Similar differences are manifest in their relative levels of public services.

The purpose here is to suggest that the conceptualization of socioeconomic structure is becoming increasingly complicated and sophisticated with the expansion of systematic inquiry into sociopolitical relationships. The comparative state and local policy studies lay out some suggestive hypotheses and possible relationships. They also

[29]Hofferbert, "Socioeconomic Dimensions."

lay out the groundwork for the exploration of differential social structures.

Within the context of policy studies specifically, however, many different arguments support the necessity for clarity in the conceptualization of socioeconomic influences. Several authors have suggested the strong possibility that the structures of determination will vary from one policy area to another.[30] Not only will different aspects of society and political systems be relevant to different policies, but also the mix of relevant social and political variables will be different from one policy area to another.[31]

To summarize, then, Dawson and Robinson captured the imagination of students of state and local politics. The line of inquiry begun with their article has been reinforced and significantly advanced by other studies.[32] Although political scientists have given much of their attention to the iconoclastic demonstration of the low importance of political-system variables to policy outputs, in the long run the greatest theoretical contribution of Dawson and Robinson comes from the expanded vistas provided by looking carefully at social structures and how they relate to policy.

In the succeeding chapters we shall see how the analysis of social structure has advanced our knowledge of the policy process, at least in the American context. However, some additional measurement problems must be discussed first. In the society-politics-policy model, conceptual and measurement problems have not been confined to the first sector, inputs (Figure IV-1). Equally awkward and difficult problems confront us when we begin to attach numbers to the content of the middle box in the systems diagram—the political process.

[30]Theodore Lowi, "American Business, Public Policy, Case-Studies, and Political Theory," *World Politics* 6 (1964): 677-715; Robert H. Salisbury, "The Analysis of Public Policy: A Search for Theories and Roles," in *Political Science and Public Policy*, ed. Austin Ranney (Chicago: Markham Publishing Co., 1968), pp. 151-178; Richard I. Hofferbert, "Elite Influence in State Policy Formation: A Model for Comparative Inquiry," *Polity* 2 (1970): 316-344.

[31]Sharkansky and Hofferbert, "Dimensions of State Politics."

[32]See Dye, *Politics, Economics, and Public* and the essays in Herbert Jacob and Kenneth N. Vines, eds., *Politics in the American States*, 2nd ed. (Boston: Little, Brown and Co., 1971).

Conceptualization and Measurement
of the Political Process

The systems model suggests a set of classifications into which one may fit related features of the policy process and for which the student of that process seeks real-world counterparts. I have noted the classical concern with the intersection between society and politics. The systems framework simplifies the problem faced by classical scholars as well as by contemporary analysts. In many respects much of classical political philosophy failed to make any distinction whatever between the social and the political. In some epochs the distinction would have been without any genuine difference. For most eras, however, trying to separate what is political from what is social has been a nagging problem for both normative and empirical scholars.

From the purely operational standpoint, for example, it is reasonable to treat levels of industrialization or income as causes and to treat governmental expenditures for industrial development or welfare as effects. But in a modern, highly politicized, planned economy, the levels are as much a function of the expenditures as the expenditures are of the levels. Does a high educational level of the populace lead to more expenditures for the public schools, or should the equation be reversed? At a somewhat higher level of abstraction, can we treat the economic growth of the United States as determined by our governmental structures, or should we see the structures a product of the growth? Surely the railroads opened the West. Railroad policy was consciously devised by political decision-makers at both the state level and the national throughout the nineteenth and twentieth centuries. Yet the economic consequences of that policy have conditioned the subsequent actions of policy-makers in a host of seemingly unrelated areas.

This problem of measuring policy consequences has not yet been solved by students of the policy process. What has evolved, nevertheless, is an increase in attention to a specific and discrete set of attributes that can qualify on a common-sense basis as significant characteristics of state and local governmental structures. Measuring some of these characteristics has opened the door to an exploration of their comparative importance in determining policy performance. The features of state and local political systems that have been investigated are those relating most directly to the intellectual position established in earlier decades of political inquiry. Though techniques of measurement and the research focus have been somewhat different at the state and at the local level, the differences are within a common focus. The concerns of structural reformers and those seeking more responsible party systems are clearly visible in the features of political systems that have been measured most carefully.

Executive Influence

Concern with the governor's role in the policy-making process has fixed itself primarily on the formal attributes of the executive structure. From the time of the president's Committee on Administrative Management in 1939 down through the "Little Hoover Commissions" of the 1940s and '50s and up to the present, much reform-oriented discussion has dealt with the need for centralizing and rationalizing the state executive's role in the policy process. This discussion has resulted in specific proposals for strengthening the office; among them: the executive budget, expanded appointive powers, and various combinations of veto authority. To the extent that a systematic effort has been made to account for the executive's influence in the policy process, the effort has tended to dwell upon variations with respect to these structural characteristics. The questions have been asked: What difference does executive authority make regarding policy? Does a state with a "strong" governor enact different policies from a state with a "weak" governor?

Ideally, if an analyst were investigating the influence of a governor upon state public policy, he would want to know the frequency with which the governor "had his own way," how often he got enacted the types of policies he desired. The data on which to base this estimate would include not only those legislative proposals the governor had recommended, but also those he would have recommended had he not anticipated adverse legislator response. Further, the analyst would want some estimate of the relative importance the governor attached to all items in his program. Some progress has been made along these lines.[33] The problem of anticipated reactions, however, is

[33]Ira Sharkansky, "Agency Requests, Gubernatorial Support and Budget Success in State Legislatures," *American Political Science Review* 62 (1968): 1220-

yet to be confronted in any systematic research. And most of the work in the comparative studies has concentrated upon measuring the formal aspects of gubernatorial power.

Joseph Schlesinger's is the best-known effort to construct an index of formal gubernatorial power.[34] He assigned points to the governors on the basis of four formal features of their office: budget powers, appointive powers, tenure potential, and veto powers. Scores derived from these items were combined by Schlesinger in a composite index of formal gubernatorial power. He provided an interval scale with scores ranging from 19 for New York to 7 each for Mississippi, South Carolina, Texas, and North Carolina. The states' ratings are given in Table IV-3. It should be borne in mind that Schlesinger makes no case that this index measures the ability of a governor to "get his own way" in the process of policy-making. The measure is of *formal* power, and formal power may be of varying relevance in real situations.

By means of interview data, Thad Beyle checked the extent to which gubernatorial perceptions of power match up with the Schlesinger index.[35] Beyle also examined what other attributes of the office governors would like to change in order to expand their policy-making roles. Generally, a pretty good match appeared between Schlesinger's items and each governor's perception of his appointive influence, the salience of his veto power, and the relevance of his tenure and budget powers. The governors perceived the limitations on their appointive powers as the most constraining. However, governors also saw a need for other powers not included in the Schlesinger index, especially authority to reorganize agencies by executive order. Beyle's essay suggests not the limitations of the Schlesinger index so much as the means of reordering and weighting its components.

1231; Ira Sharkansky and Augustus B. Turnbull, III, "Budget-Making in Georgia and Wisconsin: A Test of a Model," *Midwest Journal of Political Science* 13 (1969): 631-645.

[34]Joseph A. Schlesinger, "The Politics of the Executive," in *Politics in the American States,* ed. Jacob and Vines. Figures used in my discussion are based upon the first version of Schlesinger's essay in *Politics in the American States,* 1st ed., 1965.

[35]Thad L. Beyle, "The Governor's Formal Powers: A View from the Governor's Chair," *Public Administration Review* 16 (1968): 540-545.

Table IV-3   Formal Gubernatorial Power Scores for the States: 1964

State	Power Index	State	Power Index
New York	19	Oklahoma	13
Illinois	18	Georgia	12
New Jersey	18	Indiana	12
California	17	Iowa	12
Pennsylvania	17	Massachusetts	12
Virginia	17	Nebraska	12
Washington	17	Wisconsin	12
Maryland	16	Arkansas	11
Missouri	16	Kansas	11
Montana	16	Maine	11
Oregon	16	New Mexico	11
Utah	16	South Dakota	11
Wyoming	16	Arizona	10
Alabama	15	Delaware	10
Connecticut	15	New Hampshire	10
Ohio	15	North Carolina	10
Colorado	14	Rhode Island	10
Idaho	14	Vermont	10
Kentucky	14	Florida	8
Michigan	14	West Virginia	8
Minnesota	14	Mississippi	7
Nevada	14	North Dakota	7
Tennessee	14	South Carolina	7
Louisiana	13	Texas	7

SOURCE: Joseph A. Schlesinger, "The Politics of the Executive," in *Politics in the American States*, ed. Herbert Jacob and Kenneth N. Vines (Boston: Little, Brown and Co., 1965), p. 229. Reprinted by permission.

He also suggests that the index might include a few additional gubernatorial powers.

Legislative Structure

The structural reform tradition looms large with respect to legislative studies. The characteristic of legislatures that has received the greatest amount of attention from reformers has usually been the one most frequently investigated in terms of its policy effects. This, of course, is legislative apportionment.

Probably no other feature of American state government has been the subject of so much acrimonious debate as apportionment. Moreover, the lack of numerical equality in state representative systems has often been considered the primary cause of the states' providing no higher levels or broader ranges of public services than they do. This distress over appointment notwithstanding, remarkably little research was done until recent years to check the specific causes or consequences of malapportionment. Part of this lapse can be attributed to the absence of any broadly accepted measure of apportionment equality.

Several efforts have been made to devise an acceptable metric. In its apportionment decisions, the Supreme Court seems to have placed reliance upon the ratio of the smallest to the largest single member district in a state.[36] Thus, if one district in a state has a population of 175,000 people and another has a population of 1,750 —a not uncommon situation prior to the 1960s—the malapportionment ratio would be 100.

Scholars and practitioners alike have taken issue with this measure. It says nothing about how most of the people in the state are represented, even numerically. It says nothing about the representativeness of a potential majority in the legislature. It merely specifies a range, with no reference to the pattern of distribution within that range. One could draw an analogy with a comparable form of income distribution. If one member of a population had an income of $500 a year and another had an income of $500,000, the ratio of most to least would be 1,000. Yet it could well be that, with the exception of these two, all members of the population had incomes between $7,500 and $9,000. It could then be argued that there was substantial equality of income for nearly all members of the population. Far more distressing to the true egalitarian would be a situation in which incomes spread themselves evenly between $4,500 and $45,000, although the ratio here of most to least would be only 10.

In one index of apportionment, the analyst assigns a score to each state on the basis of a minimum percentage of the state's total

[36]Dye, *Politics, Economics, and Public,* p. 63.

population that could elect a majority of the legislators.[37] He begins with the least populous legislative district and adds the populations of each larger district until one more than half of the legislative districts are included.

In another index, the analyst attempts to take account of the presumed urban-rural conflict in state legislative-apportionment systems.[38] Total population of the state is divided by the number of legislative districts. This ideal average is then compared with the actual population of the legislative districts in the state's urban areas. The resulting ratios for the two legislative houses are averaged to produce a score measuring the degree of urban representation in the state legislature.

Still a third measure has been constructed by Glendon Schubert and Charles Press.[39] This scoring procedure is too technically involved to be explained in full here, but essentially it combines a measure of the relative distribution of district populations with measures of the spread of populations (the skewness or the normality of the distribution as well as the kurtosis, the flatness or the peakedness of the population curve). Table IV-4 arrays the states according to the Schubert-Press scoring technique.

The variation in the values of these three scoring procedures have led scholars in the field to investigate their policy correlates separately. However, the scores are sufficiently comparable to give confidence that the main features of apportionment have probably been covered with all of them collectively.

Aside from the ethical and political problems of apportionment, one of the main causes of dismay among those wanting to improve the quality and efficiency of American state legislatures has been the amateurishness of legislators. Scarcely a year goes by without an article in a popular magazine painting a pitiful picture of state legislatures—and drawing the conclusion that their inadequacies can be at-

[37]Manning O. Dauer and Robert G. Kelsay, "Unrepresentative States," *National Municipal Review* 44 (1955): 551-575.

[38]Paul T. David and Ralph Eisenberg, *Devaluation of the Urban and Suburban Vote* (Charlottesville: Bureau of Public Administration, University of Virginia, 1961).

[39]Glendon Schubert and Charles Press, "Measuring Malapportionment," *American Political Science Review* 58 (1964): 302-327. See also pp. 966-970.

Table IV-4   Apportionment Scores for the States: 1962

State	Score	State	Score
Ohio	90.3	Montana	46.8
Oregon	89.0	Missouri	46.2
New Hampshire	88.0	Idaho	45.1
Nebraska	80.9	Michigan	44.1
Massachusetts	80.4	Virginia	43.8
Utah	73.4	Mississippi	42.4
Maine	73.2	Rhode Island	42.3
Tennessee	71.8	Louisiana	40.4
Pennsylvania	71.0	Texas	40.0
Indiana	69.8	Arizona	39.6
Arkansas	69.2	North Dakota	39.3
New York	69.2	Maryland	30.5
West Virginia	67.2	Connecticut	27.4
South Dakota	62.7	Nevada	25.3
Washington	62.6	New Mexico	23.7
Wyoming	62.3	California	20.2
New Jersey	60.2	Florida	17.3
Wisconsin	58.5	Iowa	15.0
North Carolina	58.3	Kentucky	13.9
South Carolina	56.4	Alabama	12.3
Colorado	54.7	Oklahoma	11.9
Delaware	50.6	Kansas	11.5
Illinois	47.2	Minnesota	1.8
Vermont	46.9	Georgia	−4.9

SOURCE: Glendon Schubert and Charles Press, "Measuring Malapportionment," *American Political Science Review* 58 (1964): 969. Reprinted by permission.

tributed to their basically amateur composition. Various structural factors are blamed for this ineptness—low salaries, poor research facilities, short terms, inadequate length of sessions. Related to these structural factors is the additional fact that roughly 50 per cent of the legislators in any given session are freshmen. Some of the earliest empirical studies of state legislatures were concerned with this very problem.[40] Textbooks on state and local government are often rich in

[40]See Charles S. Hyneman, "Tenure and Turnover of Legislative Personnel," *The Annals of the American Academy of Political and Social Science* 195 (1938): 21-32.

anecdotes pointing to the buffoonery—and chicanery—in daily evidence, presumably, within state legislatures.[41]

Although amateurism may be widespread in state legislatures, ample variation in the degree of professionalism among them allows relatively refined comparisons. In the 1964-1965 legislative term, actual realized compensation ranged from $25,000 in Michigan to $200 in New Hampshire.[42] Some legislatures meet nearly year round; others meet for short biennial terms. Until recently, for example, Indiana's legislature met only sixty-one days every second year. Some states provide a private office with secretarial assistance for each legislator; others provide no work space aside from the legislator's desk in the chamber. Some legislators must use public telephones and share a small secretarial pool. Some must rely on private interest groups to draft bills; others have available the facilities of a well-stocked state library, professional legislative reference assistants, and able counsel from state university bureaus of public administration.

A good index of legislative professionalism would be sensitive to these important differences. It would also provide some objective means for weighting the specific components of the index. By using factor analysis, John Grumm has come close to fulfilling these requirements by combining several indicators of legislative activity and services.[43] Grumm includes in his index the compensation of legislators, the length of sessions, the expenditures for legislative services and operations, and a measure called "legislative services." His findings are portrayed in Table IV-5. This index represents a significant step forward in the measurement of a main dimension of legislative structure. It finds its justification not so much in an elaborate systems theory as in the assumptions of legislative reformers. Nonetheless, it is a useful device in summarizing a characteristic of the institutional situation that is, a priori, appealing as a possible determinant of the policy performance of legislatures.

[41]Duane Lockard, *The Politics of State and Local Government* (New York: Macmillan, 1963), pp. 308-309.

[42]John G. Grumm and Calvin W. Clark, *Compensation for Legislators in the Fifty States* (Kansas City, Missouri: Citizens Conference on State Legislatures, 1966).

[43]Grumm, "Effects of Legislative Structure."

Table IV-5   Legislative Professionalism Scores for the States: 1965

State	Score	State	Score
New York	2.8	Oklahoma	− .2
Massachusetts	2.4	Iowa	− .2
California	2.2	Alabama	− .2
Pennsylvania	1.8	Nebraska	− .3
New Jersey	1.3	Kentucky	− .3
Michigan	1.3	West Virginia	− .4
Illinois	.8	Rhode Island	− .4
Texas	.7	Kansas	− .4
Florida	.6	Indiana	− .4
Delaware	.6	Colorado	− .4
Georgia	.5	Nevada	− .5
Wisconsin	.4	Maine	− .5
Louisiana	.4	Arkansas	− .6
South Carolina	.3	Virginia	− .7
Ohio	.3	South Dakota	− .9
North Carolina	.3	Vermont	−1.0
Maryland	.3	New Mexico	−1.0
Connecticut	.3	Utah	−1.3
Oregon	.2	Tennessee	−1.3
Missouri	.2	North Dakota	−1.3
Minnesota	.1	Idaho	−1.3
Mississippi	.0	New Hampshire	−1.5
Arizona	.0	Montana	−1.7
Washington	− .1	Wyoming	−2.0

SOURCE: John Grumm, "Structure and Policy in the Legislature" (Paper presented at the 1967 annual meeting of the Southwest Social Science Association, Dallas, March, 1967). Reprinted by permission.

Other common attributes of the legislative situation that have been subjected to measurement by students of comparative policy-making include the distribution of partisan identification of legislators and other features related to partisan composition such as the electoral competitiveness of the districts from which legislators come, the division between legislative houses and the governorship in terms of party control, and so forth. Little more has been done, however, other than to construct these fairly simple and obvious indicators in order to capture in a theoretically interesting manner the important dimensions of legislative activity. Especially disturbing is how little attention has been given to the relative consequentiality of legislatures themselves as compared with governors or administrative structures or other sources of policy input. Again, as with the studies of legislator behavior, these indices of legislative structure still do not provide us with a means for assessing the role of the legislature in the total policy process. Some steps have been taken in this direction in the analysis of executive influence, but as we shall see shortly these, too, do not get around the whole problem.

Patterns of Political Activity

In addition to descriptive measurements of the formal characteristics of the legislative situation, the comparative-policy literature contains several tests of the policy consequences of certain features of the political situation within which governors and legislators interact. In this respect, three particular aspects of the political situation have consumed most of the scholars' interest: voter turnout, interparty competitiveness, and the partisan structure of policy-making bodies. No one claims that such an abbreviated list of characteristics offers a comprehensive picture of anything that might legitimately be called "a system of political participation." After a bit of wandering through these studies, however, one finds ample justification for giving attention to these different aspects of political activity. Each, in its own right, has been credited with having an independent effect upon the pattern of policies in the states. Each has been viewed as a determinant of the other. The assumption has been that turnout, competitiveness, and partisan composition are part of a single dimension of politically relevant activity.

Considerable attention has been paid to the determinants of these aspects of the political process at the individual, city, and state levels. For example, political scientists and sociologists have examined the relationship between a host of personal and social characteristics that might tend to inhibit or encourage citizens to show up at the polls on election day.[44] The same influences have been examined

[44]Lester W. Milbrath, "Political Participation in the States," in *Politics in the American States,* ed. Jacob and Vines, pp. 25-81.

with an eye to their effect upon the party preferences of voters and the degree of party support in particular geographic areas.[45] Their effect upon interparty competition has also been studied.[46] Yet despite these efforts, unsettled problems of measurement remain.

These studies and the whole literature of which they are a part tend to leave out the more radical modes of activity and expression that are currently growing in frequency and that have obvious political and policy relevance. Protest marches and urban disorders can certainly be viewed as forms of political participation. The indices of participation that Lester Milbrath and others have used, therefore —and which are used in most comparative-policy studies—may be subject to the challenge that they are unduly biased toward "middle class" behavioral forms.

It is difficult to study all the intricacies of individual citizens' political participation. If such "micro" data were to be the basis of comparative analysis at the aggregate (for example, state) level, the problems of data collection alone, not to mention conceptual difficulties, would be nearly astronomical. To compare individual survey responses by state it would be necessary for the number of people sampled in each state to be nearly as large as the number included in most national surveys. That is, in order to have the same degree of accuracy in estimating the patterns of political participation of individual Nevadans that George Gallup has in discussing the political attitudes and actions of Americans generally, one would have to interview nearly as many Nevadans as Gallup does Americans. To make equally accurate estimates about the residents of all fifty states, one would have to interview fifty times as many people as are included in the national sample. Neither the resources nor the motivation to do a sample survey of 75,000 people has yet presented itself to the task.[47]

[45]Austin Ranney, "Parties in State Politics," in *Politics in the American States,* ed. Jacob and Vines, pp. 82-121.

[46]Dawson and Robinson, "Inter-Party Competition"; Robert T. Golembiewski, "A Taxonomic Approach to Political Party Strength," *Western Political Quarterly* 11 (1958): 495-519.

[47]Some effort, by Frank Munger and his associates has been made to estimate attitudes toward particular policy issues on a state-by-state basis. While their data cannot be regarded as conclusive, they do allow for some interesting

Despite the absence of data, however, it is possible to make some assumptions about the interrelatedness of party and other popular control variables.[48] Variables associated with turnout are also associated with competitiveness and partisan orientation at the state level.

Voter turnout is not a particularly difficult datum with which to work. Nor is the partisan composition of legislative bodies—with the exception of Nebraska and Minnesota, which have nominally non-partisan legislatures. Serious problems do arise, however—the theoretical clarity of Key's early work to the contrary—in attempts to measure interparty competitiveness, and a sizable amount of literature has dealt specifically with this facet of political life in the American states.[49] The objective of these studies has been to derive a single index that takes account of both the relative magnitude of support for the two major parties and their alternation in winning elections in each state. Most indices of interparty competitiveness have been derived from scores based on average party performance over several years. A good deal of the discussion has centered around the offices chosen for the composite indices, the span of time employed in the indices, and the relative emphasis given to magnitudes of party strength versus alternation in office.

---

estimates of the effects of opinion on policy. Munger and Michael Mezey, "Participation and Party Competition as Determinants of State Policy: The Old Politics and the New" (Paper presented at the annual meeting of the New York Political Science Association, Poughkeepsie, N. Y., March, 1968); Ronald Weber, "Dimensions of State Party Systems" (Paper presented at the annual meeting of the Northeastern Political Science Association, Hartford, Conn., November, 1969). Research based on sample surveys in thirteen states during the 1968 election is currently being conducted in the Comparative State Election Project, directed by Professor James Prothro, the University of North Carolina.

[48]Sharkansky and Hofferbert, "Dimensions of State Politics."

[49]Austin Ranney and Willmoore Kendall, "The American Party Systems," *American Political Science Review* 48 (1954): 477-485; Joseph A. Schlesinger, "A Two-Dimensional Scheme for Classifying the States According to Degree of Inter-Party Competition," *American Political Science Review* 49 (1955): 1120-1128; Golembiewski, "A Taxonomic"; Richard I. Hofferbert, "Classification of American State Party Systems," *Journal of Politics* 26 (1964): 550-567; David G. Pfeiffer, "The Measurement of Inter-Party Competition and Systemic Stability," *American Political Science Review* 61 (1967): 457-467.

Although various indices have been employed in several studies, I would propose that, given the available data, they may all be impractical. In no intrastate or organizational sense are the measures of interparty competitiveness measures of party strength. Competitiveness and organizational strength may be highly correlated, but they are not identical. The distinction is vital if one is investigating the effect of party systems upon policy outcomes. The contrasting examples of Connecticut and Massachusetts illustrate this shortcoming. Although both states score similarly on most indices of two-party competitiveness, Connecticut has perennially had much more tightly organized hierarchies in its parties than has Massachusetts.[50] Party officials in Connecticut are crucial figures in matters of campaign finance and organization; they are customarily active and influential in the policy process. None of these circumstances applies in Massachusetts. Although candidates from both parties in Massachusetts are often involved in hotly contested elections, the parties themselves are little more than loosely organized ethnic and socioeconomic alliances.

To the problem of indexing organizational potency is added the problem of timing: there are no "natural" periods suitable for aggregation in which to construct a composite index of competitiveness. How can we be sure one year is as important as another and thereby be justified in weighting them equally? Could it not be argued that the 1948 or 1960 election gave a much more valid picture of the presidential electorate than the 1936 or 1964 national contest? And how can we be certain that one office ought to be equated with another in determining average party strength? In the literature that attempts to account for the effects of competitiveness upon policy, these questions have not been resolved. As in the case of apportionment, however, what findings do exist tend to be iconoclastic, and as such have dramatized the activities taking place in the comparative-policy field.

Local Governmental Structures

At the local level a somewhat different set of characteristics as policy determinants has been the object of attention. Partly because

[50]Lockard, *New England State Politics*, chaps. 5, 6, 9, 10.

of the flexibility with which local government can be formally re-organized, a somewhat more extended range of structural experimentation has been carried out at the local level than at the state level. Most of the reform impetus generated within the Progressive movement was in reaction to the apparent deficiencies of local governments. Organizational inadequacies were held responsible for the incidence of graft and the declining quality of urban life. Thus, we have experienced greater experimentation with local governmental forms. The reform tradition and its objectives, furthermore, have had a certain constancy from the early years of the century to the present. These objectives have manifested themselves in terms of suggestions for reform: at-large election of councilmen, nonpartisan elections, and the council-manager system of government.

Political scientists making comparative studies of local government have given over much of their attention to the middle-class bases of support for reform objectives. The justification for reform is usually in terms of implementing administrative efficiency and serving the needs of the "community at large"—instead of the specific needs of selected groups of political favorites. Indices constructed and used in comparative analysis are largely based on the presence or absence of particular reform characteristics in cities of varying size and social composition.

The assorted characteristics of state and local governments and patterns of political participation have not been fully analyzed to determine their interdependence. Without such analysis it is not easy to speak with sophistication about state and local "political systems." It is reasonable to assume that not all the attributes discussed so far in this chapter are aspects of one thing—that they vary in common directions and that they are somehow functionally connected. The examination of the relationships and the dimensionality of governmental and political characteristics has been attempted. These efforts follow closely the modes of analysis used to plot the socioeconomic dimensions of the states.

Multidimensional Indices of State Political Structure

Following arguments analogous to those for looking at social structure in multidimensional terms, Sharkansky and I factor analyzed

Table IV-6   Political Variables Factor Analyzed*

Participation and Party

† 1. Per cent voting-age population voting for governor
2. Per cent voting-age population voting for U.S. representative
† 3. Number of items on Milbrath's list of suffrage regulations on which a state scores as a "facilitator"
† 4. Per cent of gubernatorial vote won by major party
5. Per cent of congressional vote won by major party
† 6. Per cent of seats in lower house of state legislature held by major party
7. Per cent of seats in upper house of state legislature held by major party
‡ 8. Number of years during 1952-1962 when major party controlled governor's office
† 9. Number of years during 1954-1962 when major party controlled lower house of legislature
‡ 10. Number of years during 1954-1962 when major party controlled upper house of legislature

Institutions and Personnel

‡ 11. Dauer-Kelsay index of legislative apportionment
‡ 12. David-Eisenberg index of legislative apportionment
‡ 13. Schubert-Press index of legis-legislative apportionment
‡ 14. Number of state legislators

† 15. Legislators' compensation
† 16. Total expenditures on legislative services per legislator (minus compensation)
‡*17. Number of legislative committees
† 18. Number of bills introduced into the legislature
19. Number of bills passed by the legislature
‡*20. Proportion of bills introduced that were passed
‡*21. Number of days in the legislative session
‡*22. Term of judges on state court of last resort
‡*23. Minimum-age requirement for judges on appeals courts
‡*24. Minimum-age requirement for judges on trial courts
† 25. Compensation of judges on court of last resort
‡*26. Minimum term for state judges to be eligible for pension
27. Number of state employees per 10,000 population
28. Average salary of state employees
‡*29. Per cent of state employees covered by state personnel system
‡ 30. Schlesinger index of gubernatorial formal power
‡ 31. Number of separately elected executive officials in state government

‡ 32. Number of state plus local government employees per 10,000 population

‡ 33. Average salary of state plus local government employees

‡ 34. Per cent of state and local government employees covered by government-supported health and hospital insurance

‡ 35. Per cent of state and local government employees covered by government-supported life insurance

36. Number of words in state constitution

‡ 37. Number of amendments in state constitution

‡ 38. Date of state constitution's ratification

† 39. Population per local governmental unit

Fiscal Structure

‡ 40. Per cent of state and local government revenues collected from real-property taxes

‡ 41. Per cent of state and local government revenues collected from individual income taxes

‡ 42. Per cent of state and local government revenues collected from general sales taxes

43. Per cent of state and local government revenues collected from excise taxes

‡ 44. Per cent of state and local government revenues collected from current service charges

45. Per cent of state government revenue received as federal aid

† 46. Per cent of state and local government revenue received as federal aid

47. Per cent of state and local government revenue raised by state government

† 48. Per cent of state and local government revenue spent by state agencies

49. Per cent of state and local government revenue raised by local governments

50. Per cent of local revenue received from the state government

† 51. Per cent of state aid to localities allocated on the basis of fixed criteria of population or the amount of certain taxes collected locally

52. Per cent of state aid to localities allocated on the basis of need

‡ 53. State aid to localities per capita

*Unless indicated otherwise, the data pertain to 1962.
†Variables surviving test for high loading on a single factor. (All † variables also meet the test of those being noted with ‡.)
‡Variables surviving test for high intercorrelations among substantively similar variables.
Sources of data noted in Ira Sharkansky and Richard I. Hofferbert, "Dimensions of State Politics, Economics, and Public Policy," *American Political Science Review* 63 (1969): 867-879.

a variety of aspects of state political processes.[51] Indicators of local-governmental forms were not included, but most of the most commonly employed attributes of state processes were. The variables examined are presented in Table IV-6.

In selecting the items for construction of the political indices, we tried to include a comprehensive list of characteristics that have long been of concern to political scientists.[52] We chose measures of voter participation and party competition; features of the legislative, judicial, and executive branches of state government; and the individual and mutual aspects of state, local, and intergovernmental fiscal structures. The items themselves are often complicated, and we discussed them at greater length in the original sources than is convenient here. Something should be said, however, about the guidelines followed.

The measures of voter turnout and party competition' assess prominent aspects of the electoral process, involving contests for both governor and United States representative. The measures of party competition include both the spread of the vote received in recent elections and the distribution of legislative and gubernatorial control between parties and over time.

The variables indicating government structures, personnel, and revenues tap several aspects of state and local government that may influence the perception of and the responsiveness to citizen interests. The variables pertaining to the legislature include the three

[51]Sharkansky and Hofferbert, "Dimensions of State Politics."

[52]To maintain prima facie relevance, we used factor analysis in "stages" first to select from among a large collection those variables that load highly on principal factors and then to define the loadings of these variables on factors that contain only those highly loaded components. In this way, the factor technique produced relatively "pure" factors, devoid of large numbers of variables that contribute only weakly to the principal factors. Many variables loaded low on two principal factors, and several loaded about equally on each principal factor. To simplify these factors for the purposes of clarity and further analysis, we eliminated all variables loading below .5 on both principal factors and those loading at least .5 on one but above .4 on the other factor in each sector. The variables surviving this elimination are noted as such in Table IV-6. We then made separate factor analyses of the variables that remained after this culling procedure. The results are in Table IV-7. The values derived from this final set of analyses constitute the bases for constructing indices of the political sectors of the model.

separate indices of apportionment equity, plus the number of legislators, the length of the legislature's session, the number of committees, the salary of members and total expenditures for legislative services, and the number of bills introduced and passed at a recent session. Other scholars have used these variables to assess the representativeness of state legislatures, their "professionalism," and their activism. Several of the variables pertaining to the executive branch assess the magnitude and professionalism of the civil service and the formal nature of leadership in the executive branch. They also show the relative number of employees and their conditions of work. Two variables relative to executive leadership are the score of each state's governor on Schlesinger's index of formal authority, and the number of administrative officials who are directly elected. The age and length of the state constitution and the number of its amendments have been used by one scholar to assess the activism of state interest groups and their orientation toward constitution building.[53] Also examined are terms, official qualifications, compensation and pension opportunities of the state judiciaries; these should denote some pertinent aspects of judicial professionalism.

Sharkansky and I measured state and local tax systems by the proportion of revenues raised from the principal taxes. Each tax has a distinctive impact upon a particular segment of the population,[54] thus, the composition of state and local revenue systems may reflect the political strength of different economic groups, and affect the relationship between each group of taxpayers and state and local governments.

Several measures of intergovernmental relationships assess the mutual dependence of state and local governments and the role of federal agencies in financing public services. These variables permit an answer to the question: "Which government pays the bills?" Federal, state, and local taxes vary in their progressivity-regressivity. A state that relies heavily on locally financed services may generate a different type of response among taxpayers than one that relies on state or federal revenues. It is also likely that each level of govern-

[53]Lewis A. Froman, Jr., "Some Effects of Interest Group Strength in State Politics," *American Political Science Review* 60 (1966): 952-962.
[54]See George A. Bishop, "The Tax Burden by Income Class, 1958," *National Tax Journal* 14 (1961): 41-58.

ment differs in its responsiveness to demands. Thus a state that emphasizes services financed by federal or state agencies may present a different complexion of need-gratifications than one that is localist in orientation. Finally, the state supervision of "avoided" programs is likely to differ from that of programs financed locally. Heavy reliance on federal and state revenues, therefore, may have administrative implications that influence other dimensions of state politics.

No two of our political variables measure the same phenomena in exactly the same manner. It is possible, however, that our penchant for a comprehensive list of indicators overloaded the factor analysis in favor of phenomena—for example, party competition, legislative composition—that have been the subject of several earlier measurements. In order to guard against this kind of overloading, Sharkansky and I computed a matrix of simple correlation coefficients between all of our political variables. In those cases where variables measuring similar phenomena showed high coefficients of correlation ($r > .7$), we omitted one of the highly intercorrelated pair from the factor analysis. The forty-one variables surviving this first screening process are indicated in Table IV-6 and were entered into a preliminary factor analysis. This analysis was used to identify those variables that loaded high on two or more factors or did not load high on any factor. A second factor analysis was performed without these ambiguities and irrelevancies, and produced the two principal factors reported in Table IV-7.

The first principal factor is labeled "Professionalism-Local Reliance." It draws its name from the positively loaded measures of judicial and legislative compensation, expenditures on legislative services, and legislative activity; and from the *negatively loaded* measures of local-government reliance upon *state* government expenditures and *federal* aids. States scoring high on this factor show high salaries for judges and legislators, well-financed legislative staffs, and primary reliance on locally raised and spent revenues. The inverse juxtaposition in Factor 1 of professionalism in government and the use of state and federal aids makes sense in terms of functions that intergovernmental payments are reputed to serve. They are often defended as devices that are used most by governments that redistribute resources from *have* to *have-not* jurisdictions—and, indeed, the recipients have apparent need for assistance. Factor 1 suggests that

Table IV-7   Loadings of Political Variables
              on Two Principal Factors

Variables*	Factor 1: Professionalism- Local Reliance	Factor 2: Competition- Turnout
Compensation of judges (25)	.90	.04
Compensation of legislators (15)	.86	.14
Legislative service expenditures (16)	.82	.02
Number of bills introduced (18)	.81	—.13
State and local revenue from federal government (46)	—.76	—.29
State and local revenue spent by state agencies (48)	—.73	—.33
Lower-house seats of major party (6)	—.28	—.86
Gubernatorial election turnout (1)	.03	.83
Gubernatorial vote for major party (4)	—.08	—.78
Liberal suffrage laws (3)	—.01	.72
Lower-house tenure of major party (9)	—.06	—.62
Per Cent of Total Variance	36.7	28.8

*The parenthesized numbers correspond to the variable numbers in Table IV-6.

states making much use of intergovernmental assistance have judicial and legislative institutions that are less well-developed than average.

Factor 2 "Competition-Turnout"—has as its highest-loaded variables the measures of voter turnout in a gubernatorial election, an index of suffrage liberality, and, negatively, one-party dominance in the state legislature and in the recent elections for governor.[55] The competition-turnout dimension supplies some post hoc justification for the many studies of state politics that have dwelt almost entirely on electoral processes and interparty struggles. Books and articles by V. O. Key, Duane Lockard, and John Fenton, among others, view party competition and electoral behavior as the primary

[55]In interpreting the results of the factor analysis, a loading of .7 will be considered high.

stuff of politics.[56] Our factor analyses suggest that an electoral-party
dimension has indeed some importance as a distinct component of
state politics.

The scores for the individual states on the two political process
factors are listed in Table IV-8. The test of the value of these
indices will have to wait a bit. Whether or not they have some value
for policy analysis rests on how well they tap aspects of political
systems that are helpful in explaining policy differences between the
states. Even without a demonstration of the policy consequences of
professionalism-local reliance or of competition-turnout, however,
the very fact of demonstrated multidimensionality offers a richer
conception of the political process than is possible with a scatteration
of discrete elements.

Conclusion

This chapter has attempted to justify conceptualization of social
and political processes in multidimensional terms. It is argued that
many aspects of the policy system would be obscured without such
an approach to analysis. The indices offered should serve to enrich
the conceptualization of the first two sectors of the systems model—
inputs and political process—even in the simple form it is being
used here.

Before moving on to a specific examination of the relationships
between these two sectors of the model and the third sector—outputs
or policy performance—it would be well to examine the interdependence of social and political processes. Consistent with the systems
model most commonly employed in comparative analysis, much attention has been directed at discovering the social and economic circumstances that may account for differences in the political attributes
discussed in the preceding pages. In systems terms, many students
have asked "What is the effect of environment on the structure of
the political process?" Chapter V is addressed to this question.

[56]Key, *Southern Politics;* Key, *American State Politics: An Introduction* (New
York: Alfred A. Knopf, 1956); Lockard, *New England State Politics;* John H.
Fenton, *Politics in the Border States* (New Orleans: Hauser Press, 1957); and
Fenton, *Midwest Politics* (New York: Holt, Rinehart and Winston, 1966).

Table IV-8   Political Process Factor Scores for the States

State	Professionalism- Local Reliance	State	Competition- Turnout
New York	4.2	Utah	1.6
California	2.1	Nebraska	1.5
Massachusetts	1.6	Idaho	1.3
Pennsylvania	1.6	Minnesota	1.3
Michigan	1.4	Indiana	1.2
Illinois	1.2	Montana	1.2
New Jersey	1.0	Illinois	1.0
Ohio	.6	Wisconsin	1.0
Wisconsin	.6	Oregon	.9
Maryland	.5	New Jersey	.8
Minnesota	.4	North Dakota	.8
Florida	.3	Colorado	.7
Texas	.3	Washington	.7
Connecticut	.2	Michigan	.6
Delaware	.1	California	.4
Georgia	.1	Connecticut	.4
Missouri	.1	Kansas	.4
Arizona	.0	Wyoming	.4
Indiana	.0	Iowa	.3
Louisiana	.0	Missouri	.3
South Carolina	.0	West Virginia	.3
Iowa	— .2	Delaware	.2
Kansas	— .2	New Hampshire	.2
Mississippi	— .2	Ohio	.2
Nevada	— .2	Pennsylvania	.2
North Carolina	— .2	Rhode Island	.2
Oregon	— .2	Massachusetts	.1
Virginia	— .2	Maine	.0
Washington	— .2	Arizona	— .1
Colorado	— .3	South Dakota	— .1
Nebraska	— .3	Nevada	— .2
Rhode Island	— .3	North Carolina	— .2
Alabama	— .4	Oklahoma	— .3
Maine	— .6	Kentucky	— .4
Tennessee	— .6	Maryland	— .4
Kentucky	— .7	Vermont	— .5
New Mexico	— .7	Florida	— .6
West Virginia	— .7	New Mexico	— .6
Arkansas	— .8	New York	— .6
New Hampshire	— .8	Tennessee	— .6
Oklahoma	— .8	Texas	— .6
North Dakota	— .9	Virginia	—1.0
Idaho	—1.0	Louisiana	—1.2
South Dakota	—1.0	Arkansas	—1.4
Utah	—1.0	Mississippi	—1.8
Montana	—1.1	Alabama	—2.5
Wyoming	—1.4	Georgia	—2.5
Vermont	—1.5	South Carolina	—2.8

chapter V

The Context of
Political Processes

Introduction

If the total policy process—environment, institutions, and outputs
—is taken as the focus of comparative inquiry, one can proceed with
explanations of it in terms of *contexts*. Policy is made in many contexts. The task of policy research is to examine them as they relate
to policy outputs, and the first step is a matter of measurement.
Chapter IV discussed how both the socioeconomic and the political
contexts have been measured. No claim to final accuracy is made
for the measures used by scholars in the field, but their progress
thus far is encouraging.

The next step is to see how the contexts of policy (as measured) relate to one another and, in turn, to the policy itself. This
chapter takes that step. It does not yet address itself to the determinants of policy. Rather, here the object is to see how the socioeconomic context—the source of inputs for the systems model—
relates to the political context—to the institutional setting within
which policy statements are codified. Later I shall examine research
that relates these to the policy outputs themselves.

Socioeconomic Correlates
of Political Practices

As noted in the last chapter, nation-level indicators have been used to demonstrate the relationship between economic development and the structure of "democratic" political institutions. These studies take their main impetus from Lipset's 1959 article on the "Social Requisites of Democracy."[1] The work of Cutright, Neubauer, and Smith expands but does not significantly alter the main thrust of Lipset's thesis—that with higher levels of urbanization, industrialization, and wealth come a higher frequency of such institutions as competitive parties, peaceful alternation in office, and operative representational systems.[2] Socioeconomic development is a significant context for "democracy." The ranges of developmental variation, however, are sufficiently broad to challenge any totally deterministic model of socioeconomic effects upon democratic political systems. A formal similarity obtains between these studies and the efforts to examine the interdependence of socioeconomic and political contexts at the subnational level.

Within the context of the fifty states and the policy-systems model that has been most widely employed, a fairly rigorous and cumulative body of research has grown up in recent years. Many analysts have attempted to assess the relationship between different levels and forms of state and local socioeconomic development and the various structural arrangements and patterns of political activity discussed in Chapter IV.

The setting for the present discussion, then, is this: public policy is responsive to a number of contexts; one context is the socioeconomic environment—for example, industrialization and affluence;

[1] Seymour Martin Lipset, "Some Social Requisites of Democracy: Economic Development and Political Legitimacy," *American Political Science Review* 53 (1959): 69-105.

[2] Phillips Cutright, "National Political Development: Measurement and Analysis," *American Sociological Review* 28 (1963): 253-264; Deane E. Neubauer, "Some Conditions of Democracy," *American Political Science Review* 61 (1967): 1002-1009; Arthur K. Smith, "Socio-Economic Development and Political Democracy: A Causal Analysis," *Midwest Journal of Political Science* 12 (1969): 95-125.

another is the political process—executive and legislative procedures and partisan patterns are examples; the socioeconomic and the political contexts of policy are themselves interdependent. It is best to understand this interdependence before examining the contextual effects on policy.

Contextual relationships found at the subnational level may not be the same as those found at the cross-national level, even though formal comparisons are apparent. Variations within the American states in political patterns and structural forms are necessarily narrow when compared with those found between all nations. The contexts that differentiate the fifty states may not be the same as those that differentiate nations. The states are constrained in their governmental processes by requirements of a national constitution and by the diffusion and emulation that necessarily characterize a national political system. Nevertheless, the findings that emerge from the state inquiry, when placed in the systems framework, are highly suggestive for comparative policy studies at other levels.

Correlates of Executive Structure

Schlesinger's essay illustrates how hard it is to unravel the conditions producing particular executive arrangements within the states.[a] While he presents the rationale and data for his index of formal gubernatorial power, he makes other observations about the development and patterns of state executive structures. He discusses patronage versus merit appointments, for example.

Schlesinger found that states that rely primarily on patronage have a definite tendency toward low per capita state employment. Where state government occupies a larger relative position within the total sociopolitical setting, it places a greater reliance upon competitive examinations and "nonpolitical" methods of personnel selection.[1] Schlesinger also determined that states with merit systems but also with a small proportion of state employees—that is, states

[a]Joseph A. Schlesinger, "The Politics of the Executive," in *Politics in the American States,* ed. Herbert Jacob and Kenneth N. Vines (Boston: Little, Brown and Co., 1965), pp. 207-237.
[1]Ibid., p. 217.

as deviant cases from the preceding hypothesis—generally had adopted their merit systems prior to 1920, as part of the package of Progressive reforms. Thus, decades later, the context of a particular era continues to manifest itself in practices followed in the political process.

The question of appointment versus merit systems also relates to the direct election of state officials, an issue that has received a good measure of attention from reform groups. The long ballot declined in popularity toward the end of the last century. Few of the positions that have been added to the state governmental hierarchy in recent decades have been made elective. Today's elective-appointive pattern is for those administrative officials of key importance in an earlier era to be the ones that continue to be elected—secretaries of state, attorneys general—while those directing departments added during the twentieth century—welfare, education, highways—tend to be appointed, usually with some consideration given to more or less objective indicators of professional competence.[5]

With respect to formal gubernatorial powers, Schlesinger discovered that states with more competitive party systems are normally those that also endow their governors with greater legal authority.[6] As seen from Table V-1, some relationship also exists between the average income and urbanization level of the states and the tendency to endow governors with greater formal power. Income and urbanization, in fact, appear to be more important than

Table V-1   Correlation Between Formal Gubernatorial Power and Selected Socioeconomic Characteristics of the States: 1960

	Per Capita Income	Per Cent Urban	Manufacturing Employment	Industrialization	Affluence
	r =	r =	r =	r =	r =
Gubernatorial Power (Schlesinger Index)	.50	.49	.21	.38	.39

[5]Ibid., p. 214.
[6]Ibid., p. 231.

the more general structures of industrialization or affluence, as measured by the scoring procedure discussed in Chapter IV.

Most of the theory employed in the comparative studies of state politics addresses itself only superficially to reasons for the relationship between such contextual features as socioeconomic development and the efforts to create greater, more professionally oriented executive authority. Nonetheless, the most appropriate lines of reasoning are not very hard to pick out. Consistent with Schlesinger's findings on the scope of state governmental employment and the relationship that income and urbanization have to formal gubernatorial powers, one could assert quite readily that the more urban, economically complex, and interdependent states deal with a broader range and a more intricate structure of public problems. Competitive, urbanized, and wealthy states are in general more complicated to live in and to govern. The complexities of modern social and political life seem to demand centralized leadership, and some sacrifice in classical democratic control is one price that must be paid for durable and effective leadership and policy coordination. Governors are granted more extensive appointive powers. They are given longer terms. No state in recent decades has shortened the term of its governor; several have lengthened it. The admirer of the Athenian Forum or the New England town meeting must view these changes as one more cost of urban society.

The greater the degree of interdependence and complexity of problems handled by any organization, the greater the need for clarity of leadership and centralization of performance auditing. The model American small town, even well into the twentieth century, did not ask much of outside governments. Its people defined their needs in terms of local resources. State and federal governments had little immediacy for the small-town resident.[7] Further, these towns and the surrounding countryside posed no substantial challenges for policy-makers. In a simpler age, laissez-faire was a practical option. As states increased in their complexity and problems and as policy mechanisms responded with regulations and services to handle these problems, it is not at all surprising that a corresponding effort—

---

[7]In 1910, 54 per cent of the American population lived in communities of less than 2,500 population. By 1970 the percentage had dropped to 26.5.

admittedly a somewhat legalistic one—evolved to create executive mechanisms that would facilitate coordination.

Correlates of Legislative Structure

The same logic that was applied to the executive structure should hold with respect to the professionalism of legislative bodies. And, indeed, as Table V-2 illustrates, a modest correlation does exist between legislative professionalism and the income, manufacturing employment, and urbanization of the states. The correlation with the industrialization factor scores is even more striking. A view of the legislative halls of California or New York compared with those of Kansas, or even those of a moderately industrialized state like Indiana, reveals marked differences. New York and California legislators are provided with a professional staff, individual office space, and ancillary services that warrant incumbency being a member's primary occupation. At the time these data were assembled, Indiana's legislators, although spending considerable time between sessions on legislatively related business, met formally only sixty-one days every two years. While they now meet more often, their only office is still their desk in the chamber. They are not provided with an individual telephone or staff assistant. The Indiana pattern is

Table V-2   Correlation Between Legislative Structure and
            Selected Socioeconomic Characteristics of the States: 1960

	Per Capita Income	Per Cent Urban	Manufacturing Employment	Industrialization	Affluence
	r=	r=	r=	r=	r=
Legislative Professionalism (Grumm Index)	.44	.58	.52	.72	.03
Apportionment Score (Schubert-Press Index)	.11	.20	.31	.19	.02

more the rule than the exception—and it is clearly associated to some extent with the levels of a state's industrial complexity and the social interdependence of its residents.

It is equally interesting to note that there is almost no discernible relationship between legislative professionalism and the affluence of the states (r = .03). Again, to return to the methods by which these indices of social structure are constructed, it must be borne in mind that, given the factor analysis used, a state's industrialization score is computed by holding the affluence feature constant. Affluence, in turn, is measured by holding the industrialization feature constant. This procedure helps one sort through a lot of complexity. It might well be expected that the professionalism of state legislatures would be largely a matter of affluence. Can the states afford such legislative services? Is there pressure from an educated electorate, one of the features of the affluence index, for "sophistication" in government? Apparently, these social "pressures" are not as important as are those created by the concentration of industry and the intricate social orders that accompany it. Management of an industrial state requires professionalized governmental structures; it is not a matter of available wealth or an educated populace.

Regarding the distribution of legislative seats, there is a fairly straightforward justification for expecting strong relationships between socioeconomic indicators and the degree of malapportionment, especially in urbanized states. The states that have urbanized most rapidly in the past several decades should be the most poorly apportioned, at least prior to the series of relevant Supreme Court decisions in the early 1960s. Because most states resisted reapportionment, the most urbanized would seem to be the ones with the greatest degree of imbalance. Surprisingly, the data reveal few pronounced relationships between socioeconomic development and the equity of apportionment. Table V-2 shows only slight relationships between the apportionment score and either the individual socioeconomic variables or the comprehensive indices of industrialization and affluence. True, these relationships are in the expected direction. But they hardly illustrate a strong connection between state socioeconomic structure and equity in the allocation of legislative seats.

Malapportionment, therefore, appears to be determined largely by idiosyncratic factors. The socioeconomic context does not seem to be relevant. If apportionment has a bearing on policy—to suggest here a point that will be discussed later—it is not because of the indirect effect of social structure.

Correlates of Political Activity

In moving from a consideration of fairly formal institutional aspects of state political systems and their relationships to social-structure phenomena into the realm of political behavior and party systems, a few considerations that necessarily span both domains should be mentioned. Some of the early concerns of political scientists about formal structures of government carry over logically into the realm of parties and elections. A clear example is their concern with the divided partisan control of the different branches of state government.

It is anathema to the operation of a "responsible two-party system" that differences in party control should occur between the two houses of a bicameral legislature or between the governor's office and one or both houses of the legislature. It has been assumed that divided control is a function of several phenomena, but especially of malapportionment and party competitiveness.[8] In a malapportioned legislative situation, we should expect the retention of outdated legislative districts to benefit the party that enjoyed a majority in earlier years. If a former minority party wins the governorship, malapportionment should minimize its chances of also carrying both houses of the legislature. Conventionally, malapportionment has been assumed to work to the disadvantage of the Democrats in the post-1930s elections; in other words, because of their rural base, the Republicans should have benefited from it.[9] On those occasions where the Democrats have been able to compile a statewide majority adequate to elect a governor, they have not always been able to overcome the loaded dice of legislative districting. No systematic

[8]V. O. Key, Jr., *American State Politics: An Introduction* (New York: Alfred A. Knopf, 1956), p. 53.
[9]Ibid., p. 57.

relationship, however, has been found between the level of malapportionment and the frequency of divided control.[10] This finding raises a serious question about the assertion that Democratic governors face opposition-controlled legislatures with greater frequency than do their Republican counterparts. No supportive evidence has been found for such a partisan differentiation in the frequency of divided control.[11] Therefore, two aspects of the political context that would appear to relate logically are, in fact, quite independent of each other.

Conventional expectations are supported, however, with respect to the relationship between competitiveness and the frequency of divided control. In his review of legislative studies, Dye found that governors who have won by small margins are more likely than those elected by wide margins to face opposition legislatures.[12] This circumstance is explainable in common-sense terms. One-party states by definition will not elect people to office of different parties. As the vote for the two parties converges, the likelihood of the legislative and gubernatorial victors bearing opposite labels increases.

In the case of divided control, one attribute of the political process is clearly dependent upon another. Other political characteristics, however, may be independent of one another, but mutually dependent upon socioeconomic forces. Students of the policy process have given considerable attention to the various attributes of political activity and the relationship of these attributes to socioeconomic characteristics.[13] Competition has received a large share of this attention.

Table V-3 presents the simple correlations of several indicators of party competition and voter turnout with five measures of socio-

[10]Richard I. Hofferbert, "The Relationship Between Public Policy and Some Structural and Environmental Variables in the American States," *American Political Science Review* 60 (1966): 73-82.

[11]Ibid.

[12]Thomas R. Dye, "State Legislative Politics," in *Politics in the American States*, ed. Jacob and Vines, p. 154.

[13]Robert T. Golembiewski, "A Taxonomic Approach to Political Party Strength," *Western Political Quarterly* 11 (1958): 495-519; Thomas W. Casstevens and Charles Press, "The Context of Democratic Competition in American State Politics," *American Journal of Sociology* 68 (1963): 536-543; Lester W. Milbrath, "Political Participation in the States," in *Politics in the American States*, ed. Jacob and Vines, pp. 25-60.

Table V-3   Correlation Between Party Competition,* Voter Turnout, and Selected Socioeconomic Characteristics of the States

	Per Capita Income	Median School Years, Adult Population	Per Cent Urban	Manufacturing Employment	Per Cent Black
Voter Turnout, President, 1960	.56	.58	.23	.20	−.88
Voter Turnout, Governor, 1962**	.62	.61	.33	.16	−.81
Competition, President, 1960	.43	.27	.25	.17	−.38
Competition, Governor, 1962	.34	.37	.23	.18	−.57
Per Cent Democratic, President, 1960	−.06	−.44	.21	.30	.56
Per Cent Democratic, Governor, 1962	−.49	−.61	−.31	.02	−.61

*Competition is measured as two times the percentage of total votes cast for the losing candidate.
**Thirty-seven states held gubernatorial elections in 1962.

economic development. These findings are consistent with the earlier findings reported by Dawson and Robinson. The particular variables that correlate with indicators of competition—namely, income, education, and race—are also the ones that correlate highly with voter participation in gubernatorial and presidential elections. Urbanization and industrialization do not appear as consequential in this regard as do income, education, and race. And the same pattern is true with respect to the negative relations of income and education to Democratic party control. Clearly, strong interrelationships between participation, competitiveness, and partisanship explain the common direction of correlations between the independent socioeconomic variables and the dependent political variables. They are

all saying something in common. This is the logic behind the procedures for the multivariable index construction that Sharkansky and I
employed. Dye demonstrated that no pair-wise correlation drops
below .56 within a list of nine such indicators. Most of the relationships are in the range of .70 to .80.[14]

Socioeconomic Dimensionality and Political Activity

It is interesting for theoretical purposes to explore the fact that
income, education, and race seem to explain more of the political
differences between the states than is explained by urbanization and
industrialization. Except for race, these are the socioeconomic attributes studied by Dye in his groundbreaking volume. James Elliott,
having been stimulated by Dawson and Robinson's finding of high
correlations between economic attributes of the states and the degree
of interparty competition, has drawn upon a large body of economic-
development literature to assist the political-science community. In
so doing, he reveals some of the problems of economic analysis that
pertain to this research setting.

Elliott makes the assumption that economic development is a
single dimension of social change. He states, "Exceptions notwithstanding, economic development *means* industrialization, urbanization, and rising per capita incomes."[15] Yet if economic development
is all these things, one would expect various indicators of it to relate
to any particular set of political variables in a common manner. But
income, education, and race correlate much more highly with state
political activity than do urbanization or industrialization. This
prompts questions about what lines of theory are to be employed
to explain the relationships.

Wealth, education, and race are obviously of more consequence
to voting than population location or occupational composition of a
state (Table V-3). Although Dye did not include a measure of the
nonwhite population in his book, it can easily be included with the

[14]Thomas R. Dye, *Politics, Economics, and the Public: Policy Outcomes in
the American States* (Chicago: Rand McNally, 1966), p. 72.
[15]James R. Elliott, "A Comment on Inter-Party Competition, Economic Variables, and Welfare Policies in the American States," *Journal of Politics* 27
(1965): 186.

income and education measures as a high correlate of the variables included in his analysis. In all states, per cent black correlates negatively with indicators of interparty competitiveness and turnout. It correlates positively with per cent Democratic, regardless of the office chosen for investigation. This finding, of course, is a reflection of the high concentration of blacks in the southern states. The point of the argument here is that indicators of nonwhite population, education, and income are outcroppings of fundamentally different attributes of the social structure than are industrialization and urbanization—a point discussed earlier with respect to the socioeconomic dimensions of the states.[16] That research found industrialization to be consistently less relevant to voting indicators than affluence. How rich and how well educated a state's population is turn out to be more important to the patterns of voter participation than are where people live or how they make a living. The affluence measure is the one that most clearly delineates the North-South dimension.[17] And the affluence index is heavily affected by indicators of education, wealth, and ethnicity. Table V-4 shows that it is affluence—not urbanization or manufacturing activity—that distinguishes differences in political participation. Industrialization, on the other hand, is heavily affected by indicators of manufacturing employment and urbanization. Dye's study, while providing an innovative compendium of findings and rigorously tested hypotheses, does not take adequate account of the possible multidimensionality of the economic-development process that he discusses—a problem to be considered more fully in Chapter VI in the examination of the determinants of state-policy outputs.

[16]Richard I. Hofferbert, "Socioeconomic Dimensions of the American States: 1890-1960," *Midwest Journal of Political Science* 12 (1968): 401-418; Ira Sharkansky and Richard I. Hofferbert, "Dimensions of State Politics, Economics, and Public Policy," *American Political Science Review* 63 (1969): 867-880. See also chap. IV of this volume.

[17]In my 1968 article affluence was misleadingly labeled "cultural enrichment." The changed label is discussed in Hofferbert and Ira Sharkansky, "Social Structure and Politics in Subnational Systems: A Comparison in Four Nations" (Paper prepared for the Conference on Comparative Legislative Systems, Durham, N. C., February, 1970, pp. 17-18).

Table V-4   Correlation Between Party Competition, Voter Turnout,
             and Industrialization and Affluence of the States

	Industrialization	*Affluence*
	r=	r=
Voter Turnout, President, 1960	.21	.64
Voter Turnout, Governor, 1962	.24	.67
Competition, President, 1960	.21	.38
Competition, Governor, 1962	.21	.30
Per Cent Democratic, President, 1960	.35	.41
Per Cent Democratic, Governor, 1962	.11	.62

Correlates of Local Governmental Structures

Although specific contents differ, inquiry at the local level cor-
responds to the type of questions that have been asked concerning
state governmental and political patterns. The historical and theoretical background of local reform movements diverges somewhat from
that of the state-level movements. The "public-regarding" ethos and
the middle-class bias of the local reform movements have been
discussed at length by several contemporary students of urban
governmental structure.[18] This line of analysis has guided most of the

[18]James Q. Wilson and Edward C. Banfield, "Public-Regardingness as a Value
Premise in Voting Behavior," *American Political Science Review* 58 (1964):
876-887; Raymond E. Wolfinger and John Osgood Field, "Political Ethos and
the Structure of City Government," *American Political Science Review* 60
(1966): 306-326; Robert L. Lineberry and Edmund P. Fowler, "Reformism
and Public Policies in American Cities," *American Political Science Review*
61 (1967): 701-716.

comparative studies of social structure and urban governmental institutions.

Urban governmental-reform movements persist today in many guises. Their most striking beginnings, however, are in the Progressive era of the first and second decade of this century. The heritage of the muckrakers persists in the matters that concern today's more "objective" scholars. "The cure for democracy is more democracy," or so goes the paraphrase of the Progressive's guiding assumption. The Progressives sought efficiency through civil-service reform. They sought public honesty through the initiative, the referendum, and the recall. They reserved their most vicious criticisms for political parties, for the seeds of urban venality and ineptitude were to be found in the intervention of political parties between the people and public officeholders. Ward organizations were to be broken by at-large elections. Party control was to be further undermined by non-partisan elections and the council-manager system of city government.

The zeal is gone, but the reform movement continues in the National Municipal League and assorted other organizations with similar interests. The assumption—then and now—is that one can govern a city by businesslike methods—that "politics" has no place in local government. Middle-class values of efficiency and rationality can replace ethnic and economic rivalries as the dynamic of city politics.

Those who have sought systematically and comparatively to study local politics have been influenced by this tradition. The values of scientific inquiry have superseded the moral commitments of the reform groups. But the questions asked in studies of comparative local politics still have their theoretical roots in the reform movements. The consequence for research has been a series of studies that has sought to correlate reform structures with the extent of middle-class dominance in local communities.[19]

John Kessel finds the frequency with which the manager plan has been adopted correlates with a number of environmental char-

[19]Most of the relevant hypotheses employed have been stimulated by Edward C. Banfield and James Q. Wilson, *City Politics* (Cambridge, Mass.: Harvard University Press, 1963) and their influential article. (See Wilson and Banfield, "Public-Regardingness" on the ethos of city politics.)

acteristics.[20] The manager plan is most often instituted in rapidly growing communities, in cities located in one-party states or states without strong formal party organizations, and in communities with a high percentage of native-born citizens. Moreover, the manager plan is found more commonly in cities dominated by tertiary rather than by secondary economic activity. "Middle class" communities appear to view this local-government reform instrument more favorably.

Raymond Wolfinger and John Osgood Field examine the same hypotheses explored by Kessel, but with additional indicators of structure, including at-large versus ward and partisan versus nonpartisan elections.[21] They also expand considerably the list of independent variables. Their list of socioeconomic features includes city size, region, ethnicity, income, level of education, and the percentage of white-collar workers. They also treat as a dependent variable the civil-service coverage of urban employees. They are guided by Edward Banfield and James Q. Wilson's "public-regarding" and "private-regarding" framework. This distinction arises from a study that found a correlation between the upper-middle-class social composition of cities and the willingness of voters to approve referenda that, although costly, would advance community well-being. Banfield and Wilson argue that such communities contain what can be called a "public-regarding ethos," which contrasts with the "private-regarding ethos" of lower-class cities.

Wolfinger and Field conclude that the "ethos theory" of middle-class impact does not help explain urban governmental structures. By subdividing the regions of the nation and by examining the environment-structure relationships within these regions, Wolfinger and Field find that the environment-structure hypotheses do not hold in the South, the West, nor the Northeast. "The Midwest provides the best evidence for the ethos theory, but even there the differences between 'public-regarding' and 'private-regarding' cities are small and uneven."[22] Differences between regions were clearly more conse-

[20]John H. Kessel, "Government Structure and Political Environment: A Statistical Note about American Cities," *American Political Science Review* 56 (1962): 615-620.

[21]Wolfinger and Field, "Political Ethos."

[22]Ibid., p. 326

quential than differences within any region, broken down by socio-economic structure. Wolfinger and Field suggest that the predominance of regional differences is explained not by inter-regional socio-economic differences, but rather by the historical sequence in which urban governmental institutions were founded. The greater frequency of reformed governments in the northern Midwest and western cities is a function of their having been founded, or their having experienced their major growth, at a time when Progressive ideology was most visible and prominent. Older cities have simply persisted in their prior, unreformed state. And it happens that the older cities are located in the East, the South, and, to a lesser extent, in the southern Midwest.

Robert Lineberry and Edmund Fowler, in a carefully constructed and insightful piece of research, deal with a set of propositions similar to that examined by Wolfinger and Field.[23] They find significant socioeconomic differences obtain between reformed and unreformed cities. The larger the city, the greater the likelihood of reformed structure. The faster the growth rate, the more likely the city is to use the manager plan. Their explanation is that very large cities have unreformed institutions and may be declining in population. The ethnic composition and population characteristics of the reformed cities, however, lead them to believe that the thesis posing a connection between reformed structures and white middle-class havens should be significantly amended. White middle-class communities do not have a monopoly on reformed institutions of city governance. But, they say, neither do particular regions of the country.

Comprehensive Relationships

One of the flaws in the research discussed in the preceding pages of this chapter is their generally piecemeal manner of investigating sociopolitical relationships. Chapter IV contained a discussion of one effort to construct more comprehensive indicators of the political process in the American subnational setting. The indicators of

[23]Lineberry and Fowler, "Reformism and Public Policies."

professionalism-local reliance and competition-turnout seemed to accommodate the core concepts of most discussions of the political process, and the indicators of industrialization and affluence seemed to tap the major socioeconomic dimensions of the American states. The appropriate next step is to explore how the political phenomena appear to be conditioned by the socioeconomic dimensions.

A strong association exists between competition-turnout and the affluence dimension of state economics, as Table V-5 shows. Evidently, citizens are more likely to participate in politics and parties are most likely to compete with one another where the residents are well-educated and relatively wealthy. Of course, this finding is not new. Nonetheless, it is a very important relationship in the political and economic systems of American states, and it is highlighted by the use of techniques that sort out the intricacies of several indicators and how they interconnect.[24]

Another strong relationship is that between the professionalism-local reliance dimension of state politics and the industrialization dimension of state economics. It is apparently the value of industrial output and the incidence of industrial employment—instead of education, wealth, or ethnicity—that have the most to do with the development of legislative and judicial professionalization and the ten-

Table V-5   Coefficients of Simple Correlation
Between Socioeconomic and Political Factors

Political Factors	Socioeconomic Factors	
	Industrialization	Affluence
Professionalism-Local Reliance	.73	.14
Competition-Turnout	.11	.66

[24]The strength of relationships between the political and economic factors is stronger than that customarily obtained with individual variables. The correlations described here are .73 and .66. Only two out of the forty-eight simple correlations between economic and political variables that Dye reports in his study reach the level of .66 and none reach .73 (see his chap. 3). The underlying dimensions that are tapped by factor analysis appear to be more salient representations of the economic-political nexus than are apparent in studies using single variables.

dency of local authorities to rely on their own economic resources. These findings corroborate some of those portrayed in Table V-2, and much the same reasoning holds here. It may be that a large industrial tax base and an urbanized population permit government to rely on locally raised revenues. An industrial economy may also encourage states to develop professional, active policy-making institutions in response to comparable models in the private sector.

Conclusion

The major social distinctions between the states—their affluence and their industrialization—have visible consequences for their political systems. The most industrial states find a reflection of the managerial ethos in their governmental activities. The most affluent states manifest the closest approximation of the democratic ideal of high voter participation and hotly contested elections. Yet if we conceive of the political system as a mechanism for producing some kind of consequences, and if we conceive of public policies as the means of attaining these consequences, then it is perhaps dysfunctional to engage in elaborate disputes about the context of the middle box in the systems paradigm until we make some determination as to how relevant that middle box is to policy. It may turn out that the institutional forms—both governmental and political—are not related to policy. Political and governmental differences may be inconsequential for differences in outputs. If governmental structural arrangements have no effect on policy, then we may view disputes about the context of the political process as irrelevant. It is to this theoretically more interesting and quantitively larger body of studies of the context of policy to which attention is now directed.

chapter VI

The Context
of Public Policy

Introduction

The "systems model" simplifies the policy process. Scores of interacting, convoluted events and circumstances lie behind any product
of governmental activity. Interest groups form and persist, disappear
and reappear. Party fortunes rise and fall. Offices change hands.
Societies experience evolution and revolution, decline and decay.
Libraries are filled with volumes relevant to how and why public
policies are as they are. And yet our knowledge remains incomplete.
The movement to comparative inquiry constitutes a new departure
in policy analysis. Progress toward understanding the policy process,
however, is contingent upon the further development of analytical
techniques and upon much more theoretical sophistication. Whether
the systems model survives is of less consequence than the fact that
policy analysts are now comparing societal contexts of policy
processes.

For comparative analysis to proceed rigorously, it is necessary,
just as it was in the study of the first two sectors of the model—
"inputs" and "political process"—to pin numbers on the "outputs."

Has "policy" been measured in such a manner that comparative analysis can at least get off the ground?

Once again, the conceptual examples necessarily are from policy studies of state and local government. The reader should not interpret this as a conscious decision to ignore national policy-making. Rather, the argument is that theory is advanced most rapidly by comparison of system performance. Comparison requires several instances. If the objective is to build a general statement, several cases are needed. This analytical procedure contrasts with a desire to understand "Congress" or the "Presidency"; the problems involved in that kind of an approach have been extensively reviewed in Chapter II. As a consequence of the requirements for comparative analysis, I am arguing that the policy systems of the states and their localities provide a much more scientifically enticing laboratory than does the single national setting.

Measures of State and Local Policy

To turn to the last sector of the model of inquiry used in comparative policy studies, we shall first consider how "outputs" or "policy" has been measured. Comparative studies of policy-making have customarily relied almost exclusively on revenue and spending data. In many respects, this premise is perfectly sound, as long as interpretations of findings are not extended beyond the denotative capacity of the data. For example, a measure of per capita state and local spending does indicate something about the general level of involvement of state and local governments in the affairs of their citizens. But spending figures do not tell us anything about the quality of state administration, the fairness of policies in distributing public goods, or the efficiency with which funds are used. Per capita spending for police protection indicates something about the responses of policy-makers to the need for public order. But it does not indicate that public order is necessarily better preserved in communities with high spending rates. Indeed, it may well be the reverse—that is, policy-makers may be responding to high crime rates with increased appropriations for police protection. Per pupil expenditures for public education may be a fairly good index of policy-makers' concern for the intellectual betterment of the young. We cannot be sure, however, that any particular Johnny will read better in a state that spends $600 a year for each pupil than if he resides in a state spending only $350.[1] Money cannot be assumed to equal services.

From the standpoint of ease and rigor of analysis, the advantages of relying on spending and revenue figures are obvious. In the United States financial data are conveniently available in reasonably consistent form for several decades. They are recorded in a manner that facilitates interstate comparison. Precise intervals may be employed, making possible the application of refined techniques of statistical manipulation. And insofar as the findings so derived make theoretical sense, there is no reason at all for not exploiting such information. Even so, the storehouse of financial data available at any governmental level has not begun to be fully exploited by the political science community.

Some significant areas of public policy, nevertheless, are not readily measurable by financial figures. For example, regulatory policies cannot be assessed in terms of dollars and cents, and, obviously, if one is to get anywhere near a comprehensive picture of the patterns of policy in American communities, civil-rights legislation, public-utilities regulation, labor law, and divorce statutes cannot be ignored. Some efforts to achieve this comprehensive picture, however, have been made and will be reviewed later in this chapter.

All the policy studies cited here reveal a certain bias and simplicity in the implicit definition of what constitutes "public policy." Robert Salisbury recognizes this weakness, and he therefore distinguishes between the substance of governmental outputs, the general frame of authoritative rules, and the orientations of policy-makers toward action.[2] All are legitimate focuses for students of public

[1] Ira Sharkansky has examined the relationship between various indicators of state spending and some, admittedly crude, indicators of state services (approximations of policy impact). Sharkansky, "Government Expenditures and Public Policies in the American States," *American Political Science Review* 61 (1967): 1066-1077. His findings are discouraging for those who might assume a direct relationship between expenditures and policy effects.

[2] Robert H. Salisbury, "The Analysis of Public Policy: A Search for Theories and Roles," in *Political Science and Public Policy,* ed. Austin Ranney (Chicago: Markham Publishing Co., 1968). pp. 152-153.

policy. Quite evidently, the comparative studies of state and local policy have opted for the substantive approach. Ample sources of data and hypotheses have kept a good many scholars busy dealing with the very obvious, definitionally central outputs of governmental institutions and political interactions.

Still, the ambiguity of what is "policy" causes some problems in the treatment of particular variables as independent rather than dependent in the policy model. Dye, for example, treats the median adult educational level as an independent variable having an impact upon public expenditures for education. In any single, temporal context, this makes sense. However, there is an obvious relationship between the policy indicator at one time—educational expenditures —and the presumed independent variable—adult educational level— at a subsequent time.

Much policy analysis is necessarily a snapshot from which temporal processes are inferred. Ideally, a motion picture of the sociopolitical process would be more appropriate. Yet undue caution can render any group of scholars inert. Until more temporally sensitive models are constructed, however, none of the findings can stand without significant qualification.[3]

The Impact of Political
Processes and Social Structure

The most controversial finding of the comparative state and local policy studies has been the repeated demonstration that nearly all the effects on policy that have often been attributed to variations in the political context—for example, apportionment or party competitiveness—are in fact caused by differences in the socioeconomic context. In spite of widespread misgivings, most students of American policies have welcomed the move to a more systematic comparative analysis of outputs. While many critics hail the opening of theoretical vistas that has occurred with the focus on socioeconomic determinants, they quite reasonably remain cautious about some of

[3]Richard I. Hofferbert, "Socioeconomic Dimensions of the American States: 1890-1960," *Midwest Journal of Political Science* 12 (1968): 401-418.

the negative implications. Considerable skepticism continues toward some of the studies that devalue the relevance of state political systems and governmental structures to public policy. Yet the clear effect of the comparative works has been to shift the burden of proof. Enough evidence is available to make us doubt that such facets of state political structures as competitiveness, partisanship, turnout, or apportionment have direct relationships to patterns of public policy. This assertion, however, seems to me to be of relatively short-range consequence and of fairly slight theoretical interest. That most comparative state policy studies *do* show a close relationship between the level of policy activity and the socioeconomic structure is the really interesting aspect of modern policy analysis.

Dye's finding of occasional strong socioeconomic-policy correlations is, at first blush, somewhat disquieting to most political scientists. Their skills are often more sharply developed for dealing with other types of data. They are usually more comfortable talking about governmental institutions, elections, and parties than about "social structure." Furthermore, these findings may be disturbing for their normative implications. To assert that the policies of the American states are the result of "immutable social and historical forces" is to read out of our vision questions of morality, leadership, and human judgment. No one, however, is arguing such a rigorously deterministic interpretation. Socioeconomic-policy correlations should be placed in perspective.

Dye examined the policy impact of four measures of economic development, and found that between them and each of fifty-four measures of public policy multiple correlation coefficients ranged from .27 to .90.[4] From 2.0 per cent to 81.0 per cent of the variance in these policy indicators, therefore, could be attributed to the joint impact of four economic variables.[5] Moreover, of fifty-four multiple correlation coefficients, only twenty-two were above .70. Only a little more than a third of Dye's policy measures have half or more of their variance explained by the socioeconomic indicators. The mul-

---

[4]Thomas R. Dye, *Politics, Economics, and the Public: Policy Outcomes in the American States* (Chicago: Rand McNally, 1966), pp. 286-287.

[5]See Dye's lucid discussion of the use of correlational techniques in *Politics, Economics, and the Public,* chap. 2.

tiple R of the fifty-four coefficients, moreover, averages to 60.62, indicating that the mean per cent of the variance in any policy indicator explained by the four economic measures is 36.57.

This 36.57 per cent is a significant gain over what we knew prior to Dye's research. Nevertheless, it clearly shows that—insofar as these fifty-four policy indicators are representative of our universe of dependent variables—we still have an average two-thirds of the variance in policy to be accounted for by something other than these particular socioeconomic indicators. Some clarification results from employing other levels of policy activity.

Sharkansky has found rather divergent levels of association between social and political variables and policy at the state level as opposed to a mixture of state and local figures.[6] While it can be argued that local governmental activities take place at the legal sufferance of the states, it is too much of a logical jump to assume that local policies constitute a part of a composite policy structure consciously devised at both levels by actors who consider fully the nature of the mix. State legislators and city councilmen are each aware of policies enacted by the other, but their joint effect is probably marginal at most specific points of decision.

The case for examining state figures only or for aggregating state and local policy indicators is frequently encountered in the comparative-policy literature. Sharkansky's point is important if one is concerned with the actions of specific groups of decision-makers. If, on the other hand, policy-makers—at whatever level—are viewed as operating within an environment of finite demands and supports, it follows that provision of services by local government alters the inputs into the state system just as state provisions alter inputs into the local system. Sharkansky's criticism, however, applies in another sense. The political-system variables (for example, apportionment or party systems) that have been studied and found inconsequential for policy are all based on gubernatorial and legislative election returns, state legislative apportionment, and so forth. And yet such findings as Dye's or some I have reported elsewhere use these indicators and compare them with policy measures that are

[6]Ira Sharkansky, "Economic and Political Correlates of State Government Expenditures," *Midwest Journal of Political Science* 11 (1967): 173-192.

substantially affected by aggregations of local decisions.[7] And no indicator of local-political-system variation has been included in these analyses of state and local policy. On the other hand, Dye examined certain policy activities at the local level exclusively and found structures of government to be far less consequential than environmental variables.[8]

Dawson and Robinson's initial article, as noted before, is the landmark in the field.[9] It was the first to employ in a direct and straightforward manner the systems model. It was one of the first efforts by political scientists to employ correlational analysis to examine the determinants of policy. And its most consequential effect was to turn analysts' attention from the political context to the more theoretically enticing and, in the long run, comparatively more interesting socioeconomic context of policy.

Dawson has followed the original article with an essay in which he presents one of the few efforts to examine the society-party-policy model over time.[10] He studied the relationship between indicators of state and local policy, interparty competition, and socioeconomic conditions for three time periods: 1914-1929, 1930-1945, and 1946-1963. The hypothesis examined is that interparty competition and political participation operate as intervening variables linking socio-

[7]Dye, Politics, Economics, and Public; Richard I. Hofferbert, "The Relationship Between Public Policy and Some Structural and Environmental Variables in the American States," American Political Science Review 60 (1966): 73-82.
[8]Thomas R. Dye, "Governmental Structure, Urban Environment, and Educational Policy," Midwest Journal of Political Science 11 (1967): 353-380. See also, Robert L. Lineberry and Edmund P. Fowler, "Reformism and Public Policies in American Cities," American Political Science Review 61 (1967): 701-716.
[9]Richard E. Dawson and James A. Robinson, "Inter-Party Competition, Economic Variables, and Welfare Policies in the American States," Journal of Politics 25 (1963): 265-289. The argument presented in the Journal article is repeated and elaborated in their chapter in Politics in the American States, ed. Herbert Jacob and Kenneth N. Vines (Boston: Little, Brown and Co., 1965), pp. 371-410.
[10]Richard E. Dawson, "Social Development, Party Competition, and Policy," in The American Party Systems: Stages of Political Development, ed. William Nisbet Chambers and Walter Dean Burnham (New York: Oxford University Press, 1967), pp. 203-237.

economic conditions to policy outputs. Dawson offers a stimulating and elaborate theory of the way in which the political party may operate as an articulator and communicator of demands within a socioeconomically developed set of circumstances. Party, according to this hypothesis, would operate as the conversion mechanism in the model. Society changes. This changes party systems. The party systems serve directly to influence policy.

In the final analysis, Dawson's evidence leads to a rejection of this model. Socioeconomic conditions correlate strongly with state policy outputs for all three time periods. Interparty competition, however, correlates strongly with policy only in the last period. The correlation between socioeconomic conditions and party competition is weak in the first time period, strong in the second and third. The correlations between interparty competition and policy outputs is weak in the first time period, moderate in the second, and strong in the third. This variation in the linkage, together with the consistently strong direct relationship between socioeconomic conditions and policy outputs, moves Dawson to make the following summation:

> The developmental findings do not allow us to affirm that inter-party competition has played any role in the development of more liberal policies. What they do suggest is that wealthy, urbanized, and ethnically diversified states tend to be more liberal in their public policies, regardless of the level of party competition.

He concludes:

> . . . the level of inter-party competition is not the crucial factor, intervening between socio-economic factors and policy outputs, that our original hypotheses and theory suggested. A fairly strong association between party competition and policy outputs exists during the final period analyzed here, but the indications are that the relationship is probably spurious. High levels of party competition and liberal state policies both seem to be related independently to highly developed socio-economic conditions.[11]

By the time Dawson's essay was published, a number of additional articles had appeared that predicted and supported the asser-

[11]Ibid., p. 237.

tion of independence between political and policy variables when the environmental characteristics are held constant. The favorite independent structural variable, in addition to interparty competition, has been malapportionment. And, as mentioned earlier, most research has found no significant relationships between patterns of policy and the malapportionment of state legislatures.[12]

At the local level, Dye discovered a similar low salience of the political context when environmental variables are held constant.[13] Employing data from sixty-seven large cities, he examined the relative impact on educational policies of urban governmental variables compared with socioeconomic environmental variables. The structural variables employed were: method of selecting school-board members and school-tax assessors, degree of governmental control over budgets, and reformed nature of city government. Socioeconomic variables included wealth, white-collar employment, property value, and racial composition. Educational-policy variables included school expenditures and taxes, local proportion of financial support, teachers' salaries, teacher-pupil ratios, dropout rates, and private-school enrollments. The social context is fairly clearly related to school policies; the political context is not.

Spending and overall measures such as dropout rates do not say how policy benefits are shared in a community. Nor do they consider intrastate distributions, community control, racial integration, or a host of policies of great importance to the quality of

[12]Herbert Jacob, "The Consequences of Malapportionment: A Note of Caution," *Social Forces* 43 (1964): 256-261; Thomas R. Dye, "Malapportionment and Public Policy in the States," *Journal of Politics* 27 (1965): 586-601; Richard I. Hofferbert, "The Relationship Between Public Policy and Some Structural and Environmental Variables in the American States," *American Political Science Review* 60 (1966): 73-82; David Brady and Douglas Edmonds, "The Effects of Malapportionment on Policy Output in the American States" (Paper presented at the Annual Meeting of the Midwest Conference of Political Scientists, Chicago, 1966). For some modification, see also John G. Grumm, "The Effects of Legislative Structure on Legislative Performance," in *State and Urban Politics*, ed. Richard I. Hofferbert and Ira Sharkansky (Boston: Little, Brown and Co., 1971), pp. 248-322; Jack L. Walker, "The Diffusion of Innovation Among the American States," *American Political Science Review* 63 (1969): 880-899.

[13]Dye, "Governmental Structure."

education. Some suggestive work has been done with respect to distributional considerations. In yet another study, Dye determined that inequality—that is, the concentration of wealth in the hands of a few—is negatively related to levels of per capita income, family income, urbanization, industrialization, and the education levels of state populations.[14] The poorest states are those with the most sharply graded distributions of income. Inequality is positively related to the proportion of state population that is nonwhite, as might be expected given the relationship between the nonwhite population and various indicators of state wealth. Employing the Hofferbert indices of industrialization and affluence, Dye also found that a negative relationship obtains between these socioeconomic indicators and inequality.

Certain political variables are also related to inequality. The more unequal the distribution of wealth, the lower the level of party competition and voter participation and the higher the level of Democratic party success.[15] With respect to policy, Dye discovered that the measure of income inequality does not predict as well as does per capita income. Income predicts certain standard policy indicators better than does inequality, industrialization, or affluence.

Dye has confirmed these findings in yet another article concerning inequality and various policy measures.[16] In addition to using the measure of income equality, Dye in this latter essay also used the income differentials of whites and nonwhites, and racial differentials of educational attainment, occupational categories, and unemployment. Looking at what he calls "income discrimination," Dye examined the ratio of black and white incomes on professional jobs and craftsmen jobs. His object was to study the "environment

[14]Thomas R. Dye, "Income Inequality and American State Politics," *American Political Science Review* 63 (1969): 157-162.

[15]As Dennis Riley and Jack Walker point out in a communication regarding Dye's article, most of these relationships are accounted for by the concentration of socioeconomic characteristics peculiar to the southern states. Dye properly responds to this criticism, however, by citing the problems of "region" as a substitute for more precise measures of characteristics that happen to be regionally concentrated. Riley and Walker, "Communications," *American Political Science Review* 63 (1969): 900-903; Thomas R. Dye, "Communications," *American Political Science Review* 63 (1969): 903.

[16]Thomas R. Dye, "Inequality and Civil Rights Policy in the States," *Journal of Politics* 31 (1969): 1080-1097.

analysis of case studies, some inquiry into elite socialization and background, and careful examination of the institutional situations within which elites operate.

The argument from convenience, however, is not the only defense for studying elite behavior with a full awareness of the relevance of environmental conditions. The concepts in terms of which elite behavior is usually examined—"leadership," "initiative," and so forth—assume some knowledgeability about the environment in which such behavior takes place. Too often these concepts are operationalized with little sensitivity to their varying substantive implications when shifted from one environment to another. Manifestly comparable actions may have varying social implications when placed in different settings. A simple example would be the advocacy of open-housing legislation in communities with different proportions of second generation white immigrants and blacks. "Leadership" might be an appropriate concept in a community with one immigrant/black ratio, but quite inappropriate where the ratio is different.

The model, as discussed so far, seeks both to convey the independent effect of each sector of variables and to account for the development or cumulative effects, or both, of multiple levels of determination. In the same sense that we might think of "interim" levels—(b), (c), (d)—having effects independent of prior or more "basic" variables, so the more "basic" variables may have effects that are original and direct—effects that "bypass" the interim conduits of determination. Historical conditions certainly have molded governmental institutions irrespective of socioeconomic composition or the range of mass political behavior that exists within and between the states. And, as indicated in the earlier discussion, social development and mass behavior may influence elite behavior and policy directly, irrespective of existing variation in governmental institutions. The same may be said of region as a set of historical phenomena operating independently of other sectors of the model. It is the possibility of such routes as these that is portrayed by the solid arrows outside and above the main funnel.

The reason for placing all the developmental arrows within the funnel and putting the "bypass" arrows outside is because the "normal" processes in the creation of policy will be expected to be composed of the relatively constant historical-social-mass political-

of inequality," and he did so by looking not only at the usual list of environmental variables but by expanding the customary list of policy indicators to include scores for civil-rights legislation and grants under the programs administered by the Office of Economic Opportunity.[17] Dye found that inequality is inversely related to the comprehensiveness of civil-rights legislation, that inequality is not as closely related to civil-rights policy as is the level of family income, and that median family income seems to have a greater bearing on civil-rights policy than any of the measures of inequality. These findings are consistent with those in Dye's earlier study of income inequalities. Employing different aspects of the socioeconomic context, he seeks to explain the civil-rights scores, aid-to-dependent-children payments, and the ratio of police to population. Generally, the correlations with the socioeconomic indicators are small, although income still has the highest in all instances. Dye concludes:

> On the whole, inequality in the states appears to be less influential than levels of economic development in determining policy outcomes. This is true even in policy fields conceptually linked to inequality—civil-rights legislation, anti-poverty programs, and law and order. . . .
>
> . . . Inequality in America is linked to both economic underdevelopment and the presence of a large racial minority. The political consequences of inequality are reflected in lower voter turnout rates and reduced party competition in the states. However, inequality is not directly reflected in public policy. . . .[18]

Thus, from Dye's standpoint, differentials between population subsets have consequences for voting behavior and party systems, but have little measurable relevance to patterns of public policy pursued by the states.

Brian Fry and Richard Winters also address themselves to the question of distributional considerations.[19] They seek to explain the

[17]The civil-rights legislation score was comprised from items presented by Duane Lockard, *Toward Equal Opportunity* (New York: Macmillan, 1968), p. 21.

[18]Dye, "Inequality and Civil Rights Policy," pp. 1095, 1097.

[19]Brian R. Fry and Richard F. Winters, "The Politics of Redistribution," *American Political Science Review* 64 (1970): 508-522.

ratio of expenditure benefits to tax burdens for the three lowest income classes in the states. They place an additional feature— distribution of benefits—in the standard policy-analysis model, and they maintain they have demonstrated some independent effect of "political variables" upon distributional policies. What they are calling "political variables" is a rather mixed lot, including participation, party competitiveness, legislative salaries, malapportionment, party cohesion, governor's formal powers, policy innovation, and legislative professionalism. Questions can be raised as to whether these are all "political variables" or if they are not in themselves indicators of policy. The thrust of their analysis is to keep open the relevance of variations in the political process to the policies of state and local governments.

The necessity for more theoretically refined conceptualizations of policy is underscored also by Sharkansky's study of expenditures and service indicators.[20] Sharkansky analyzed the relationships between expenditures and indicators of "public services" in the states.[21] He observed the relationships between spending and the measures of public services at single time points and he also took a look at the relationships between increases in expenditure and increases in the quality or quantity of public services.[22] For causes, Sharkansky studied total state and local expenditures per capita, state. and local expenditures per $1,000 of personal income, and the percentage of total governmental expenditures going to particular major functions. He also reviewed federal aid, total number of state and local employees, public salaries, intergovernmental transfers, per capita income, and population. Using sixty-eight variables, Sharkansky measured different aspects of public services. Some tapped amounts of

[20]Sharkansky, "Government Expenditures."

[21]In effect, the "expenditure"/"service" distinction is equivalent to David Easton's distinction between "outputs" and "outcomes" of the policy system. Easton, *A Systems Analysis of Political Life* (New York: John Wiley and Sons, 1965).

[22]An additional aspect of policy analysis should be pointed out. We must concern ourselves not only with a mix of the activities of the various governments, but also, in many instances, with a mixed private-public system of providing services. Governments may adjust their policy behavior in some areas to accommodate the programs of private institutions within their boundaries.

benefits; some weighed services in relation to population; some quantified service utilization; and some gauged activities that policies were designed to control or effect. Usually, the correlations Sharkansky found between expenditures and his indicators of service were pretty low. The analysis of change patterns showed even fewer relationships. Neither levels of expenditures nor changes in expenditures appeared related to service levels. What does the public get for its money? The question is not answered. The implication is profound. Indicators of output and services, however, are too crude to suggest that governments should stop spending money.

Comprehensive Sociopolitical-
Policy Relationships

Although one cannot yet answer the question, "What does the public get for its tax dollar?" it is possible to take a comprehensive view of the policy process that sorts through some of the complexity and focuses on some central aspects of "outputs" and equally consequential elements of "services." In the same research that yielded the comprehensive indicators of competition-turnout and professionalism-local reliance, Sharkansky and I explored the dimensions of state and local policy.

Public Policy Factors

The list of policy measures is limited in conception to the expenditures for and outputs of prime public services. It is not designed to measure "everything government does." Some measures of government activity seem better conceived as measures of state politics than as measures of policy.[23] In the factor analysis of state

---

[23]Chapter V presented the justifications for including measures pertaining to government personnel, structure, and revenue among the political variables. In brief, they represent features of revenue inputs and governmental structures that may affect response to citizens' needs and demands. The policy measures are narrower than the political in representing the benefits that governments actually provide their citizens within the prominent categories of service.

public policies, the variables were chosen to represent both current expenditures for major services and approximations of results from service operations. The nonexpenditure variables measure "outputs" expressed as services rendered. Table VI-1 lists the variables entered into the factor analysis of policy outputs.

The measures of educational output show the capacity of secondary schools to entice students to remain until graduation and the success of each state's residents on a nationwide examination. Presumably, the first measure assesses the schools' ability to serve the needs of the students, whether they are inclined toward college preparation or immediate placement in business or the trades. The incidence of examination passes should reflect the quality of information and the intellectual skills that state residents possess by the time they finish secondary school.

The measures of highway output record the mileage of various types of state roads in relation to population. Population seems to be the best measure of traffic needs that is readily available.[21] Therefore, the measures show the number of roads in relation to the demands of traffic. Admittedly, road location is not considered. Some states may build many miles of roads but place them unwisely with respect to centers of population, commercial needs, and so forth. The completion rate of the interstate system provides some indication of a state highway department's administrative skills and the capacity of a state to respond quickly to a major opportunity for federal assistance. The inverted death rate offers a measure of road safety; where a state scores high, it should indicate excellent standards of road design and maintenance, an adequate system of highway patrol, or both.

Output measures in the public-welfare field reflect both the generosity of payments and the coverage of each major public-assistance program. These specific programs have been in operation generally for several years, and they represent much of the work carried out by state departments of public welfare. However, the indicators do not assess such aspects of welfare as the quality or quantity of counseling services, cost-of-living differences, or the activ-

[21]See Philip H. Burch, Jr., *Highway Revenue and Expenditure Policy in the United States* (New Brunswick: Rutgers University Press, 1962), p. 23.

Table VI-1   Policy Variables Analyzed*

Education

† 1. Per cent of ninth-grade students (1959) graduating three years later
† 2. Per cent of candidates passing selective-service mental examination
3. State and local government expenditures for education per capita

Highways

4. Total road mileage per capita
† 5. Rural road mileage per rural resident
6. Municipal road mileage per urban resident
7. Per cent of designated interstate mileage completed
8. Population per highway fatality
† 9. State and local government expenditures for highways per capita

Welfare

†10. Average payment, Aid to Families of Dependent Children (AFDC)
†11. Average payment, Old Age Assistance (OAA)
†12. Average payment, Aid to the Blind (AB)
†13. Average payment, Aid to the Permanently and Totally Disabled (APTD)
14. Incidence of AFDC recipients among population with incomes of less than $2,000
†15. Incidence of OAA recipients among population with incomes of less than $2,000 and more than 65 years of age
16. Incidence of AB recipients among population with incomes of less than $2,000
17. Incidence of APTD recipients among population with incomes of less than $2,000
18. State and local government expenditures for public welfare per capita

Health

19. Proportion of white infants surviving their first year of life
20. Proportion of nonwhite infants surviving their first year of life
21. State and local government expenditures for health, hospitals, and sanitation per capita

Natural Resources

22. Visits per 10,000 population to state parks
†23. Fishing licenses sold per 10,000 population
†24. Hunting licenses sold per 10,000 population
†25. State and local government expenditures for natural resources per capita

General

26. Total state and local government general expenditures per capita

*The data pertain to 1962.
†Variables surviving test for high loading on a single factor.

ities under the later programs sponsored by the Federal Office of Economic Opportunity.

Measures of health policies assess the likelihood of white and nonwhite children surviving their first year. Admittedly, these variables cover only a small portion of health-relevant services within each state; also, they show the influence of many social and economic processes. Nevertheless, we assumed that high scores on these scales reflect the presence of health and hospital facilities that are adequate to cultural and medical needs.

Natural-resources policies are reflected in measures of the tendency of state residents to use the programs and facilities offered by state departments of parks and wildlife. High scores on these variables should signal attractive programs. The basic assumption was that an attractive program activates usage by state residents.[25]

Examination of the simple correlations among the policy measures revealed no redundancies comparable with those found in the list of political variables discussed in Chapter V. A preliminary factor analysis of the policy variables led us to eliminate ambiguities and irrelevancies that loaded high on two factors or on no factors.

[25]In collecting the data for the measures of outputs and services, the assumption was made that recorded information is a reasonably accurate reflection of fact. We recognized considerable controversy about the reliability of the data. Yet the data chosen appear to be the best available, and they enjoy wide use among social scientists. For comments about each item, the reader is referred to the sources. The sources for the political variables include: *Census of Governments, 1962; The Book of the States 1964-1965; Statistical Abstract of the United States, 1964.* The index of gubernatorial power comes from Joseph A. Schlesinger, "The Politics of the Executive," in *Politics in the American States,* ed. Jacob and Vines, pp. 207-237. The index of suffrage regulations is taken from Lester Milbrath, "Political Participation in the States," in *Politics in the American States,* ed. Jacob and Vines, pp. 25-60. The indices of legislative apportionment are from Paul T. David and Ralph Eisenberg, *Devaluation of the Urban and Suburban Vote* (Charlottesville: Bureau of Public Administration, University of Virginia, 1961), pp. 5, 15; and Glendon Schubert and Charles Press, "Measuring Malapportionment," *American Political Science Review* 58 (1964): 969. Sources for policy variables include: National Education Association, *Rankings of the States, 1963;* U.S. Bureau of Public Roads, *Annual Report, 1963;* Social Security Administration, *Social Security Bulletin: Annual Statistical Supplement, 1963; The Book of the States, 1964-1965; Statistical Abstract of the United States, 1964.*

A second factor analysis was then performed with the remaining variables. The variables retained and their loadings are shown in Table VI-2; specific scores for the states are presented in Table VI-3. The first factor—"Welfare-Education"—emphasizes liberal welfare payments, the tendency of high-school pupils to remain until graduation, and the success of state residents on the national examination.

The second principal policy factor is "Highways-Natural Resources." Its major components are measures of rural highway mileage and highway expenditures, plus measures of fish and wildlife services and expenditures for natural resources. A curious variable that is loaded highly on this factor is Old Age Assistance recipients. At first glance, it seems out of its proper place in the welfare-education factor. Aid to the aged, however, is the product of a policy process that is distinct from that of other welfare and education programs. Several rural states that have paid little attention to the average level of welfare benefits have shown consider-

Table VI-2   Loadings of Policy Variables
on Two Principal Factors

Variables*	Welfare-Education	Highways-Natural Resources
AFDC payments (10)	.91	.05
OAA payments (11)	.86	.17
High-school graduates (1)	.85	.11
AB payments (12)	.83	.04
Examination success (2)	.78	.41
APTD payments (13)	.72	—.27
Rural road mileage (5)	.11	.87
Hunting licenses (24)	—.06	.86
Highway expenditures (9)	.12	.86
Fishing licenses (23)	.04	.80
Natural-resources expenditures (25)	.31	.72
OAA recipients (15)	.04	.71
Per Cent of Total Variance	35.4	34.9

*The parenthesized numbers correspond to the variable numbers in Table VI-1.

Table VI-3 Scores for the States on Two Policy Factors

State	Welfare- Education	State	Highway-Nat- ural Resources
California	1.85	Wyoming	3.73
Massachusetts	1.45	Nevada	2.87
Wisconsin	1.44	Montana	1.85
Minnesota	1.32	Idaho	1.58
Illinois	1.26	South Dakota	1.55
New York	1.15	Vermont	1.31
New Hampshire	1.04	Utah	.69
New Jersey	1.04	Oregon	.66
North Dakota	.90	North Dakota	.61
Connecticut	.85	Minnesota	.59
Kansas	.85	Colorado	.47
Iowa	.84	Maine	.34
Washington	.79	Nebraska	.34
Oklahoma	.78	New Mexico	.27
Michigan	.76	Arizona	.18
Oregon	.74	New Hampshire	.18
Colorado	.71	Wisconsin	.10
Nebraska	.70	Arkansas	.06
Rhode Island	.64	Washington	.06
Ohio	.28	Iowa	− .06
Wyoming	.22	Kansas	− .08
New Mexico	.18	Tennessee	− 17
Indiana	.16	Mississippi	− .19
Utah	.12	Oklahoma	− .26
Pennsylvania	.08	Missouri	− .30
Idaho	− .04	California	− .34
Montana	− .06	Louisiana	− .36
South Dakota	− .07	Alabama	− .40
Maryland	− .16	Indiana	.40
Arizona	− .27	Kentucky	− .42
Missouri	− .38	West Virginia	− .42
Delaware	− .39	Texas	− .49
Maine	− .46	Georgia	− .54
Nevada	− .54	Michigan	.58
Vermont	− .62	Florida	− .59
Louisiana	.73	Virginia	− .64
Texas	− .81	Ohio	− .76
Florida	− .88	Pennsylvania	− .77
Kentucky	−1.04	Delaware	− .78
Virginia	−1.06	Maryland	− .79
North Carolina	−1.08	South Carolina	− .81
Arkansas	−1.26	Connecticut	.84
West Virginia	−1.36	North Carolina	− .86
Georgia	−1.45	Illinois	− .88
South Carolina	−1.58	New York	−1.08
Tennessee	−1.74	New Jersey	−1.12
Alabama	−1.75	Rhode Island	−1.14
Mississippi	−2.43	Massachusetts	−1.36

able concern for their aged and have made the OAA program available to many. Some of this concern may be related to the political strategy of state governmental decision-makers. Aside from welfare mothers (who are tainted with a stigma of illegitimacy), the aged are the largest group of potential welfare recipients eligible to vote.[26] The lines of reasoning suggested by this instance will be more carefully explored later.

The use of factor scores has thrown some light on the controversy over the relationships among political and economic characteristics of the states that are alleged to influence the nature of public policies. Several publications that I summarized in the earlier sections of this chapter employ individual variables to answer the central question, "How do political and economic elements relate with each other and with the nature of public policies?" Although most authors use comparable measurements and attempt to make their research additive with respect to each others', the interpretation of their findings is made difficult by the discreteness of the variables examined. The correlations reported by Dye, for example, often show differing policy relationships with industrialization and urbanization than with income and education.[27] The findings obtained when the political measures assess a certain type of voter turnout or party competition differ from the findings derived from political measures that assess the equity of apportionment or the centralization of state-local financial relationships. Likewise, findings vary with the use of expenditures or other variables that purport to measure public policy.[28]

Influences on Policy

We can now face the issue of political or economic influences on public policies with some important new tools. The six factors measure prominent dimensions of state economics, politics, and

---

[26]For a discussion of the politics of old-age assistance in Alabama, see Ira Sharkansky, *Spending in the American States* (Chicago: Rand McNally, 1968), pp. 138-141.

[27]See, for example, Dye, *Politics, Economics, and Public,* pp. 125 and 162.

[28]See Sharkansky, *Spending in American States,* chaps. 4 and 7.

public policies. They should enable us to see which types of economic and political phenomena are most relevant for which types of public policy.

The welfare-education dimension of state policy shows positive relationships with each of the political and economic factors (Table VI-4). The coefficients of partial correlation reveal that this policy factor is associated most closely with high scores on competition-turnout and affluence, with neither being significantly more important than the other. The elements of interparty competition, high voter participation, high levels of educational attainment, and wealth seem to provide the impetus—independently from other governmental and economic conditions—for public officials to provide generous welfare payments and successful educational services.[29]

Table VI-4   Coefficients of Simple, Partial, and Multiple
              Correlation, and Multiple Determination Between
              Socioeconomic, Political, and Policy Factors

	Welfare-Education	Highways-Natural Resources	Welfare Education	Highways-Natural Resources
	SIMPLE CORRELATION		PARTIAL CORRELATION*	
Professionalism-Local Reliance	.39	−.54	.26	−.24
Competition-Turnout	.68	.25	.47	−.02
Industrialization	.37	−.69	.17	−.55
Affluence	.69	.43	.43	.53
	MULTIPLE CORRELATION		MULTIPLE DETERMINATION	
Socioeconomic Factors	.77	.82	.59	.68
Political Factors	.78	.60	.61	.36
Socioeconomic + Political Factors	.83	.84	.69	.70

*Controlling for the other factors.

[29]The political and economic factors are more successful in accounting for interstate variance in the policy factors than are most individual measures of these phenomena. Table VI-4 shows simple, partial, and multiple correla-

This finding of importance for the competition-turnout factor with respect to welfare and education services provides some latter-day support for hypotheses derived from Key and others that electoral and party characteristics of state politics have something to do with the nature of services that are provided. Our findings do not, however, fit the neat, linear, single determinant structure of causality suggested by some of Key's followers. Rather, the data suggest that it is not any one element of state politics, but an underlying factor, which is only partly measured by individual variables, that exerts an independent influence on public services. The prominence of this finding is increased by the importance of the policy factor involved. Welfare and education services consume a substantial proportion of state and local government resources: 49 per cent of general expenditures and 51 per cent of government employment in 1965-1966. Policy-making in welfare and education is characterized by sharp controversies, which may explain the relation of education and welfare with electoral and partisan processes in a manner quite different from other areas of public policy.

The highway-natural resources dimension of public policy shows its primary dependence on economic factors. It is inversely and strongly related to industrialization and directly related to affluence.

---

tion coefficients between policy factors as dependent variables and the political and economic factors as independent variables. It shows that both political factors together account for 61 and 36 per cent of the variance in the policy factors. In contrast, the multiple correlation coefficients that Dye reports show that his collection of individual political variables account for 36 per cent of the variance in only fifteen out of fifty-four dependent variables, and they account for 61 per cent of the variance in only two out of the fifty-four instances. (Dye, *Politics, Economics, and Public*, pp. 286-287.) Both of our socioeconomic factors account for 59 and 68 per cent of the variance in the policy factors; the individual social and economic variables in Dye's collection, by contrast, account for 59 per cent of the variance in only fourteen of fifty-four dependent variables, and they account for 68 per cent of the variance in only eight of fifty-four dependent variables. A similar finding appears when we compare with his data the success of our economic and political factors together in explaining variance in our policy factors. We explain 69 and 70 per cent of the variance in the policy factors by means of all political and socioeconomic variables; Dye explains 69 per cent of the variance for only thirteen of fifty-four variables.

Thus it appears that *low* levels of industrial output and employment, population density, and urbanization, together with *high* levels of personal wealth and education, incline a state toward heavy investments in roads, especially in rural areas, and in active fish and wildlife programs. Wide-open spaces contain an abundance of recreational opportunities, the need for highway facilities, and the rural interests that have concentrated their political efforts in behalf of these services. Highway-natural resource policy also is inversely dependent on the professionalism-local reliance dimension of state politics, but this is secondary to its dependence on socioeconomic characteristics.

Why the lack of dependence on political factors for highway and natural resource policies? Despite conflicting interests, the particular programmatic activities involved in these policies do not fall neatly along the symbolic continua that are most commonly the objects of partisan controversy. Few issues, for example, seem to array taxpayers and the socioeconomic haves against recipients of services and the have-nots (in contrast with the case in education and welfare). This absence of cleavage may be because highways, parks, wildlife, and conservation programs are "self-financed" by means of earmarked taxes, licenses, and user fees. The recipients themselves pay for much of these benefits, thereby precluding a great deal of conflict across the lines of different social classes and ethnic groups.

Conclusion

Each of the last three chapters has discussed a series of studies that have sought to examine the relationships between the more or less separate aspects or attributes of state and local social situations, political processes, and policy performance. Good theoretical reasons exist for viewing such collections of attributes as representations, in some sense or another, of structural relationships. Factor analyses of each of the three sectors of the policy-system model attempt to come closer to a "pure" measure of these structures than is provided by any single variable or group of discrete variables. The factors, even if they do not qualify as measures of enduring "structures," at least clarify relationships among the inputs, the political process, and the outputs of the widely used model of the state policy process.

The factor analysis of social structure goes a long way toward isolating basically distinct social differences between the states. The anomaly of prosperous nonindustrial states and of poor but fairly industrial states is largely resolved by this analysis. The factor analysis of political variables reveals two underlying dimensions of state politics; these have been labeled professionalism-local reliance and competition-turnout. The distinctiveness of the competition-turnout factor testifies to the importance of this dimension in distinguishing the politics of each state. And it credits the perception of Key, Lockard, Fenton, and other political scientists who took aspects of electoral and party behavior as the focus of their own work. The factor analysis of policy variables reveals two principal dimensions of welfare-education and highway-natural resources. The examination of political and economic factors shows strong associations between competition-turnout and affluence, and between professionalism-local reliance and industrialization. (See discussion in Chapter V.) The relationships among political, economic, and policy factors show that the welfare-education dimension of state policy is significantly dependent upon the competition-turnout dimension of state politics and the affluence dimension of the state economy. A wealthy state showing high voter turnout and intense interparty competition is likely to score high on the level of welfare and educational services. The highway-natural resources dimension of policy appears most dependent upon the industrialization dimension of the states' economies. The relationship is inverse, indicating that well-developed highways and wildlife programs accompany low levels of industrialization and population concentration.

The relationships among economic, political, and policy factors are generally stronger than the relationships between individual variables that have previously been used. Thus, the underlying dimensions tapped by factor analysis strengthen as well as simplify our explanations of policy-making in the American states.

The single most important finding of this research may be its emphasis upon multidimensionality in state economics, politics, and public policy. There is no single answer to the question: "Is it politics or economics that has the greater impact on public policy?" The answer, contrary to the import of much recent research, varies with the dimensions of each phenomenon that is at issue.[30] Welfare-education policies relate most closely with the competition-turnout dimension of state politics *and* with the affluence dimension of the economy. Highway-natural resource policies show their closest (inverse) relationships with the industrialization dimension of a state's economy.[31]

While these findings add to the inquiry into political and economic contexts of public policies, they offer little encouragement to those who would seek to expand the level and scope of public services by manipulating one political or structural characteristic of state government—for example, voter turnout, party competition, or apportionment. It is apparent only that certain aspects of the political context having to do with voter turnout and interparty competition are related to certain public policies. But this does not terminate the inquiry. Factor analyses depend on the nature of the variables included in them. Although this research has included a wide range of political, economic, and policy variables in its factor analyses, it

---

[30]Charles F. Cnudde and Donald J. McCrone, "Party Competition and Welfare Policies in the American States," *American Political Science Review* 63 (1969): 858-866.

[31]One limitation of the data employed is their lack of historical perspective. A separate study of industrialization and affluence and their relationship with individual policy and electoral variables has shown that the strength of relationship is, in some cases, quite fluid over time. (See Hofferbert, "Socioeconomic Dimensions.") This fluidity, however, may be a result of simple changes in the value of isolated dependent variables and not an accurate picture of the more analytically interesting dimensions of policy and political life that Sharkansky and I have considered. I have found that the relative contribution of individual variables maintained a high degree of consistency in their loadings on the principal factors from one decade to the next, although individual variable-by-variable correlations shifted considerably. If it were possible to analyze the full component of political and service variables over extended periods of time, the same type of configuration could probably be expected. Consequently, the strength of relationship of *factors* could be fairly constant over time even though the individual variable correlations change considerably. Because of the limited availability of the political and policy data for previous years, however, this thesis must remain a matter for speculation.

is likely that further analysis—with more measures of political, economic, and policy traits—will permit more refined measures of the contexts of state policy systems.

The factors Sharkansky and I constructed leave unexplained much of the variance in state politics and policy. This unplumbed variance might be reduced by adding more variables to the factor programs. However, it may be inherent in the nature of the phenomena that much variance will remain unexplained by factor analysis. This unexplained variance may reflect the importance of particularistic, unpatterned happenings that fashion and lend excitement to political institutions.

The effort to explain why politics and policies differ from one state to the next may be helped considerably by examining the dimensions lying beneath readily measured variables. But no amount of archival search and factor analysis will account for the contributions made to the institution of policies in individual states by dynamic personalities or the force of strong traditions. The study of elite and organizational behavior, plus exploration of the values that prevail in the cultural environments of the individual states, may be essential for a thorough understanding of interstate differences in politics and public policy.

chapter VII

Leadership, Elite Activities, and Policy Processes[1]

Relationships as Processes

Knowing what we now know about the context of policy-making, is there any reason to study policy-makers? The level of affluence of the states correlates .69 with welfare-education policy scores—a clue to the process by which welfare and education policies are formulated. The correlation, however, does not tell us much about how decision-makers set levels of support—that is, about what their policy-making activity "looks like" as they draw up budgets, pass resolutions, and print bills. Nonetheless, the correlation, other things equal, tells us a great deal about the context within which welfare and education policy-makers work. The more we know about the context of policy-making, the less we need to know about policy-makers as such. Yet we then run the risk that such considerations as elite role patterns, leadership, and ideology will be treated as merely residual categories in much comparative inquiry. The direc-

[1]This chapter draws heavily upon my essay "Elite Influence in State Policy Formation: A Model for Comparative Inquiry," *Polity* 3 (March, 1970): 316-344.

tions being taken by recent analyses of aggregate data have led to a concern along these lines that has been summarized by Harmon Zeigler and Michael Baer: "... Thomas R. Dye and Richard Hofferbert [have] ignored human behavior in seeking to explain the correlates of policy outcomes."[2]

Although the comparative state studies of recent years have obviously opened new theoretical vistas for students of policy formation, they have justified the impression articulated by Zeigler and Baer. Despite the appearance of determinism in the relationships between socioeconomic development and public policy, we know that—by any reasonable definition of policy—human beings have to act for there to be a policy. It is not all a matter of context. In most instances, a fairly small group of people is proximate to the processes of deciding what is to be public policy at any point in time. Some of these people are elected by popular preference; others are appointed through legally defined means; still others participate because of their status in private groups. Policy-making elites, at least in my usage, are denoted by their proximity to points of decision, not by the mechanisms of investiture.

The obvious relevance of small groups of decision-makers in the policy processes provides ample justification for clarifying the main dimensions of elite behavior and for elevating the priority attached to them by students of comparative politics. Certainly the various studies of community decision-making and power should, notwithstanding the problems discussed in Chapter II, offer some guidance for the study of policy-makers. It is my argument that there are theoretical and technical guidelines in both the aggregate studies and in the local elite analyses that can be legitimately and fruitfully merged in the comparative study of policy processes. Without question, a clearer conceptualization of the role of influential individuals is necessary. Yet at the same time, the demonstration of the relevance of socioeconomic factors to policy patterns suggests equally strongly that a full explication of environmental contexts is essential to aid illumination of the behavior of policy-making elites. Interactional analysis (à la community studies) is insufficient without a

---

[2]L. Harmon Zeigler and Michael Baer, *Lobbying* (Belmont, Calif.: Wadsworth, 1969), p. xix.

specification of the external boundaries that define, to a greater or lesser extent, the range of probable behaviors by those doing the interacting. These boundaries are specifiable in part by means of comparative aggregate analysis. One can no longer justify the study of elite activities *in vacuo*.

New theoretical avenues have been opened by the comparative studies, and considerable doubt has been cast upon much of the conventional wisdom regarding the effect of both formal and political institutions on policy outputs. The broad contours of the research, however, have not proceeded beyond the aggregation of individual hypotheses. The relevance of particular aspects of state socioeconomic development to patterns of policy has been demonstrated with sufficient clarity to warrant their thorough investigation. The relevance to policy patterns of political-system variables long respected by political scientists has been sufficiently challenged to shift the burden of proof concerning relevance to those who would maintain that political patterns "matter" in policy determination. The linkages that account for the social-policy correlations have not been specified in more than a preliminary way. And substantial unexplained variance in policy remains even after the effects of obvious social characteristics are taken into account. In the entire body of this literature, little guidance is given on where to proceed in accounting for the impact of ideology, leadership, inertia, and that whole set of actions and attitudes broadly included under the label "elite behavior." A diagrammatic representation of the policy-formation model I propose is shown in Figure VII-1. As drawn, the scheme would appear to be unidirectional, with requisite actions and resources flowing into the open end of the funnel and resulting in a formal policy conversion. This simplicity is somewhat deceptive, for it is necessary to consider three aspects of the process, all of which can be fitted into the scheme presented in the figure. Two of the aspects are related to time; the third concerns the substantive areas of policy under consideration.

Single-Issue Processes

The first dimension pertains to the genesis and progress of specific policy alternatives within the environments of the political

Figure VII-1

MODEL FOR COMPARATIVE STUDY OF POLICY FORMATION

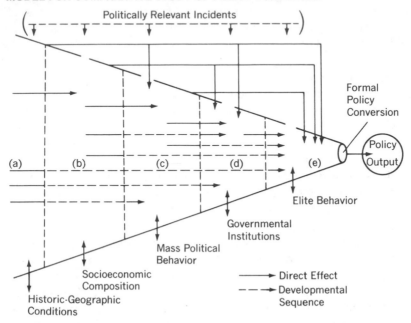

system. The time element involved at this level of analysis is the relatively short span—a matter of weeks, months, or at most a few years—encompassed by the gestation and birth of particular issues. I am concerned with the initiation and evolution of single issues— not with long-range development of a pattern of governmental policy. Examples would be an increase in welfare allotments, the creation of a new state university campus, an agreement to participate in a new federal grant-in-aid program. Policy decisions like these, however, are never made in a historical, social, or political vacuum. Policy-makers are never confronted with a clean slate, either in terms of relevant circumstances of immediate political consequence or in terms of past policy commitments. It is in regard to this aspect of policy-making that processes of incrementalism are most appropriately analyzed.

The first sector of the model (a) is intended to show that history and geography are intricately woven into the actions of contemporary policy-makers. A golden codfish hangs behind the speaker's dais in the Massachusetts House of Representatives. Cod are caught in the ocean. The proximity of the ocean and the commercial history it actuated in the Bay State have created a set of circumstances for the policy-maker in Boston that differs in meaningful ways from those of his counterpart in Helena, Montana. The ocean not only yielded the cod to line the coffers of Massachusetts fishermen, but it also was the thoroughfare that brought to the port of Boston successive waves of immigrants. These newcomers, along with their descendants, have continued to give special flavor to politics in Massachusetts. Problems of urbanization, ethnic integration, and industrialization were experienced early in Massachusetts' history. Some states further inland are only now, a century later, beginning to anticipate what seaboard states underwent in the late 1800s.

Kansas is what it is in large part because it leads the nation in wheat production. Dryland agriculture long ago involved the farmer in a politico-economic market system that generated dependencies and awarenesses not felt by more self-sufficient, consumption farmers east of the Mississippi. Nor can the remaining strains of populism in Colorado be fully comprehended unless one is familiar with the history of mining and the labor strife of the tempestuous nineties or the policies of the railroads as they opened the West.

History and geography help to condition the social and economic structures of political systems. But social structures and economic conditions can, at least analytically, be separated from the more obvious historical and geographic determinants. Neighboring states, with almost similar backgrounds and resources, have developed measurably different social and economic climates that may have independent determinative effects upon the manner in which particular issues are raised and resolved within the policy-making milieu. Depending upon one's perspective, of course, any social or economic condition can be classified as "historical." Nothing happens that is not in some sense a function of prior circumstances.

The distinction I am making is between social circumstances of direct relevance and such events as the Depression or the invention of the cotton gin. That Louisiana is disproportionately Catholic, compared with other southern states, can be analyzed in terms of its

relevance to policy-making, without overtly accounting for the trans-
plantation of the Acadians from Nova Scotia or the nature of religious life under Spanish and French rule up to 1803. The relevance
of a nonwhite population to policy-making can be understood at one
level without detailed reference to slavery, the Civil War, or the
northward exodus of blacks in the twentieth century.

On the one hand, a distinction between historical events and
current socioeconomic conditions is artificial, because of their mutual
dependence. On the other hand, such a distinction can be useful,
because at a given level of analysis we simply do not care why
socioeconomic conditions have come to be the way they are. We may
be satisfied to measure their effect upon the dependent variable—
for instance, public policy—being explained. Thus Sharkansky's dis-
covery of the effects of region—controlling for level of economic
well-being—is interesting and enlightening. But, as he admits, we
know that "region" is not a very stimulating theoretical concept.[3]
It might be seen as a substitute for another common conceptual
dodge—"political culture." The finding of independent regional impact, nevertheless, adds to our predictive capacities and leads us
to explore further what lies behind regional differences.

In a manner comparable with that in which socioeconomic
composition can be seen to have original effects, mass political behavior may influence elite decisions or governmental institutions
independently from socioeconomic determination. Markedly different
patterns of voter turnout, party structure, and associational activity
exist in socioeconomically similar jurisdictions.

Any bibliography of state and local politics studies would include as its largest set of entries discussions of governmental institutions—constitutions, legislative apportionment, length of officers'
terms, administrative forms, and so forth. One of the contributions
of recent state-politics studies has been the start toward making these
variables operational in a manner that facilitates measurement of
their relative impacts upon policies also measured in a reasonable,
precise manner.[4]

---

[3]Ira Sharkansky, *Regionalism in American Politics* (Indianapolis: Bobbs-
Merrill, 1970).
[4]See the discussion of measurement in chaps. V and VI.

The last sector of the model (e) prior to formal policy conversion is "elite behavior." One should note that all possible preconversion routes pass through this sector. Most definitions of "policy formation"—which includes nonperception or rejection of proposed alternatives—encompass some type of action connoting formal legality that must be attached to a policy output by the behavior of relevant elites. This action may be a simple imprimatur whereby legal cognizance is taken of a de facto situation. For example, a state might pass a civil-rights statute though the relevant forms of discrimination had long since disappeared. Or, at the other extreme, elite behavior may well take the form of vigorous action against strong historical and economic forces, such as the levying of the severance tax in Louisiana.[5] The point is that any combination of "pre-elite" factors may be operative on a given policy proposal, but elite response in some formal manner is a sine qua non of policy as here conceived. As I indicated earlier, the actions of formal officeholders are not the whole of relevant elite behavior. But such actions are a *necessary* condition of policy-making, and they serve as a point of departure in the search for *sufficient* conditions.

This last observation suggests that the most fruitful strategy for inquiry into the determinants of public policy would be to begin with elite behaviors and work backward through the factors conditioning them. And, indeed, the model may be viewed in this manner. If one starts with a given policy situation, the model directs attention first and foremost to the behaviors of relevant elites. From the standpoint of research tactics, however, such an approach is likely to be frustrating. Of all sectors of the model, the most difficult to measure is elite behavior. And of all possible linkages, the most difficult to formulate and observe are those between other sectors and elite behavior. In a sense, therefore, we are forced to run the risk, at least at this stage of technique and theory, of treating elite behavior as a sort of residual category. In other words, whatever variation in policies we are unable to explain by something else, we simply attribute to elite behavior—to human "static" in an otherwise neatly deterministic model. This risk can be minimized by sensitive

[5]See Allan P. Sindler, *Huey Long's Louisiana* (Baltimore: Johns Hopkins University Press, 1956), especially chap. 2.

institutional conditioning of elite behavior (even though the data and analysis at any particular moment may not be able to take full cognizance of this progression). Phenomena in categories (a), (b), (c), and (d) provide a constant backdrop for (e)—a set of circumstances with multiple relevance that the elite can overcome, suppress, or exploit, but not ignore, under normal conditions. Depending upon the time and policy involved, then, it may be hypothesized that any bypassing of interim sectors—such as (a-e), (b-d), (a-b-e)—would in some sense be a deviant case.

Some examples will clarify the type of hypotheses that the model is designed to generate from the aspect of single issues. From the discussion of the various sectors it should be clear what types of relationships are posited by the main routes within the funnel itself. However, the nature of the "bypass" relationships may need further elaboration.

We may find, for example, a direct relationship between the historical facts (a) of Reconstruction and populism that induced the southern elites of the 1890s to pass Jim Crow laws and thereby create the conditions for a low level of voter turnout (c). This relationship may be conceived either as (a-c), or to introduce the operation of feedback, (a-e-d-c), indicating a set of historic conditions to which elites responded by changing governmental institutions, which in turn had a measurable effect upon mass political behavior. Another example is the direct relationship between the residue of the Progressive era found in the tier of northern states from Wisconsin westward and such institutional hallmarks as comprehensive merit systems, initiative, and referendum. Here the linkage is between historical facts and governmental institutions, (a-d). Similarly, the relationship (b-d) may well account for the evolution of a high ratio of state to local spending in the South, a circumstance some scholars attribute to the weakness of the southern local-property-tax base. In this example, institutional and policy characteristics are responding to internal economic conditions.

The linkage between mass and elite behavior, (c-e), is the subject of most of the traditional writing on democratic systems. Further, this connection has constituted the theoretical watershed for a good deal of contemporary empirical research. The expected link between masses—opinions and actions expressed as political participation—and the behavior of the elected is what might be called the "democratic premise." It is the assumption that the behavior of those in office is somehow a response to or at least conditioned by the desires or needs, or both, of those who participated in one way or another in electing them. The elected are, in some recognizable sense, assumed to be controlled by the democratic premise.

These examples have dealt primarily with two-sector relationships. Of course, once one admits the possibility or likelihood of cumulative and developmental relationships, the limit of possible routes is set only by the combinations and permutations of the number of indicators in the various sectors. A full appreciation of the policy-making process must also include feedback, such as suggested in the first example above (a-e-d-c), which makes the possible number of combinations and permutations infinite. It is primarily the unidirectional relationships depicted in the model, however, to which initial attention could be given most readily and fruitfully.

Substructural Variation over Time

The second aspect of variation in the policy-making process is not as readily spotted in the diagrammatic presentation of the model as is the first—the resolution of single issues. Any substantive area of policy may be dependent upon an intricate pattern of social, political, and governmental resources or determinants. Assuming some stability in this pattern, we may speak of a "substructure" of policy as another aspect or dimension.

Assume, for example, that there is a high correlation at one point in time between a complex of variables roughly related to industrialization and the level of support for a particular set of policies. We may speculate as to the nature of causal connections, along the lines of analysis suggested by the first dimension of the model—single-issue determination. Other variables may also be related to the same set of policies, in greater or lesser degree than industrialization. The network of these associations would comprise what I am here calling the "substructure" of policy.

Consider the possible range of findings if we now measure the relationships at different points in time between these same environmental factors and the dependent policy variables. From decade to decade the strength of the relationship will change in magnitude. In other words, the political relevance of particular environmental phenomena will vary over time, and it is possible to accommodate such variation within the parameters of the model.

In Table VII-1 the industrialization and affluence scores are correlated with various indicators of public expenditure and mass electoral behavior. The explanatory power of these factors varies considerably from one decade to another. The relevance of industrialization to state and local expenditures on highways, for example, varies from +.44 in 1890 to −.50 in 1960. The correlation between affluence and expenditures for welfare varies from .67 in 1900 to .06 in 1960. And, as the findings in the table reveal, the aspects of state social systems associated with partisan preferences and voter turnout have been quite fluid over time.

Returning to the diagrammatic presentation in Figure VII-1, it is variation in policy substructures over time that is indicated by the two-way vertical arrows through the bottom boundary of the funnel. As the national political environment changes, one would expect modification in the structures of independent variables. It is in this sense that the model serves to alert one to the long-range developmental or dynamic aspects of the policy-making process. It seems a plausible hypothesis that certain features of the historical, socioeconomic, mass, and institutional environments have a reasonably stable and predictable impact on the directions of policy. It is equally plausible to assume that some variables gain strength in their policy impact while others decline. And long-term forces may be temporarily reduced in determinative impact, only to reassert themselves once a disturbing element of the system is removed.

The nature of the substructure itself—that is, the pattern of independent variables—may change incrementally over time, as is seen with the affluence-welfare spending correlations in Table VII-1. The nature of the substructure may also be interrupted or disturbed by incidents in the environment that "happen" and that temporarily alter the ground rules for policy-makers; this possibility is represented by the parenthesized arrows at the top of Figure VII-1. Furthermore, existing facets of the environment can, by the conscious manipulation of elites or by some nonpurposive means, become relevant to the policy-making process on a temporary basis. For instance, above-

Table VII-1 Correlations of Socioeconomic Factors and Selected Political Variables*: 1890-1960

	Total Spending	Spending for Education	Spending for Highways	Spending for Welfare	Vote Democratic for President	Voter Turnout for President**
Versus Industrialization						
1890	.31	.21	.44	.17	-.04	.14
1900	.34	-.08	.38	.36	-.38	.05
1910	.27	.05	.38	.06	-.11	.05
1920	—	—	—	—	.22	.27
1930	.38	-.03	.12	.61	-.36	.06
1940	.19	.07	-.26	.06	-.13	.17
1950	.14	.00	-.09	-.07	.15	.23
1960	-.04	-.13	-.50	.01	.35	.21
Versus Affluence						
1890	.80	.83	.44	.62	-.78	.09
1900	.82	.87	.61	.67	-.61	.36
1910	.60	.62	.52	.59	-.82	.61
1920	—	—	—	—	-.23	.57
1930	.72	.70	.52	.59	-.77	.71
1940	.70	.65	.46	.66	-.78	.84
1950	.51	.45	.35	.04	-.64	.74
1960	.80	.76	.38	.06.	-.41	.64

*All spending figures are total state and local and are computed on a per capita basis. The spending figures are for the years 1890, 1902, 1913, 1932, 1942, 1957, and 1962 respectively. In years without presidential elections, data were taken from the subsequent biennium.

**The data employed are per cent of total vote cast for the Democratic presidential candidates and the per cent of population over voting age casting ballots for president. Account has been taken of the different times at which the suffrage was made available to women.

ground testing of nuclear weapons took place in the United States for years without federal publication of figures on the extent of atmospheric pollution. Normally, atomic testing would not be within the range of state concern. Yet Minnesota policy-makers took it upon themselves to make the issue politically relevant by persuading the state health commission to take daily samples of the atmosphere and publicize the extent of pollution by the tests. The environmental fact of a national practice, normally beyond the governmental ken of the states, was made politically relevant by the actions of a state's elite.[6]

The series of tragic assassinations in recent years has, to some extent, altered the priority of gun-control legislation for many policy-makers. The likelihood that these events were intentionally designed for that effect is beyond reasonable belief. Something "happened" that significantly—if temporarily—rearranged the substructure of policy.[7]

We may observe, for example, the history of efforts to repeal capital punishment statutes. It is not uncommon for these efforts to be thwarted from time to time by a ground swell of reaction to an especially heinous crime. Although each infamous crime is unique in its character and timing, its occurrence during a campaign to repeal capital punishment has a somewhat predictable effect.

We may well wish to categorize national and international crises—for example, wars and depressions—as "politically relevant incidents." Because of their extended duration and comprehensive impact, however, we are probably on sounder ground if we consider crises of this severity as historical conditions. Their classification as such is not arbitrary, but based upon the demonstration of their long-range, relatively stable effect upon policy-making processes.

By considering the likelihood of substructural variation and the impact of politically relevant incidents, we can see that the boundaries of the model (depicted by the outlines of the funnel) are quite permeable. Thus, what may at one point in time be merely a polit-

[6]Daniel J. Elazar, *American Federalism: A View from the States* (New York: Thomas Y. Crowell, 1966), p. 61.
[7]The same line of reasoning is applicable in V. O. Key's analysis of the changed relevance of Catholicism to party orientation in some states following the nomination of Al Smith in 1928. See his "A Theory of Critical Elections," *Journal of Politics* 17 (1955): 1-18.

ically relevant incident may become a relatively fixed part of the substructure of policy in the main model.

Some policy-makers of the 1930s held such rigidly formulated conceptions of "proper" policy that they perceived the Great Depression as nothing more than a minor irritant to an established pattern of policy-making behavior. Had the Depression been less severe and of shorter duration, their view might indeed have been the general reaction. The Depression, however, was not a momentary annoyance. It was an incident that has come to qualify as a momentous historical condition in the background of current policy-making. It accelerated support for a variety of policies previously considered quite inconceivable; yet these policies are today beyond effective challenge.

Social change and politically relevant incidents can, therefore, introduce new features into the substructure of policy. Similarly, long-term substructural characteristics can lose their determinative impact either temporarily or permanently. The price of farm commodities up to the 1920s had immediate and continuing consequences for particular policies in Massachusetts; today, because of changes in the composition of the Bay State economy, farm prices are of far less direct consequence in the policy-making arenas. Comparable changes common to most states can permanently lessen the overall impact of a particular variable upon policy outputs. The passage of the Social Security Act introduced large quantities of federal assistance into the social-welfare field; the act's redistributive formulas were partly responsible for reducing the relevance of a particular state's wealth to the amount of money it spent on public assistance. (Note the decline in the relevance of affluence to welfare spending after 1940, as shown in Table VII-1.)

The boundaries of the policy-formation model, as Figure VII-1 seeks to portray, therefore, are not impenetrable. Some variables that affect it decline in relevance as others gain; still others fade out for a time and then return to their former levels of impact.

Variation Between Policy Areas

Although the model employed here is designed to apply to any substantive area of policy, it seems reasonable to assume that the specific components of the model and the paths followed in the formulation of a policy would vary considerably from one type of policy to another. The distribution of relative impact between sectors of the model is likely to vary between policies. We would also expect the stability and complexity of substructures to be different for different policies.

Our introductory discussion of the model pointed out that time is less relevant to this third aspect; nonetheless, it must be borne in mind that each area of policy is subject to variations through time regarding the factors associated with the process of issue resolution and in substructural composition.

It should not be difficult to imagine examples of how processes of initiation and formulation would be dissimilar from one policy area to another. In matters involving a high degree of technical expertise, for example, the role of the professional administrator within the institutional sector will loom relatively large. Louisiana has a peculiar set of historical characteristics that have placed it high in terms of welfare expenditures. Yet those same characteristics have not generated a similar commitment to educational excellence. Louisiana's educational policy may well be subject to the influences operative in other states showing a high percentage of students enrolled in parochial schools.

Dye's examination of the multiple impact of industrialization, income, urbanization, and education showed substantial variation from one policy area to another.[8] Based upon a consolidation of his figures, Table VII-2 shows the percentages of variance in different policy areas that are explained by these economic indicators, by certain political-system variables, and by each of these holding constant the effects of the other. We can see from this table that the joint impact of the economic and political variables ranges from 37.21 per cent on highway policy to 63.20 per cent on educational policy. The independent effect of the economic-development variables ranges from 7.56 per cent for highways to 16.97 per cent for public regulation. And the political-system variables explain only .56 per cent of the variance in highway policy, but 7.45 per cent in education policy.

[8]Thomas R. Dye, *Politics, Economics, and the Public: Policy Outcomes in American States* (Chicago: Rand McNally, 1966).

Table VII-2 Effects of Economic Development Variables
and Political System Variables on Policy Outcomes

Policy Area (with Number of Indicators)	Mean Percentage of Variance Explained by:				
	Total Effect of Economic and Political Variables	Total Effect of Economic Variables	Total Effect of Political Variables	Economic, Controlling for Political Variables	Political, Controlling for Economic Variables
Education (11)	63.20	47.33	36.24	15.68	7.45
Welfare (14)	49.56	39.56	26.62	11.83	2.43
Highways (6)	37.21	30.80	14.29	7.56	.56
Public Regulation (13)	46.10	34.92	12.39	16.97	3.69
Taxation (10)	41.34	28.62	17.47	9.80	3.06

Based on a consolidation of figures in Thomas R. Dye, *Politics, Economics, and the Public: Policy Outcomes in American States* (Chicago: Rand McNally, 1966), pp. 286-287.

If we return to the findings reported in Table VII-1, we can see that the relevance of industrialization or affluence varies not only over time but also between areas of both policy and mass political behavior. Analysis of highway policies and the factors underlying them may find Michigan in a category with Indiana, Missouri, and Wisconsin. But examination of the substructures of labor policy may put Michigan with Illinois, and perhaps New Jersey. History and political participation may play a greater role than institutions or the economy in determining the nature of civil-rights policy. The determinants of policy on highways and natural resources may be much more stable over time than the factors affecting support for welfare and education.

The most fruitful conceptualization of substructural variation between policy areas, however, is not likely to be constructed on the basis of such nominal policy categories as these. Rather, a more theoretically comprehensive group of policy sets may emerge as inquiry proceeds. Examples are present in the literature that illustrates what I have in mind. Lowi's typology of regulatory, distributive, and redistributive policies may be a useful way of separating issue areas— useful in terms of classifying policies by the processes that operate in their formulation. Or Eulau and Eyestone's distinction between "adaptive" and "control" policies may be most useful.[9] Furthermore, it is likely that some form of multivariate analysis of groups of specific indicators will be most profitable theoretically. That has been the brunt of the argument for multivariate, composite policy indicators that I emphasized in previous chapters.[10] The basic point here

[9]Theodore Lowi, "American Business, Public Policy, Case Studies, and Political Theory," *World Politics* 16 (1964): 677-715; Heinz Eulau and Robert Eyestone, "Policy Maps of City Councils and Policy Outcomes: A Developmental Analysis," *American Political Science Review* 62 (1968): 127-143.

[10]In this regard, it is well to follow the example of Eulau and Eyestone and allow the classification to emerge from familiarity with the data. Appropriately for the present discussion, they note: "Much classification activity, in the field of public-policy analysis as elsewhere, is a game. Either the inventors of classifications and typologies do not make it clear just what analytical purpose the classification is to serve, or they may even imply that by having a classification they have explained something." Eulau and Eyestone, "Policy Maps of City Councils," p. 127. Kindness evidently triumphed over gratification, as Eulau and Eyestone give us no specific citations for the games policy analysts play.

is that at any stage where generalizations about the policy processes are possible we should be attuned to the likelihood of variation in the "fit" of the generalizations from one class of policy to another.

Identification of substructures, plotting of patterns of longitudinal variation, and specification of interpolicy differences are essential in setting forth the terrain upon which policy-making elites must do their work. These three processes, however, still do not conclude the business of studying the behavior of the particular people who constitute the elites. Rather, what I have provided thus far is only the comparative setting within which advancement in elite analysis can proceed.

Conversion Processes

It can be argued that income levels, manufacturing activities, and so forth are not strictly "inputs" to the policy process—no matter how high the correlation between indicators.[11] Policies are made by people. These people are called "policy-makers" in order to locate them somewhere in the main body of the stream of things that produces policies. Policy-makers act in a publicly consequential way because of their perceptions of social need, personal political gain, sense of history, or whatever. The fact that policy-makers in rich communities produce different outputs than their counterparts in poor communities characterizes the process, but it does not tell us how it works in human terms.

The extent of socioeconomic conditioning of the policy process, furthermore, is far from complete. Sometimes—all too often, from the standpoint of scientific neatness—things do not come out the way we would expect them to. If we knew more about politicians in specific settings, our expectations might be improved.

Identification and investigation of the impact of elites is no easy task. The data on most of the dimensions of elite behavior likely to be of interest are not contained in handy volumes such as the *Book of the States* or the *Statistical Abstract*. And it is a pathetic argument in favor of studying elite behaviors that we should treat

[11]Herbert Jacob and Michael Lipsky, "Outputs, Structure, and Power: An Assessment of Changes in the Study of State and Local Politics," *Journal of Politics* 30 (1968): 510-538.

elite decision-making as the residual that is left over once we have accommodated everything else.

The study of policy-makers is necessary not only in order to expand the amount of variance in public policy outputs for which we can account, but also in order to specify the linkages that account for the variance explained by socioeconomic factors. The task facing the student of comparative state politics is twofold. First, he must account for the "why" of the relationships between social development and policy that have been discovered by such scholars as Dye and Dawson and Robinson. Secondly, he must attempt to account for the variance left unexplained by that particular mode of inquiry.

Overall, the studies summarized in Chapter VI demonstrate the benefit to be gained from a careful, comparative analysis of the nature and relevance of social structure to the policy performance of states and localities. The model I have proposed seeks to help integrate that knowledge. However, as Dye notes, the assertion that the relationship between socioeconomic structure and policy is "direct" is, to say the least, misleading and premature.[12] Certainly no one can argue that once a community reaches a certain level of socioeconomic development particular patterns of public policy simply emerge full-blown from the social structure. We continue to have governments. We continue to have politicians. Politicians deliberate and dispute and, on occasion, decide. None of the correlation coefficients thus far computed accounts for anything approaching the total variation in any particular area of policy. Considerable attention, therefore, has to be given to what takes place in the process. We need to examine processes not only to account for the unexplained variance, but also to specify the mechanisms by which socioeconomic forces are transformed into policy outputs. The correlation coefficient is a clue to the processes by which policies are formulated. But a full explanation necessitates a specification of connections as well as conditions. Herbert Jacob and Michael Lipsky[13] stress that income, urbanization, industrialization, and education are not themselves inputs. In systems terms such conditions

[12]Dye, *Politics, Economics, and Public,* pp. 229ff.
[13]Jacob and Lipsky, "Outputs, Structure, and Power."

may create the activity that leads to the articulation of demands and supports, but the conditions should not be confused with the process. Social structural indicators are but rough surrogates for activities. We cannot assume a one-to-one relationship. "Social structure, political culture, political institutions, and elite perceptions intervene between a given environment . . . and the articulation of demand."[14]

Lineberry and Fowler as well as Greenstone and Peterson argue that policy processes in reformed cities operate under a fundamentally different set of rules than do those in unreformed cities.[15] Terry Clark's study of fifty-one communities further supports such a distinction.[16] On the basis of a combination of interview and aggregate data, Clark found reformed governments to be more centralized than unreformed governments in their decision-making mechanisms. Lineberry and Fowler's data indicate that reformed governments (perhaps because of their centralization) are also less sensitive to particularistic needs of segmented portions of the community. Jacob and Lipsky's criticisms and these studies suggest that social and political structures affect the perceptual mechanisms of policy-makers in such a way that they are responsive to certain types of claims and unresponsive to others. These studies also argue against an early dismissal of the role of individual policy-makers from whatever models of the policy process are formulated.

Innovation and Incrementalism

No matter how constraining the resources of the socioeconomic and political environments, there appears always to be some room for the impact of leadership and individual policy-making initiative. Innovation itself makes this abundantly clear. Policies get made.

[14]Ibid., p. 514.
[15]Robert L. Lineberry and Edmund P. Fowler, "Reformism and Public Policies in American Cities," *American Political Science Review* 61 (1967): 701-716; J. David Greenstone and Paul Peterson, "Reformers, Machines, and the War on Poverty," in *City Politics and Public Policy,* ed. James Q. Wilson (New York: John Wiley and Sons, 1968), pp. 267-292.
[16]Terry N. Clark, "Community Structure, Decision-Making, Budget Expenditures and Urban Renewal in Fifty-one American Communities," *American Sociological Review* 33 (1968): 576-591.

They are not formulated "automatically." Much of the explanation for particular decisions rests on the preferences of decision-makers.

Some clues to the methods used by policy-makers are provided in Jack Walker's study of innovation among the states.[17] This article introduces a significant additional facet to the list of determinants of policy patterns in the states—patterns of emulation and diffusion from one state to another. Walker is concerned not with levels of policy activity but with the initiation of programs (as opposed to the level of support once a policy is established). His is a vital study in the analysis of what determines the range of types of policy activity within a state.

Walker used the concepts of emulation and diffusion in a decision-making context to account for the spread of innovations across the states. He examined eighty-six different programs enacted by at least twenty state legislatures prior to 1965. All programs were treated equally in the construction of an index of innovation. Included were six to eight different pieces of legislation in several policy areas: welfare, health, education, conservation, planning, administrative organization, highways, civil rights, corrections and police, labor, taxes, and professional regulation. Most of the programs studied were adopted in the twentieth century, but sixteen of his eighty-six policies were initiated primarily during the last half of the nineteenth century.

Walker discovered fairly strong correlations between indices of wealth and industrialization and his innovation score. Richer, more industrial states generally take the lead in policy innovation. He also observed some significant correlations between party competition and innovation and a rather strong correlation between the David-Eisenberg index of apportionment and innovation. Also, the correlation with apportionment holds up even when the socioeconomic variables are held constant—indicating that apportionment is important in setting the scope of policy activity even though it may not be important in establishing levels of support for particular policies. This assertion is reinforced by the fact that the correlation of apportionment is stronger with innovations in the 1930-1966 period than

[17]Jack L. Walker, "The Diffusion of Innovation among the American States," *American Political Science Review* 63 (1969): 880-899.

it was in the 1900-1929 period, reflecting the greater degree of mal-apportionment in the later period. Walker's theoretical contribution is to articulate the rule whereby decision-makers look for analogies between the situation with which they are dealing and the situation in some other state where a specific response to a problem has been formulated. "The constituent units of any federal system are under considerable pressure to conform with national and regional standards or accepted administrative procedures."[18]

Mechanisms of communication and information exchange are obviously relevant in the processes of policy diffusion and emulation. Walker points to the importance of professional organizations as forms of communication between state administrators. He also notes the increased mobility of politically active citizens among the states. Emulation will probably cause poorer states to accept new policies more readily than would be expected, given their socioeconomic development. In deciding how the emulation process works, one has to discover in what "league" a state has chosen to play. Walker found fairly distinct regional groupings of states. He then divided states according to their innovation scores in three periods—1879-1899, 1900-1929, and 1930-1966—and conducted a similar analysis of each. The results showed that regionalism is less distinct in the last period than it is in the earlier periods, leading to the conclusion that increased communications facilities in the last forty years have eroded the impact of region on American state politics. This line of reasoning is further substantiated when he discerned a substantial increase in the speed of innovation in recent years.

Following a similar line of inquiry into the decision rules by which policies are formulated, Sharkansky's study of the impact of prior policy activity is highly informative.[19] He correlated current expenditures with previous expenditures on a program-by-program basis. He also examined the impact of federal aid, state-local ratios of expenditures, and the scope of state government as measured by the ratio of employees to population. Sharkansky ascertained that socioeconomic variables have positive relationships with the aggregate

[18]Ibid., p. 891.
[19]Ira Sharkansky, "Economic and Political Correlates of State Government Expenditures," *Midwest Journal of Political Science* 11 (1967): 173-192.

spending of state and local governments, but negative relationships with the spending activities of state governments only. His most consequential finding was that previous expenditures (spaced over five-year periods) eliminate the explanatory power of federal aid, revenue, number of state employees, personal income, and population. When previous expenditures are controlled, the correlations between these independent variables are only about half as high as they are controlling for them and looking at the effect of previous expenditures. Sharkansky also found that subsequent rates of change in expenditures correlate negatively with the magnitude of previous changes in expenditure, indicating "that state officials are unable or unwilling to make continued increases in expenditure."[20] Changes in expenditures, therefore, tend to take place in fits and starts; periods of surge are followed by periods of lag.

The finding of high independent relationships between levels of prior spending and current spending is quite consistent with the incremental model of decision-making posited by Charles Lindblom,[21] Fenno,[22] and Wildavsky.[23] Decision-makers operate on the basis of certain rules of behavior. For example, one of the most powerful rules for routine decisions on an agency's future budget is how much the agency spent in previous years. Rarely is an agency's scope of activity dramatically reduced or increased. Such decisional rules, which are not at all dissimilar from the emulation patterns discovered by Walker, considerably reduce the information load of the decision-maker and expedite the disposition of large numbers of funding requests.

It would be a mistake, however, to assume that yesterday's policy patterns apply only to increments in established programs. Andrew Cowart's study of antipoverty expenditures demonstrates

[20]Ibid., p. 185.

[21]Charles E. Lindblom, "The Science of 'Muddling Through,'" *Public Administration Review* 19 (1959): 79-88.

[22]Richard F. Fenno, Jr., "The House Appropriations Committee as a Political System: The Problem of Integration," *American Political Science Review* 56 (1962): 310-324.

[23]Aaron Wildavsky, *The Politics of the Budgetary Process* (Boston: Little, Brown and Co., 1964).

the carry-over in decisional rules from one program area to another.[24] Cowart found the antipoverty expenditures were best explained by prior expenditures for welfare—despite efforts in the mid-1960s to get antipoverty programs established in an innovative mode through the creation of the Office of Economic Opportunity. Cowart's finding supports an incremental interpretation of policy-making and argues for examining comprehensive policy structures rather than discrete program variables. If indeed those who confront what are consciously designed to be new policy inputs respond in highly predictable, patterned ways, it suggests to the policy analyst the presence of groupings of particular programs that are perceived as alike and treated alike by policy-makers.

Elite Policy Behavior

It may be, nonetheless, that there is little to be gained from an intensive investigation of policy-makers' attitudes until further guidelines are formulated on what aspects of elite behavior should be studied. Most studies of legislative behavior and its relevance to policy are discouraging to those who expect to find variations between legislatures systematically related to policy outputs. Much of what we know about contemporary policy-making underscores the necessity for examining the policy role of executives and personnel within the bureaucratic sector of state governments.

Sharkansky has taken an important step in the comparative examination of the role of executives in the policy process.[25] His study of agency requests and gubernatorial support made two major contributions. First, by working with the budgets of many agencies in each of several states, Sharkansky constructed correlations between agency requests, gubernatorial recommendations, and legislative appropriations. The correlation coefficients so derived were used as characteristics of the state. They described the different policy

[24]Andrew T. Cowart, "Anti-Poverty Expenditures in the American States: A Comparative Analysis," *The Midwest Journal of Political Science* 13 (1969): 219-236.
[25]Ira Sharkansky, "Agency Requests, Gubernatorial Support and Budget Success in State Legislatures," *American Political Science Review* 62 (1968): 1220-1231.

processes from one state to another. States were thus compared not in terms of static, aggregate characteristics, but rather in terms of relational measures.

Sharkansky's second contribution was his operationalization of relative influences in the state governmental structure. He observed the correlation between gubernatorial recommendations and legislative appropriations, for example, as an index of gubernatorial power. The higher the correlation between the governor's wishes and the legislature's actions, the greater the gubernatorial influence. The correlation between agency requests and gubernatorial recommendations may be determined in the same manner. Sharkansky's operationalization of the relative impact of different sectors of state political systems, or of any policy systems, is a most significant advance in the study of public policy.

Sharkansky's general finding, as one might expect, is that most policy innovation comes from the administrative sector. Governors and legislatures do not recommend more than administrative agencies request. However, Sharkansky also demonstrates—somewhat surprisingly, perhaps—that several characteristics of the state governmental structure and political processes affect the relationships between the administrative, gubernatorial, and legislative sectors. Governors elected for longer terms, for example, are more successful in controlling agency requests and in obtaining legislative approval of their recommendations. Party competitiveness and voter turnout seem to strengthen agency expansionary efforts. The most important characteristic of all, however, is that high levels of state government spending and debt work in opposition to agency aspirations. Where spending and debt are already high, both governor and legislature are severe in reducing agency requests. This finding, of course, is quite consistent with the incremental explanation of policy activity.

In collaboration with Augustus B. Turnbull, III, Sharkansky later presented an intensive version of this same line of analysis.[26] The authors tested attributes of the agency-governor-legislature framework in Georgia and Wisconsin. Their analysis for Georgia included the years 1964-1969, thus spanning the administrations of

[26]Ira Sharkansky and Augustus B. Turnbull, III, "Budget-Making in Georgia and Wisconsin: A Test of a Model," *Midwest Journal of Political Science* 13 (1969): 631-645.

Carl Sanders and Lester Maddox. Wisconsin data covered 1958-1967. The authors examined twenty-six agencies in Georgia and seventeen in Wisconsin, looking only at large budget agencies. The improvement over the prior analysis comes in the ability of the researchers to study the impact of specific governors on the balance of forces in the policy process. Three alternative arrangements of the components of the research design were hypothesized: (1) agency to governor to legislature; (2) agency to governor *and* the legislature (with no direct governor-legislature link); and (3) agency to governor, agency to legislature, and governor to legislature (indicating joint relationships between the three portions of the model). The second sequence, the one that excludes the gubernatorial-legislative link, never holds. The most frequent path is agency to governor to legislature, although in the case of Wisconsin there are about equal numbers of agency to governor and legislature and governor to legislature situations—that is, the third route.

The fascinating part of this study is Sharkansky and Turnbull's analysis of the role of particular governors in the policy-making process. They observe:

> Contrary to our expectations, we found that our model works well in the administrations of both Georgia governors. The budget recommendations of Lester Maddox, despite his reputation as a political amateur unable to work within the customary political process, were followed by the General Assembly to the same degree as those of his predecessor. The critical element in the Georgia findings appears to be the strength of the governor's office bolstered during the Sanders-Maddox transition by a professional budget bureau headed by a State Budget Officer who had excellent personal relationships with key legislators.[27]

The authors suggest that the persuasive power of this administrative officer was attributable to legislative weakness rather than gubernatorial strength.

In Wisconsin, Sharkansky and Turnbull found that despite all combinations of divided government between legislature and governor during the period investigated, the division of party control between

[27]Ibid., p. 641.

governor and legislature offered no consistent explanation for changes in the patterns of influence. Therefore, the distinction between Georgia and Wisconsin along partisan lines is not particularly relevant to the policy process.

One of the virtues of Sharkansky and Turnbull's research is that it demonstrates how comparative analysis, using the agency as the unit, can illuminate quantitatively such policy-making tools as gubernatorial fiscal strategy. While a high negative correlation normally exists between the magnitude of agency requests and gubernatorial recommendations—measuring the tendency of governors to trim expansionary requests—the correlation disappeared when Wisconsin Governor Gaylord Nelson sought to justify new taxes. He allowed maximum requests to go before the legislature in order to gain support of clientele groups and to dramatize the gap between available resources and "needed" revenue. He used the agency requests and his recommendations as a strategy to build support for a tax program. This mode of analysis demonstrates how, by means of aggregate analysis, we can illuminate the context within which decisions are taken, even in specific cases.

Sharkansky and Turnbull discovered several conditions that upset the "normal budget procedures"—that is, incremental decision-making. A governor may be motivated to support agencies even to the point of overlooking normal padding and likely legislative resistance. The realization that a tax increase is inevitable may allow expansionary agency requests to go by the governor in order to bolster the governor's revenue proposals. Furthermore, agency expansionary activities may be supported because of a governor's interest in a particular program. Where an agency's responsibilities had been recently increased significantly, Sharkansky and Turnbull noted a consequent willingness by both governors and legislatures to promote its budget. Their mode of analysis also isolated predispositions toward agencies with different functions. Agencies responsible for taxation, law enforcement, and economic regulation, for example, are treated with a much more jaundiced eye by both the legislature and governor than are those that provide direct services to large segments of the population.

These studies seek to delineate the ranges of leadership and elite choice, but, they still do not promise the kind of illumination of the policy process that will help answer questions about the "power elite" or "decisions versus nondecisions." The specific actions of particular actors must be examined to find answers to these questions.

Comparative Study of Elite Behavior

Much of the investigation of the pre-elite sectors of the policy process model (or post-elite, depending upon one's perspective) can be conducted with aggregate statistics. Yet an analyst who does so might be considered the modern equivalent of the armchair philosopher, with the exception that the armchair is in front of a computer console. The most comprehensive investigations of the relevance of aggregate socioeconomic factors, for example, have accounted for a disturbingly small amount of the interstate policy variance.

It is all well and good to exhort others to conduct studies of elite behaviors. But, as the history of community power studies will attest, enlightenment does not ineluctably follow admonition. The lesson that emerges from the various efforts to study systematically the nature and function of elites at the community level ought to give both pause and guidance for a comparative framework of inquiry.

The Problem of Nondecisions

I have no desire to enter the lengthy debate that has engaged the "elitist" versus "pluralist" schools of community-power analysis. Nor does the addition of a new school, the "neo-elitist" school, to the disputation heighten my willingness to enter the fray.[28] One of the central features in the argument, however, is immediately relevant to the task of devising a rational and theoretically convincing approach to the comparative study of policy-making elites. This is the problem of "decisions" versus "nondecisions."[29]

[28]Richard M. Merelman, "On the Neo-Elitist Critique of Community Power," *American Political Science Review* 62 (1968): 451-460.

[29]The most concise theoretical statement is by Peter Bachrach and Morton S. Baratz, "Two Faces of Power," *American Political Science Review* 56 (1962): 947-953. A comprehensive critique is given by Merelman in the same issue.

It is this problem that informs most of the critiques of pluralism discussed in Chapter II. Elites—whatever their motivations—may suppress some types of issues and bar their appearance on the public agenda. Or an issue may not be placed on the public agenda simply because those whose interest it might serve may be so "duped" or "socialized" that they fail to perceive their own interests. The potential beneficiaries of a policy may not recognize the relevance of political mechanisms for the fulfillment of their needs.

Vidich and Bensman's *Small Town in Mass Society* examines the processes of nondecision-making.[30] The authors lead us to believe that no existing issues of major social importance are considered by the governing authorities of Springdale because an "Invisible Government" determines what shall and shall not be scheduled for governmental determination. And the Invisible Government does not allow anything to be scheduled that might upset the business-as-usual or low-taxes applecart. Of course, if the only evidence of the Invisible Government's hegemony is the public actions of the relevant elites, this thesis can never be tested.[31] The assumption that somebody has to be "stopping up the works" prompts Vidich and Bensman to make such patently untestable assertions as the following: "When board business touches on issues of potential conflict, each board member brings up for *subliminal assessment* the position of other members on the issue in question, i.e., who would be apt to oppose the measure and with what intensity—and avoids further mention of the topic."[32]

No one should deny that mechanisms do structure the agendas of all policy-making bodies. And it is reasonable to assume that these mechanisms are never wholly neutral. But the mechanisms can take many different forms. One form is that posited by Vidich and Bensman—that a self-serving elite suppresses conflict in areas where politicization may jeopardize its own interest. In the absence of confirming evidence, however, there is no a priori reason why this explanation should be more appealing than one of at least two alternatives.

---

[30]Arthur J. Vidich and Joseph Bensman, *Small Town in Mass Society* (Princeton: Princeton University Press, 1958).

[31]See Merelman, "On the Neo-Elitist Critique."

[32]Vidich and Bensman, *Small Town*, p. 129.

One alternative explanation for the absence of particular types of issues from the public agenda is what might be called "nonpolitical perception."[33] Members of a community or political system may simply not perceive certain aspects of their lives as being susceptible to political amelioration, regardless of how onerous the conditions of their everyday existence may be. Thus, what in one polity is a source of class indignation and the catalyst for revolution may in another be seen as merely the isolated result of shiftlessness, misfortune, or simply bad weather.

Yet a third explanation for the absence of certain considerations from the agenda of political decision-making is possible. No doubt instances occur in which the probability of gain from politicization of an issue is far outweighed by the conflict it will engender. Political relevance is perceived. No group is suppressing the issue, but those who would gain by an alternative public decision do not view the prize as worth the fight. Set in the context of Springdale, for example, it is reasonable to assume that the value attached to being a good neighbor—and the rewards of amicable intracommunity relations—is greater than the rationally perceived gain from any of the various conflicts that Vidich and Bensman believe are being put down by the Invisible Government.

Identifying Ranges of Action

It is very difficult to conceive of a research strategy focused on a single decision-making unit that would allow one to make a complete and accurate list of all nondecisions. And if this cannot be done, one certainly cannot choose between the alternative explanations for any particular nondecisions. In a comparative setting, however, some of the more bothersome aspects of the problem can be handled with reasonably satisfactory results.

The first requirement is a specification in a policy area of the range of considerations that might occupy the attention of decision-making bodies. The aggregate of systems might be communities,

---

[33]Nonpolitical perception" is very similar to the "false consensus" concept discussed by Merelman and others. See Merelman, "On the Neo-Elitist Critique," pp. 453ff.

nations, or the fifty states. If states, it is possible to discover from numerous sources the variety of approaches considered or adopted, or both, on virtually any matter of public policy. And the range of response in the states is normally quite broad, even in those governmental areas where we might initially expect uniformity.

In the instance of participation in a new federal grant-in-aid program, for example, the level and speed with which states "join up," the administrative structures they establish or employ, the interests of the personnel involved, and a host of other identifiable factors are quite variable between states. As many studies will attest, the response of legislatures and executives to urban unrest has differed dramatically from state to state.[34] Antipollution proposals have been greeted with open arms in some states and resisted vigorously in others. Abortion-law reform is a matter of hot dispute in some states and is not even publicly considered in others.

To be sure, the fifty states do not at any one time contain examples of all possible policy alternatives, either in the laws of some or on the public agendas of others. Admittedly, a culturally inclusive "mobilization of bias" may be so sufficiently inhibiting that some issues of serious consequence never get articulated or even imagined. But I would argue that an aggregation of policy-making systems such as the states is more than amply inclusive to allow for specification of ranges of interesting policies. And these ranges are broad enough to test most of the principal hypotheses of elitist and counter-elitist (and, possible, neo-elitist) theories. Once one adopts a comparative-research strategy, the problems are not so much untestability or "falsibility" as they are practicality and availability of resources to support inquiry.[35]

After specifying the range of viable alternatives within the universe of policy-making systems, it is possible to ask why one particular system pursues one path and another a different one, or

[34]Michael Lipsky and David J. Olson, "On the Politics of Riot Commissions" (Paper presented at the 1968 Annual Meeting of the American Political Science Association, Washington, D.C., September, 1968).

[35]Research currently in progress demonstrates the extent to which resources can be obtained to overcome objections based on practicality. The example of the study of ninety-six cities in the San Francisco Bay area, being conducted under Heinz Eulau's direction, comes first to mind.

why a particular issue is "hot" in one state and not in another. Why have several states adopted lotteries while many states do not even consider them? Is it because "Invisible Governments" in the latter view a lottery as anathema to their interests and therefore suppress the issue? Or is it because some people think that potential revenues from a lottery do not justify hurting the feelings of those opposed to gambling?

Having identified these and similar questions as real policy considerations in some of the polities being studied, we can identify by role those involved in their perpetuation. People with similar role characteristics, but in settings pursuing different policy patterns, can then be queried about their attitudes, efforts, and expectations regarding the policy in their domain.

My expectation is that this approach can illuminate the relevance and linkages of many of the environmental characteristics that are strongly related to patterns of policy. That is, having identified the broad, aggregate features that facilitate or inhibit particular policies, and having specified the range of policies that exists, we are guided to the individual level data that reflect the linkages and explain the deviations. To the extent that the behavior of an identified elite serves to bring the system into line with what is "expected" on the basis of its social structure, we would be explaining the correlation. To the extent that an elite prevents conformity by retarding policy or preventing the politicization of an issue, we would be speaking of "inhibiting leadership." To the extent that the actions of elites facilitate performance in excess of that which socioeconomic variables would predict, we would be speaking of "initiating leadership." And the strength of the original socioeconomic-policy correlation would be a measure of the amount of inhibition or initiation that is necessary to attain a particular level of policy activity.

Conclusion

This chapter has been somewhat speculative. It has drawn together some of the lines of our prior discussion, focusing on the place of individual policy-maker activity in relation to the contexts of policy processes. Bits and pieces of the model diagrammed early in this chapter are taken from several research settings. The approach being offered argues, basically, for viewing the behavior of individual policy-makers as taking place within various contexts. The model helps to sort out that which is contextual and that which is individual. The discussion in the previous section further suggests how the analysis of elite activity in the comparative framework moves toward resolution of a number of contentious problems in understanding the policy process. Solving these problems will contribute immeasurably to the advance of political theory. Merely conceptualizing them in a comparative framework has produced a good deal of theoretical refinement. Theoretical refinement is the subject of the concluding chapter.

chapter VIII

Theories of
the Policy Process

Introduction

Social scientists have studied a number of things having to do with
the process of making public policy. Until recent years, however, the
systematic, empirical study of policy has not been the prime concern
of many researchers. The spotlight has been on actors and institutions
rather than on policy. Legislative behavior, the study of the executive,
and inquiry into the politics of courts have relevance to explanations
about why policies are formed the way they are. But the theoretical
orientation of research in these areas has been directed toward the
determinants of the actions of incumbent officials instead of toward
determinants of the products of their activity. As a consequence,
little can be said about the comparative impact of different institutional sectors upon policy. We do not know how to weigh the effects
of executives as opposed to legislatures. We do not know with any
exactness what the long-range policy consequences of judicial pronouncements are.

Case studies have informed us greatly about the mechanisms
of policy-making, in a formal and informal sense. They have certainly
served to sensitize students of policy to the array of actors and settings

in which policy initiative and resolution take place. But they, like the institutionally oriented studies, offer no significant guidance to weighing the critical contributions of the setting within which a particular issue is posed, considered, and resolved.

The comparative studies, growing largely out of state and local inquiry, seem to hold the most promise for the scientific explanation of policy-making at the level of the political system, however it is defined. It is because of their methodological and theoretical promise that I have relied so heavily in this book on subnational studies. They carry one simple message. To understand why policies are as they are, one must look beyond individual actors and institutional settings to the sociopolitical context within which the actions occur and within which the institutions persist. Focusing upon the actors or the institutions forces the observer to accept the rules of play more or less as given, without attending to the source of the rules. One cannot consider subject matter much beyond that offered by the working materials as they are found in the particular settings being studied. Behavioral, institutional, and case analysis do not provide a clear way to identify the forces acting upon the *agenda* of policy-makers. It is society that more often than not provides the forces that structure the agenda.

The Policy Agenda

To say that we must "study society" is not to offer a very precise mandate. The proper study of man is man. So what? Why do we study society? What consequences of social variance do we expect? The answer lies in the effects of sociopolitical structure upon the options of policy-makers. In the study of public policy, attention must be given to the mechanisms for agenda-setting. The agendas of policy activity reveal the *scopes of concern* that distinguish one polity from another. Sociopolitical inquiry identifies the constraints and resources that fix the context within which policy decisions are taken.

Once an issue is placed on the agenda for political decision— once it is being debated on the floor of the legislature, deliberated in the office of a governor, and so forth—it is a theoretically easy task to discover the relevant actors and to plot their activities. This is what most decision-making analysis is all about. This is what most case studies study. But elaborate and intricate mechanisms filter issues prior to their being scheduled for consideration by legitimate policy-making bodies. As we have already noted, a "mobilization of bias," to again use Schattschneider's term, can prevent the articulation of particular types of issues and the interests they embody.[1]

Much of the critique from the antipluralist school of contemporary political science is based on a concern for the issues that do not get on the agenda of public deliberation. These criticisms and the responses to them were reviewed in Chapter II. "Pluralist" political scientists are accused of being myopic, of allowing their field of inquiry to be defined by the preferences of incumbent actors in the political process.[2] Of the infinitude of issues that could be considered in any period of time, a political system or set of systems deals with but a small proportion. And it may be that the neediest in the society are least able to affect the policy agenda.

Various explanations have been offered on why one issue rather than another gets scheduled on the agenda of public policy-makers. Some social critics argue that it is the work of "ruling elites" who filter obnoxious stimuli and thereby suppress the claims of needy groups within the society.[3] Alternative explanations for the structure of the public agenda, however, are readily available and may be contrasted with the elite explanation.[4]

One of the problems of inquiry until recent years has been the overwhelming attention given individual cases in order to test elitist and pluralist hypotheses. A research strategy that concentrates on

[1]E. E. Schattschneider, *The Semi-Sovereign People* (New York: Holt, Rinehart and Winston, 1960), chap. 2; Richard M. Merelman, "On the Neo-Elitist Critique of Community Power," *American Political Science Review* 62 (1968): 451-460.

[2]Jack Walker, "A Critique of the Elitist Theory of Democracy," *American Political Science Review* 60 (1966): 285-295.

[3]Arthur J. Vidich and Joseph Bensman, *Small Town in Mass Society* (Princeton: Princeton University Press, 1958); Peter Bachrach and Morton S. Baratz, "Decisions and Nondecisions: An Analytical Framework," *American Political Science Review* 57 (1963): 632-642.

[4]Richard I. Hofferbert, "Elite Influence in State Policy Formation: A Model for Comparative Inquiry," *Polity* 2 (1970): 316-344.

a single decision-making unit or the actions of certain individuals cannot yield a complete and accurate list of all issues *not* considered in that decision-making setting. And if this is not done, one cannot choose between competing explanations for any particular "non-decision."[5] If the options forgone cannot be listed, one certainly cannot choose between alternative explanations for why some items are selected for public deliberation and others are excluded.

In a comparative setting, however, such as is characteristic of the studies discussed in the last few chapters, some of the more bothersome aspects of the problem may be handled with reasonably satisfactory results. In one sense the comparative studies of policy determination may be viewed as efforts to account for the "context of decision" within which policies are formulated. For example, a correlation of —.51 between highway expenditures and industrialization tells us a good deal about the options available to policy-makers in states of varying degrees of industrialization.[6] It says, among other things, that policy-makers in the most industrialized areas of the nation will probably have a difficult time expanding highway expenditures much beyond a certain minimum. Their job is different from that of their counterparts in the more agrarian states. As another example of the importance of the context of decisions, it should be apparent that, given the close relationship between educational expenditure and state income, Mississippi education planners face a significantly different task in obtaining a level of public educational excellence than is faced by their counterparts in New York or California. These observations may seem trivial, yet they are of considerable importance if one is constructing a decision-making model of public policy formation. These instances suggest that the agendas of public policy-making are, in large part, functions of the social and political environment in which policy is formulated.[7]

[5]Bachrach and Baratz, "Decisions and Nondecisions"; Hofferbert, "Elite Influence."

[6]Thomas R. Dye, *Politics, Economics, and the Public: Policy Outcomes in the American States* (Chicago: Rand McNally, 1966), p. 158.

[7]Robert H. Salisbury, "The Analysis of Public Policy: A Search for Theories and Roles," in *Political Science and Public Policy,* ed. Austin Ranney (Chicago: Markham Publishing Co., 1968), pp. 151-178, argues, for example, that it may well be in the definition of the agenda that political-process variables will be more striking than socioeconomic variables. Specific research tactics in this

Coming to the problem from an intellectual heritage quite
different from most political scientists, Herbert Simon observes:

> The theory of political behavior is concerned, then, with
> three aspects of the decision-making process. It must expound
> the rules that govern the shift and persistence of attention on
> the particular issues that occupy the political arena. It must
> state the principles that govern the invention or design of
> potential courses of political action. And it must set forth
> the conditions that determine which actions will be chosen.[8]

Expounding "the rules that govern the shift and persistence of attention," I am arguing, may be a function of salient differences in the
sociopolitical environment. I am suggesting further that the comparative framework adopted by the students of state and local policies
provides the mechanism for specifying many of the rules that govern
the "shift and persistence of attention" on the part of policy-makers.
It is this determination of the focus of policy-makers' attention that
is most troublesome to students of small-group decision-making.
Continuing the comparative approach should provide significant
answers to many questions about elite decision-making.

The comparative studies, however, suggest that socioeconomic
determination, while present and measurable, is far from total. Significant room is left for the impact of individual leadership and for
particular, idiosyncratic events.[9] Eulau and Eyestone stress this point:

> ... the systematic study of public policy cannot be content
> with correlating indicators of environmental challenges or indi-
> cators of resource capability to policy outcomes. Rather it was
> our assumption that policy development is greatly influenced
> by the predilections, preferences, orientations and expectations
> of policy-makers—in short by the political process itself.[10]

---

regard are discussed in Hofferbert, "Elite Influence" and in the previous
chapter.

[8]Herbert A. Simon, "Political Research: The Decision-Making Framework," in
Varieties of Political Theory, ed. David Easton (Englewood Cliffs, N. J.:
Prentice-Hall, 1966), pp. 15-24.

[9]Hofferbert, "Elite Influence," pp. 333-336.

[10]Heinz Eulau and Robert Eyestone, "Policy Maps of City Councils and Policy
Outcomes: A Developmental Analysis," *American Political Science Review*
62 (1968): 143.

The study of external resources and constraints, then, provides a specification of the ranges and conditions within which particular and successive groups of decision-makers operate.

In the studies I have summarized, two factors have been identified as constraints on policy-makers. First is the socioeconomic and political environment within a jurisdiction; social and political factors limit the magnitude and forms of outputs that policy-makers can devise and produce. The second is what Sharkansky calls the "routines" that government officials find useful; these patterns of action, summarized by the term "incrementalism," structure and simplify the environment of the policy-maker.[11] Both economic constraints and the constraints of routine decision processes can limit an official's capacity for innovation.[12]

The relevance to policy of these constraints can vary both across time and between policy areas. Some areas of public policy are more environmentally determined than others. Some are more dependent upon incremental decision-making than others.[13] Moreover, the impact of prior policy activities—the "routines" of officeholders—can vary over time and from one policy area to another. Certainly the constraints of incremental decision-making were temporarily set aside in many public-policy areas during the Great Depression. Massive shifts of responsibility for various policies occurred from one level of government to another. Further, as contrasted with nationwide phenomena such as the Depression, particularistic shifts in the relevance of the incremental model can occur. A particular governor with a particular set of favorite programs under favorable but transient conditions can well make a significant difference in public policy. The massive expansion of the State University of New York between 1962 and 1968, for example, is attributed by many to the effectiveness of Governor Nelson Rockefeller and the man he re-

[11]Ira Sharkansky, *The Routines of Politics* (New York: Van Nostrand Reinhold Co., 1970).

[12]Ira Sharkansky and Richard I. Hofferbert, "Dimensions of State Politics, Economics, and Public Policy," *American Political Science Review* 63 (1969): 867-880.

[13]Ira Sharkansky and Augustus B. Turnbull, III, "Budget-Making in Georgia and Wisconsin: A Test of a Model," *Midwest Journal of Political Science* 13 (1969); 631-645; Hofferbert, "Elite Influence."

cruited to be chancellor. In the absence of these two individuals, coupled with New York's previously lagging position in higher education, the growth probably would not have taken place.

Without question, therefore, particularistic situations either within one or several policy systems make it possible to illuminate the context of decision—the externalities of the agenda. Individual phenomena and the one-time occurrence, nevertheless, are manifested within generally durable frameworks that set constraints and provide finite resources for policy-makers.

We must remember, however, that the shape of a determination will differ from one policy area to another. Given the scores of programs pursued by any political system, this might well be a caveat that precludes comprehensive generalizations. Yet the task is not so forbidding as it might seem at first glance. Several efforts have been made to group programs into meaningful policy clusters. "Meaningful," in this case, is determined by the extent to which a classification scheme for policies produces clusters of programs that share common determinative processes.

Conclusion: Typologies of Policies

Several authors have presented typologies for policies.[14] Salisbury convincingly downgrades the theoretical utility of the labels attached to programs by policy-makers. Because a program has the word "education" in its title does not necessarily mean that it is wise for the student of policy to lump this program with all others that have "education" in the headnotes of their enabling acts. No relationship may exist, for example, between excellence in vocational education within correctional institutions and the vigor with which a state pursues community-college programs. The same may hold for different "transportation" programs. One community may have poor highways but good mass-transit services. Each program has its own objectives and serves a somewhat different segment of the population.

[14]Theodore Lowi, "American Business, Public Policy, Case Studies, and Political Theory," *World Politics* 16 (1964), 677-715; Salisbury, "Analysis of Public Policy"; Lewis Froman, Jr., "An Analysis of Public Policies in Cities," *Journal of Politics* 29 (1967): 94-108.

Lowi and Salisbury both offer typologies of policies based on estimates of the apparent *intent* and *clientele* of the policies. Such an assessment is behind Lowi's "distributive," "regulatory," and "redistributive" classification scheme. Salisbury, on the basis of the same process of reasoning, has added "self-regulative" policies. A similar process of assessing aims and clientele yields Eulau and Eyestone's distinction between "adaptive" and "control" policies.[15]

I am assuming that these classification schemes are designed to guide and aid in the explanation of why outputs of the political process are as they are. It is a purpose that views the product of the political process as the authoritative statement—the act, the appropriation, the statement of intent. Criticisms of typologies and of the strategies employed in their invention necessarily assume common purposes between the classifier and the critic. My argument in this context is that to begin the classification of policies by assessing aims and clientele is not likely to result in typologies of maximum explanatory utility. If, however, the purpose of policy classification is to guide research into the societal consequences or *impact* of programs, then the approach of Lowi, Salisbury, Eulau, and Eyestone is probably appropriate. In systems terms, this would be the entry into the feedback loop, from "output" to "outcome" and back into the system by means of policy impact on sociopolitical inputs.[16]

I take it, however, that such is not the intention of the essays in question. To date, little empirical work has been fruitfully conducted with any of these typologies. Eulau and his associates are pursuing their own research, and it may well be the exception. But those few studies that have sought to unravel the mutual association between programs have not produced clusters that neatly fit the labels or patterns of Lowi's or the others' schemes.[17] In a comparative context, one test of the vitality of a policy typology is the covariance of indicators under a common label. The evidence is as yet incomplete regarding the typologies discussed here. It is disturbing, however, at least with respect to the Lowi scheme, that the bait has

[15]Eulau and Eyestone, "Policy Maps," p. 127.
[16]David Easton, *A Systems Analysis of Political Life* (New York: John Wiley and Sons, 1965).
[17]See, for example, the factor analyses of policy indicators discussed in chap. VI.

not been taken by other researchers. Lowi's insightful review is often
noted in critical essays, but there is no instance in the literature I
have read where his classification scheme has been examined with
specific data and tested propositions.

What is clear and yet often ignored is that the processes of
determination *are different* from one set of policies to another. What
constitutes a "set" of policies is still vague, but patterns of covariance do distinguish some programs from others.[18] Dye groups policies
in terms of standard nominal categories—education, welfare, highways, and so forth.[19] He does not test for the mutual inclusivity and
exclusivity of indicators used in each set, but even these loose groupings show different patterns of covariance with his independent social
and political variables.

My suggestion with respect to the construction of typologies,
or schemes of classification, for policies is that policies be grouped
in terms of their mutual covariance, discovered in a comparative context. Typologies, in other words, should be constructed not in terms
of some a priori assessment of aims or clientele or in terms of key
words employed in the enabling statutes, but rather in terms of common structures of determination and the comparative covariance of
specific indicators. If welfare policies are determined by the same phenomena as teachers' salaries and if indeed those states that pay teachers more also pay out more for welfare, then these policies belong to a
common set. From the standpoint of explanation, no purpose is served
in separating programs in these two areas. If, on the other hand,
general-assistance programs are determined by different structures
than aid-to-dependent-children programs and if states that are generous in general assistance are not generous in aiding dependent
children, then—again from the standpoint of explaining outputs—
there is no point in placing both general assistance and ADC under
the heading "welfare."

Empirically constructed categories of policy, derived by identifying covariance among indicators, will provide a more theoretically

[18]Hofferbert, "Elite Influence"; Sharkansky and Hofferbert, "Dimensions of
State Politics"; Andrew T. Cowart, "Anti-Poverty Expenditures in the American States: A Comparative Analysis," *Midwest Journal of Political Science*
13 (1969): 219-236.

[19]Dye, *Politics, Economics, and Public.*

interesting treatment of dependent variables in the policy model. Similar work remains, however, in the conceptualization of social environmental phenomena. Social theorists have not done their work with the specific needs of policy analysts in mind.

Social Structure

It now seems appropriate to reassess and, perhaps, to reorient our thinking about social structure. Quite a lot—though by no means enough—attention has been given to operationalizing process and policy indicators. The main theoretical impact of this work lies in its ability to force our attention to the structures and consequences of the social environment. The studies discussed in Chapters V and VI suggest the kinds of social attributes that are likely to aid in the exploration of variance in political structures and policies. Forays into the field of social data, however, have a chaotic appearance to them. Lists of dozens of variables with minimal attention to theoretical mutuality are the norm in the literature. Data reduction is needed. Factor analysis and the multidimensional approach it involves offers some promise in this task of clarification.

When we look outward from the political to the social system in attempting to proceed with a rational format of data reduction, the same formal taxonomic problems seen with policies confront us. How is the multitude of interconnected attributes to be organized so as to provide maximum explanatory power in the policy model? Fortunately, political and social theorists have been thinking about the relevance of society to politics for a long time. The classical heritage has not been wasted. The question of how, when, and why the society intersects with the political system has long been in the minds of many political philosophers. Contemporary students of social change, economic development, and comparative politics, are very much interested in the hypothetical and actual relationships between structures of society and the performance of political systems. The rapidly expanding number of new nation-states since World War II has captured much of our attention in this respect. The comparative-policy studies, even though confined to the American context, should provide some stimulating guidance for the study of comparative politics in general.

It has been possible in the context of the subnational American policy studies to structure a rough hierarchy of questions for comparative inquiry. The degree of contextual homogeneity that exists in the American setting—compared with the wide diversity that would be encountered by multinational research design—has allowed for a relatively orderly progression of research. The time and techniques are now appropriate to move out of that context—to ask some of the same types of questions in quite dissimiliar settings. While it may no longer be terribly exciting to ask how important interparty competition or apportionment are in structuring policy, compared with the influence of socioeconomic structure, we can readily envision a provocative set of questions on the cross-national relevance of national political traits to policies produced. Do parliamentary governments create significantly different policies from presidential or authoritarian regimes? Is the time between instigation and enactment longer in one system than in another? Do social-structural phenomena operate the same way in other policy systems as they do in the United States? These are questions that should lead to lively research in a broad comparative mode.

Students of domestic policy also can borrow from comparative theory for purposes of enriching their own inquiry. Integration theory, developed largely in a cross-national context, is directly relevant to an explanation of the staying power of differences between subnational jurisdictions in the United States.[20] Do cross-local migratory and economic connections structure the patterns of policy innovation and change in the United States? How much local peculiarity in public services can be expected as the economy and society become ever more intricately woven together? Does the role of rural capitalism in the United States compare in terms of its policy consequences with its role as evolved elsewhere and studied by such

[20]Richard I. Hofferbert and Ira Sharkansky, "Social Structure and Politics in Subnational Systems: A Comparison in Four Nations" (Paper prepared for the Conference on Comparative Legislative Systems, Durham, N. C., February, 1970). See also Jack L. Walker, "The Diffusion of Innovations among the American States," *American Political Science Review* 63 (September, 1969): 880-899.

students as Barrington Moore?[21] The links to policy analysis of the modest theory he offers are not glaringly visible, but they are there. Conceptualizations of social change, modernization, and the importance of traditional cleavages—so carefully examined in comparative political theory—readily fit into the model of sociopolitical policy determination that has occupied center stage in the recent comparative-policy studies.[22] Students of comparative politics rarely cite the American policy studies and students of American policy rarely cite comparative theory. But the two can be happily married to the technology and propositional framework used in the policy studies.

Comparative policy analysis, growing from, improving upon, and perhaps ultimately discarding the approaches and techniques discussed in this volume, promises to be a domain of scholarly activity that will rapidly grow in prominence in the years to come.

[21]Barrington Moore, Jr., *Social Origins of Dictatorship and Democracy* (Boston: Little, Brown and Co., 1966).

[22]Reinhard Bendix, "Tradition and Modernity Reconsidered," *Comparative Studies in Society and History* 9 (1967): 292-346.

Index

227-234
processes, 225-257
role of history in, 228-230
setting the agenda for, 44
single issue processes in, 227-234
substructure change over time in,
    234-238
theories of the process of,
    258-269
use of case studies of, 89-140
Political activity
correlates of, 189-192
and socioeconomic dimension-
    ality, 192-194
Political participation, 169-172, 176,
    191, 207
Political structure
apportionment as, 208
impact on policy, 203-212
multidimensional measures of,
    173-180
tax systems and, 177
Polsby, Nelson W., 81n, 82n
Pool, Ithiel, 93-94, 95, 106-119, 135,
    137, 138
Power elite. *See* Community power,
    elite approach to
Presidency, 48-50, 53, 54-57
Press, Charles, 165-166, 190n, 215n
Presthus, Robert, 86n, 87
Pritchett, C. Herman, 66-67
Professionalism-Local Reliance
    Factor, 178-180, 181, 198, 219-
    221
Public policy
change over time in, 11
comparative studies of, 141-142
comprehensive sociopolitical
    relationships with, 212-221
conversion of, 242-248
definitions of, 3-8, 202-203
factor analysis and, 212-221
historical and economic
    determinants of, 133-134,
    218-221
interparty competitiveness as
    determinant of, 144-145
measurement of state and local,
    201-203
nondecisions as, 5

political process and social
    structure impact on, 203-212
as product of government
    activity, 5
role of interest groups in
    formulating, 134-136
study of by political scientists,
    8-10
symbolic action in, 136, 138
typologies of, 241-242, 264-267
variation among levels of
    government in, 11
Public services as policy indicators,
    211-212
Public welfare policy, 213-214,
    216-218

Raiffa, Howard, 51n
Ranney, Austin, 28n, 91n, 170n, 171n
Ransone, Coleman B., Jr., 48n
Rieselbach, Leroy N., 30n
Rigby, Gerald, 66n
Riley, Dennis, 209n
Robinson, James A., 32n, 48n, 138n,
    142n, 143-144, 146, 147, 170n,
    206-207
Roll calls, 39-40
Rossi, Peter, 77n, 81n
Rossiter, Clinton, 47-50
Rostow, Walt W., 151n
Rudolph, Lloyd, 152n
Rudolph, Susanne, 152n
Rummel, Rudolph, 152n, 153n

Salisbury, Robert H., 4n, 5n, 64-65,
    159n, 202, 261n, 264n, 265
Schattschneider, E. E., 31n, 76, 78,
    86n, 108n, 260n
Schlesinger, Joseph A., 162, 163, 171n,
    177, 184-185, 215n
Schmidthauser, John, 68
Schubert, Glendon, 59n, 61-62, 65-66,
    69-70, 71n, 72, 165-166, 215n
Schultze, Robert O., 80n
Schwartz, Richard D., 153n
Sechrest, Lee. 153n
Shannon. Lyle. 149
Sharkansky, Ira, 12n, 17n, 146n, 152,
    155n, 159n, 161n, 162n, 171n,
    175n, 176n, 193n, 202n, 205-